Oklahoma Labyrinths — a path to inner peace

by **Gail Peck**
Linda Yeingst and Phyllis Pennington

Hawks
Publishing
COMPANY
4005 NW 29, Oklahoma City, OK 73107
(405) 943-2741, wisdom110@hotmail.com

Oklahoma Labyrinths — a path to inner peace
© 7 Hawks Publishing Company
November 11, 2007

ISBN 978-0-9800900-0-0

Although this book was published in the fall of 2008, research of individual labyrinths and their unique stories was mainly conducted in 2007. Numerical statistics and titles of those interviewed reflect that time frame, honoring Oklahoma's centennial year and its 100th birthday.

Cover art and all Tonkawa photos by Ken Crowder
Inside front cover photo and
Chapter 2 title page photo by Marty Kermeen

Contents

Chapter 4 – Oklahoma Labyrinths

*This book is dedicated
to the divine essence of immortal man,
to labyrinths past, present and future
and to the ancient wisdom they impart.*

**Visualize your quest,
enter the circle
and discover yourself.**

*   *   *

Oklahoma Labyrinths — a path to inner peace
is a testament to the wondrous power of creation
encouraging readers to journey back to self.

Written in honor of the Oklahoma Centennial and to
recognize the sacredness the Sooner State offers
residents and visitors, this book connects to ancient
wisdom through a joyous path of self-reflection.

The authors wish to acknowledge all the gracious
individuals, churches, parks, retreats, seminaries,
schools, camps and hospitals who shared their
time, talents, hospitality, labyrinths and spirituality to manifest the birth of this publication.

We especially want to thank the labyrinths
themselves, those who design, build, maintain and
cherish their quintessence, and anyone who has
ever walked a unicursal path.

Meditative Prayer in the Labyrinth of Life

Labyrinths can be quite informative if walked with an open mind and an attitude of love, seeking answers to questions our soul has yet to remember or that we have not learned how to ask. Sitting humbly in the center or listening while spiraling its informative circuits, these sacred circles enlighten any who grace their artistic form.

Below is what one author learned from the subject of this book about its main character during a recent labyrinth communion:

"Reminiscent of an ancient talisman or mystical mandala, we magnify luck, afford protection, contribute to success, attract prominence, infer invincibility, uncover hidden treasure. Such a powerful medallion image reflects happiness, joy, prosperity, ancient wisdom and inner peace.

A common misconception is that labyrinths and mazes are synonymous. Both can be circular and have twists and turns, but labyrinths possess no dead ends (all paths lead to the center goal). There are more differences than similarities. A labyrinth solves all the problems a maze creates.

I can solve your problems as well if you only ask, allow and listen. A labyrinth serenely grants the following assistance:

• Offers the opportunity to experience Divinity through meditation, prayer, focus, education, art, universal knowledge, self-expression and creativity.
• Expands awareness of Christ Consciousness through love, compassion, gratitude, caring, service, understanding, healing, counseling and sharing unique talents.
• Advances higher consciousness and provides a spiritual connection to the primal source of All That Is.
• Enhances both personal and group visions of a peaceful, unified world.
• Bridges the gap between cultural mores and encourages acceptance of all aspects of diversity.
• Acknowledges ancient wisdom by creating an atmosphere of loving support and fellowship as humans expand their awareness of transcendent roles in the global community.

- Establishes a solid foundation and radiating center of truth for those seeking a spiritual path.
- Combines polarity and oneness.
- Symbolizes duality on the trip inward and unity on the way home.
- Discovers the key to unlocking hidden secrets.
- Awards the leisure to commune with nature.
- Honors and respects all spiritual paths and different viewpoints.
- Places opposites in juxtaposition for greater understanding.
- Cherishes simple accomplishments for these are the building blocks of skyscrapers.
- Advocates nourishment of dreams.
- Helps overcome obstacles impeding fulfillment of one's greatest desires.
- Encourages exploration of inner-dimensional realms.
- Serves as a roadmap on the journey of life, providing guidance, direction, opportunity and showcasing reason, passion and creativity.
- Fans the fire of passion so human angels may follow their hearts.
- Instructs travelers to visualize success and it will come.
- Admonishes forward movement and the courage to continue.
- Replaces obstructions and blockages with clarity.
- Suggests that everyone seize the moment as well as enjoy it.
- Cultivates the superlative genius of Universal Mind.
- Calms emotional waters with the flames of forgiveness.
- Soars high above the paralysis of judgment.
- Celebrates the triumphant rebirth of harmony and oneness between heaven and earth.
- Clears the cobwebs of deceit and embraces the honesty of friendship.

I am a sacred friend with whom you can converse easily mixing meditation with prayer as we share a journey of creation in a circle of perfection. Together, we experience the continuous evolutionary spiral, completing a divine connection, performing meditative prayer in the labyrinth of life."

Chapter 1
A Path to Inner Peace

Labyrinthine Revival

Labyrinths represent humanity's arduous journey through the cycles of time. The winding path spiraling to the center parallels the earth's rotation identifying the center as the source of man's spiritual connection — the temple of the eternal soul.

The goal is no longer to transcend the earthly realms, but to join them in a new creation: heaven on earth.

Secrets unfold inside this mystical circle; the Great Mystery has been revealed.

A primordial symbol that follows a path of renewal and presents a mirror image, it can be walked not only with feet, but also with hands, hearts, minds and souls.

Everyone treads the path of experience, twisting and turning toward a premiere, and often elusive, goal. Inner wisdom awaits.

"As we rounded the corner into the 21st century, it seems we are beginning to understand the importance of integrating mind, body and spirit to achieve true health and well-being. We are beginning to recognize the inexorable connection between all things and the ultimate oneness of being. The current interest in labyrinths and the practice of using them for walking meditation is evidence of this spiritual revolution," said Helen Curry, former president of The Labyrinth Society and author of *The Way of the Labyrinth*.

They are excellent tools for bringing into alignment the many aspects of our being and teaching us we are all on the same path, Curry said, adding these intriguing and intricate designs have a unique ability to capture our imaginations, our hearts and our spirits.

A 350-year absence since the Middle Ages has been erased with a resurgence in labyrinths in the last three decades (since the 1980s) and now there are more unicursal paths in the United States than any other country.

Rev. Lauren Artress, of Grace Cathedral in San Francisco, estimates about 5,000 are located worldwide with 4,000 of those in the U.S. Presently, 1,918 are listed on the Worldwide Labyrinth Locator for the United States and 428 elsewhere in the world. Less than 20 are listed for Oklahoma and we discovered 70.

The French Catholic home of the most renown labyrinth at Chartres Cathedral recently reopened its 800-year-old path for walking mainly due to American interest.

Most major cities in the United States, Canada, Britain, Australia, New Zealand and parts of Europe and Russia sport labyrinths. As part of the revival, these revered symbols are being created or restored in Sweden, Finland, Denmark, England, Austria, Germany, Holland and Switzerland.

North American models joined the evolutionary cycle in the early 1990s. Five of the top nine world labyrinth designers reside in the United States and include some of the world's most prolific labyrinth makers.

Many historians believe the United States movement is more spiritually oriented than in Britain or Europe and arose from interest in dowsing to sense earth energies and sacred geometry.

From their inception, labyrinths have been associated with spiritual forces and energetic ley lines. Origin points are less than definitive. Their rich 4,000-year history meanders throughout time, much like the winding path.

History suggests these sacred circles emerge at intervals of change and breakdowns in traditional, social and religious structures, and when worship of feminine deities is on the rise.

"It's a device for protection and guidance during difficulty and struggle," noted designer Sig Lonegren, who dowsed the ley lines at the Sparrow Hawk labyrinth in Tahlequah. "They teach peace, tolerance and understanding."

Their visibility is evident amid a preference for more introspective beliefs and mystical and contemplative religions which promise salvation or ascension through sacrifice, esoteric practices or a spiritual journey. Labyrinths characterize a symbolic path for that journey as well as a tool for initiation into the mysteries.

This pattern of renewal surfaced in eras of prosperity and economic development and periods of cultural and technological renaissance coinciding with enhanced spiritual movements.

In the past, the resurgence of sacred circles preceded times of trouble and hardship and typically appeared on the cusp between stages of expansion and growth and those of chaos and decline. Witness the labyrinth's emergence from the first to the fifth centuries in Rome, the 12th-14th centuries in Italy and France and again in late 19th century Europe. The current revival reflects another such transcendence.

Sacred Symbolism

The word "labyrinth" derives from an ancient Greek word *labyrs* or double-headed axe; a dual meaning to cut away or sever unnecessary bondage.

To free the shackles of a self-imposed prison. The labyrinth of the mind can be a powerful instrument offering opportunity for ascension or limiting restraints.

Within the labyrinth's sacred spirals, people meditate and pray to a Supreme Being, many gods and goddesses, to a single god or goddess, to an abstract power of light and love or to the divine core within every individual. Encompassing multiple forms of existence, some chant or silently repeat mantras, many ask a question, others await intuitive answers.

One of the authors said she sometimes asks, "What is the most important thing for me to know right now?" upon entering the path.

Labyrinths awaken mankind to the presence of the Divine and have encircled the world's traditions since the Bronze Age. Featured in pre-Christian, Christian and modern societies in both religious and secular settings, these images support unity and wholeness, not separation.

Their inner reflective journey shelters a comforting place and permits safe passage for finding deeper spiritual meaning renewing a connection with the power and sanctity of the earth.

Just like a mantra (a word or syllable characterizing a celestial aspect spoken aloud or in the mind of concentration), unicursal paths correspond to creative energy and align seekers with the vibration of the cosmos itself.

For those who walked these mystical illuminations in the great ancient cathedrals, the sacred geometry of the buildings ensured they saw jeweled colors glittering from the windows, casting hues of rainbow light over circular passageways.

Color has always been an important detail in labyrinth design. Medieval architects embraced this knowledge, creating glorious stained glass windows that showered the revered circles with rainbows and gold-leaf reflections from nearby statues, synthesizing a shimmering kaleidoscope of colors.

Sacred geometry is the study of the way spirit integrates into matter. Echoing and amplifying the geometry of nature and planetary movements helps to align the resonance of body, mind and spirit with the harmonic frequencies of heaven above and earth below — as above, so below.

Spaces built honoring these factors enable those utilizing them to resonate (vibrate) at an elevated rate, maximizing the possibility of connection to the One, God, Prime Creator, Universal Mind or whatever one chooses to call a Supreme Being.

All the earth is sacred, some locations just seem more alive allowing effortless spiritual communion, enhancing divine wisdom. Such sites are usually aligned astronomically, constructed via sacred geometry and positioned over energetic ley lines.

"Ley" is the old Saxon word for "cleared path." Modern vernacular calls them "lines of power" and notes they have been used for thousands of years to guide humanity to invisible pathways of energy, combining man, nature and cosmic forces.

Labyrinths call forth an ancient power spiraling to the center of our souls. The spiral is a symbol containing all the accumulated experience and wisdom of the earth's people and the center represents the source of all knowledge — the focal point of quintessence.

In mystical thought, the center of the labyrinth signifies the origin of life, the synthesis of primordial and creative insight. Concentrated with infinite energy, a central point is complete in itself, a totality of perfection, essence of the godhead, an ultimate and eternal state of being containing all meaning, radiating divine eminence.

The spiral is among the most sacred signs known to humanity. It symbolizes the timeless and universal flow of energy, representing a return to source, encircling all aspects between heaven and earth, divining cosmic communion.

Gerald Schroeder called the spiral an elliptical, not an optical illusion, in his book *The Science of God: the Convergence of Scientific and Biblical Wisdom.*

"A swirling vortex that has no end, always moving closer to but never reaching the origin. Finite in length, but infinite in origin. The circle is a special case of spiral with a zero growth rate."

Schroeder also wrote the graceful curve of the nautilus seashell occurs in nature more often than any other shape. "Its lines trace out an exponential spiral. Each successive swirl is wider by a seemingly arbitrary but fixed factor. This curve is repeated in the seeds of a sunflower, the curves of tusks and the spread of stars in spiral galaxies, such as the Milky Way. Graphically, it also describes the relation between Genesis time and earth time as the universe expanded out from its point-like creation of the Big Bang."

Dynamic forces of cosmic and microcosmic life, spiral forms are seen in nature from celestial galaxies to whirlwinds and whirlpools, from coiled serpents or conical shells to human fingertips and the double helix structure of DNA at the heart of every cell.

In art, spirals are one of the most common decorative themes. Carved on megaliths, spirals suggest a labyrinthine journey to the afterlife, with a return ticket. The spiraling snakes on the medical caduceus image (and double spirals in general) imply a balance of opposing principles — the meaning of the yin-yang motif, another form of double spiral.

Vortex forces in wind, water or fire command ascent, descent or the rotating energy that drives the cosmos. By adding whirling momentum to a circular form, the spiral also connotes time, the cyclic rhythms of the seasons, birth and death, waning and waxing of the moon, and the sun.

Like the yogic "serpent" at the base of the spine, the spring-like coil of a spiral harbors latent power. The uncoiling spiral is phallic and male, the involved spiral is female, identifying the double spiral as a fertility symbol.

The spiral as an open and flowing line intimates extension, evolution and continuity, uninterrupted movement, the rhythmic breathing of life itself.

The symbolism of these winding meditation tools conveys a rich tradition. Each detail of construction expresses eloquence. The artistic outer form of the holy labyrinth circle is a geometrical design whose essence invokes the spiritual force within and embraces permanence.

Uniting wholeness, completeness, totality and eternal perfection, circles are the only mathematical shape without divisions and alike at every point along its closed curve.

An embodiment of God, the undisputed center of the universe, the circle can also represent a sphere and is potentially without beginning or end. In mystical thought, this makes it the most important and universal of all geometric designs.

Spheres depict totality, absolute authority, dominion and are a popular art figure signifying the universal qualities of truth, fame, fortune, abundance, justice and communication. The globe is an attribute of omnipresent divinities and a crowned orb (epitomized by the philosopher's stone in alchemy) exemplifies the key to spiritual enlightenment.

The circle is implicit in many other significant emblems, including the wheel, disk, ring, clock, sun, moon and zodiac. To the ancients, the observed cosmos presented itself inescapably as circular — not only the planets themselves, including the presumed flat disk of the earth circled by waters, but also their cyclical movements and the recurring cycles of the seasons. They symbolized solar or creative and fertile cosmic forces.

Traditional symbols illustrate an elemental power that transcends boundaries. The interpretation of this power varies considerably around the world, throughout history, among civilizations, and reveals insights into philosophy, religion, mysticism, art, literature, cultural mores and societal ideology.

Such figures form a visual shorthand for ideas with an emblematic extension of function and meaning. They reinforce hidden thoughts and suppositions about human life in detailed images with swift, simple and memorable characters. These universal archetypes also erase limits since they crystallize ideas without confining them.

Symbols have great imaginative resonance and often complex, ambiguous meanings subject to interpretation. Some encapsulate the most ancient and fundamental beliefs humans have about the cosmos, their place in it, how they behave and what they should honor and revere. Many have psychological impact. Emotion is the essential element.

Even symbols that embody simpler ideas heighten the significance of the ordinary object chosen as a symbol, icon, totem or message, expanding its sphere of influence and increasing understanding.

As a form of communication, images long predated writing. Carved, painted or worked into effigies, clothing or ornaments, images that had become familiar symbols through repetition were used for magical purposes, to ward off evil or to entreat or placate the gods.

Intangible, abstract depictions also evolved as popular designs to control societies, heighten awareness and inspire loyalty, obedience, aggression, love or fear.

A coherent system of idyllic characters could enhance harmony among the citizens of a community, themselves and the cosmos. It could inspire collective action and reunite man with his inner illumination.

But what does all this symbolism mean to the seeker of divine wisdom? Perhaps nothing, perhaps everything.

Architects of sacred geometry frequently attempted the impossible: to square the circle (create a square whose perimeter equals the circumference of a circle).

The square represents the physical; the circle the spiritual. It's simply not possible to put physical perimeters on a spiritual creation.

Phillips Theological Seminary, Tulsa

Pathways of Consciousness

Labyrinthine spirals through time edify and enlighten mystical journeys enabling seekers of spiritual truth to find elusive answers among the inner universe of their souls. Sacred circles provide pathways to higher levels of consciousness where questioning explorers can awaken untapped luminescence.

Infinite gifts of spirit abide inside the peaceful path of Oneness as man discovers his individual connection to celestial radiance. People are presently pursuing a more fulfilling relationship with their Creator. There is no wrong way to interact or worship with whatever one chooses to call the Source of All Creation: Universal Mind, Prime Creator, The Force, Spirit, All That Is or God.

The very word "human" epitomizes this. "Hu" is an ancient name for God. So homo sapiens are God-man or God in man, created in the image of divinity — limitless potential waiting to unfurl.

Stagnant shadows of the past have led us on this magnificent odyssey. God-man stands as a towering temple, a spiral bridge between heaven and earth. A supreme being coalescing into effervescent sparkles of light.

This spiritual quest has inspired man to expand his mind. Scientists theorize humans use less than 10 percent of their brain. Quantum physicists are one experiment away from unveiling scientific evidence to support the unused portion of human brain power is where psyche (not psychic) abilities originate.

The key, as in everything else, is balance. When the four components of the human brain merge, miracles will become commonplace. Most recognize only three aspects of the psyche: id, ego, superego or conscious, unconscious, superconscious.

An advanced answer involves conscious awareness, unconscious filter, supra (higher) consciousness and universal mind.

These four correspond with the four parts of the body. Conscious awareness relates to the physical or corporal body; unconscious filter to the emotional or astral body. Supraconsciousness equates to our higher God selves and etheric body. Universal Mind is the Ultimate Source, Prime Creator (God) and represents the mental or causal body.

Humans are multi-dimensional beings capable of functioning in various dimensions of existence simultaneously. Herein lies the illusion. Spiritual brain enlightenment is indeed a quantum leap, transcending visionary appearances.

Spirit is everywhere... in everything... and can often appear magical if we only open to our divine essence and enjoy the beauty around, above, below and within us.

Only those who can reverse their senses to hear with their minds, see with their hearts and smell with their souls can taste the truth and feel the wisdom of love and laughter. Inner peace transcends the illuminated path of enlightenment. Hearts and minds must unite with body and soul to reflect truth and light through the healing power of love. Humans who join in this epic quest continually enjoy a magical moment of expanded consciousness.

As God-man travels the path of Oneness, surrounded by inner peace, he constantly communes with his divinity and no longer feels the need to hunt for answers. They seek him. The answers become the questor. He moves from searching to knowing.

Spiritual teacher Ram Dass explained it well when he said, "The need for reasoning is dramatically reduced and the universe becomes a mystery to be experienced, not a riddle to be solved. It becomes virtually impossible to find anything negative about existence; everything seems absolutely perfect."

Perhaps, we can equate the passages of the labyrinth to the Biblical reference when Jesus said there were many mansions in his Father's house. Mansions could be levels of consciousness.

Heaven is expansion. The transcendence of limiting beliefs; the center of the labyrinth. All problems are only perceived until we create them. The word "heaven" originates from the Greek *ouranos* meaning expansion. Heaven is the growth of consciousness, the evolution of humanity's oneness.

"In my Father's house are many mansions. I go to prepare a place so that where I am, there ye may be also." Jesus never said heaven was a physical place. He referred to it as "within" and "at hand." Note the "I am" reference in the aforementioned John 14:3 verse. The second coming of Christ is a transformation of human consciousness (Christ Consciousness), a shift from linear time to spiritual presence, from thinking to consciousness, not the arrival of some emissary.

The labyrinth says God = truth = freedom = Presence = essence. The truth of your divine essence shall set you free. It allows us to embrace the spectacular and swim upstream against the current of mediocrity.

The next evolutionary step is to master our divinity.

It only makes sense when you "get it." When you experience that "AHA!" moment. You can read every book in the library, research the whole internet, talk to all six billion people on the planet. None of that matters until you internalize your I AM Consciousness and feel what it means to Become One with the Universe.

Labyrinths bring humans (God-man) back to the light of consciousness, to the present, the presence of a Supreme Being. Just like God, the whole is always visible.

Dr. Lauren Artress wrote in *Walking a Sacred Path*: "The labyrinth is gracious and generous with its gifts for all who enter. It reintroduces the much-needed walking meditation back into the Christian tradition. It gives everyone a tool for spiritual experience. It heals and consoles, supports and confronts, and helps us remember the ancient path where others have trod before us. The labyrinth allows us to experience the rhythm of our souls. It weaves us together in the joy and mercy of God's grace."

An interpretation of grace has sometimes puzzled the common man. Not any more. The labyrinth provides a simple definition. Grace is what has been given. Granted would probably suffice here, too. So, grace is the love of God we have been given or granted. Or the gifts (blessings) God has granted (bestowed) upon his children.

The gift of divine grace is beyond human imagination. German physicist Albert Einstein had a few things to say about imagination. He said it was more powerful than knowledge and was a precursor to life's coming attractions.

Similar to dreams, says the labyrinth, but with your eyes open. Something in the dream is always real until we awaken from our illusory sense of self, described by Einstein as "an optical illusion of consciousness."

Eckhart Tolle wrote about dreams in *A New Earth — Awakening to Your Life's Purpose*. "There is the dream, and there is the dreamer of the dream. The dream is a short-lived play of forms. It is the world, relatively real but not absolutely real. Then there is the dreamer, the absolute reality in which the forms come and go. The dreamer is not the person. The person is part of the dream. The dreamer is the substratum in which the dream appears, that which makes the dream possible. It is the absolute behind the relative, the timeless behind time, the consciousness in and behind form. The dreamer is consciousness itself — who you are. To awaken within the dream is our purpose now. When we are awake within the dream, the ego-centered earth-drama comes to an end and a more benign and wondrous dream arises. This is the new earth."

Dreams are emblematic of man's inner thoughts and unful-filled aspirations. Symbols of divine consciousness, labyrinths and dreams merge abstract awareness inside the mind of God. The labyrinth is a representative design that gives power to inspiration and questions our ability to characterize the space between thoughts and differentiate order from chaos.

Note the word "quest" in question. Mission, crusade, voyage, expedition, journey, search, pursuit, exploration, excursion — all meanings of the word quest. These words also apply to a laby-rinth.

Interaction with a sacred circle can enhance the quest to decode what Einstein really meant in his infamous equation $E=mc^2$. No, he did not secretly mean Einstein creating mass con-fusion times itself.

The esoteric meaning of $E=mc^2$ is Everyone (each of us on Earth) is equal to Mastery of Consciousness using the expo-nential powers of Spirit and Hu-Man. God expressing himself through us and man expressing himself as a co-creator with God. The power of God exemplifying mass consciousness combined with God-man.

Energy = mass consciousness using the two powers of love and forgiveness.

Labyrinths connect the physical to the spiritual through divine intelligence and cosmic cosmology as they spiral to the heart of infinity inside the center of the human soul. The circuits of these sacred circles curl around a central focal point just like the flow of blood in the corporal body. The joy of God-man's pulsating life force emanates from the heart and returns for replenishing as it nourishes and sustains the body's circulatory system.

A new cognizance flows into the vital substance and per-meates our divine essence. This new pristine higher level of consciousness is not the world we were born into. The familiar third dimensional format has ascended the evolutionary ladder to quantum or holographic principles. Linear time has been replaced with spirals of transitory immortality. The rational mind is no longer in control. Heart-centered actions fuel the perpet-ual spiritual fire of passionate emotion. Wisdom embraces love; heart and mind meld.

Spirals of energetic excitement swirl through the circuits of the body and its corresponding creative labyrinthine companion. Moving in expanding circles at rapidly increasing levels, the coiled helix transmutes negativity and increases evolutionary momentum. Symbols of animated change, wisdom and encoded knowledge, the spiral unites its exploratory components into harmonic resonance. The medical caduceus emblem and human DNA epitomize creative intelligence.

Step inside the moving meditation of a labyrinth and allow dynamic spirals of planetary understanding to support the ever-changing reality instead of suppressing relevant neoteric information. Become a new child of the universe as God-man freely spirals adventurous sacred circles of creation. Celebrate the effervescent circuits encoded with enlightened compassion, joyous blessings, insightful gratitude, divine healing, spiritual nourishment, mystical opportunities and unconditional love.

Labyrinths exude creative potential. They mirror the human soul and reflect the Seven Steps of Creation: illumination, faith, imagination, understanding and will, spiritual discernment, wisdom and love (the union of our thinking and feeling natures), and resting in God's presence.

As God-man awakens his spiritual consciousness and witnesses the dawning of an inner divine light of illumination and wisdom, he pierces self-limiting concepts. Awareness stimulates manifestation desires. This calm, peaceful place of Spirit communicates man's readiness to accept a renewed faith.

"The substance of things hoped for, the evidence of things not seen," is how the Bible describes faith. The second step in the creation process empowers humans to look beyond appearances knowing there are greater forces in the universe than the eye can see. Faith enables God-man to reach into the realm of the invisible and grasp the esoteric substance of etheric existentialism.

A more intimate acquaintance with this invisible matrix convinces man that all things are possible and leads to the third imaginative step forming substance. Derived from a Latin word meaning "to be present," substance contains essential elements and connects faith to imagination. It is the energy field that holds matter together. This substantive energy field forms the invisible matrix of life and gives form to visible matter.

To create anything we desire, the imagination reaches into the invisible ethers of substance and shapes idealistic forms and images. It deposits unexpressed possibilities into the human mind so manifest forms may appear. But only if God-man has fully integrated the first two steps of the creative process. An illuminated essence and sustained faith draw the invisible substance formed by the imagination into the physical realm.

The fourth step in the creation process represents the faculties of understanding and will, which function best when intertwined. Understanding increases its value when aware discernment is expressed via determined strength. A strong purpose is more powerful when grounded in understanding. Mix in some divine aspects and spiritual understanding enhances God-man's ability to perceive and synthesize ideas.

Spiritual discernment is the fifth step in this process. The ability to choose, evaluate and make wise decisions helps unveil the truth behind the mask. Proper nourishment and cultivation of ideas is paramount if we are to ascertain unblemished integrity. Faith in the illuminated process of imagination, understanding and will, added to etheric insight, guides mankind to tender wise decisions and align with inner potential.

A union of wisdom and love (our thinking and feeling natures) epitomizes step six. Such a coalescing of ideas weds the masculine thinking, reasoning, expressive quality with the female emotional, feeling, receptive temperament. Thinking applies knowledge of mental intellect while emotions draw on experiences of the heart. Both must unite to manifest our creations and bless the rhythmic beat of divine consciousness.

The final step in the creation process joins the universe and spiritual man resting in God's presence. Ideas and patterns of form were created in the previous six steps. Tier seven allows evaluation of the creative process, the seeking of spiritual truth and a peaceful state of inner knowing.

These dynamic laws of creation activate any forms man has initiated through focused thought. The first six steps represent physical attainment and development while step seven leaves His children nestled in the presence of God, nourished with divine inspiration.

The same celestial inspiration and spiritual nourishment labyrinths provide. It is time to claim our divine inheritance and shift the vibrational matrix of the collective unconscious. Life is meant to be enjoyed, not endured.

Accept new DNA coding of Divine Nutritional Acceptance and let Love stand for

> L uminous
> O palescent
> V ibrant
> E nergy

There are no limitations, no shackling boundaries, no unobtainable goals. Only you can limit yourself by limiting your thoughts. What if? Suppose... Why can't we? Simply consider the possibility as you travel labyrinthine pathways of higher consciousness.

College Student Shares First Labyrinthine Journey

"My first experience with a labyrinth was a little poetic, but that's how it affected me. Upon stepping into the labyrinth, I noticed the way my feet marched in harmony with the beating of my heart, as though it were carving itself into the crushed gravel path like a friend to walk with me on the journey ahead.

"But we were not alone. The path was filled with people who had come for the Medieval Fair. Parents and their children, and younger adults like me, took in the scene together. I saw around me the stride of the children; their methodology was not like mine. I walked the guided direction, slow and steady with my beating heart — in a straight line. They took the road less traveled, going perpendicular to the path, crossing its boundaries, running, skipping, fleeing each other's gazes, high-fiveing trees as they made their way into the middle.

"It occurred to me then that this experience was much like life itself — a visual example. The children, without the constraints of the world, broke the labyrinth's rules. Stepped out of turn and were without life's discipline. They were making the path without needing to know how. The younger adults like myself walked the same. We had a journey to make, we needed lines to follow and a guided pace to walk. We had a long way to go and needed to take it slow.

"The parents of the children stood nearby and watched. They let their children roam in their way, knowing that someday they would be taking the path as I do now. But they had already made their paths in life and now stood on the sidelines rooting for the 20-something kids to find their way to the middle and back out again.

"We didn't finish meandering that day, a minotaur held us back. Work. School. Friends. Obligations. But isn't that so like life? I realized later that I should've kept walking. I realize now that all I needed was that beating heart."

— **Brittany Burden**
OU Student

Labyrinth or Maze?

Just as mythology and history often merge, so do labyrinths and mazes. The ancient world understood the labyrinth's purpose as a tool for journeys of initiation, healing, pilgrimage and prophecy. A maze was a game.

Although mazes and labyrinths have distinctly different meanings, the words have incorrectly been used interchangeably throughout history. Puzzle mazes descended from labyrinths and have existed for only about 500 years. Labyrinths originated 4,000 years ago. The main difference between the two is a labyrinth has a single path, spiraling unimpeded to the center and aspects of meditation and ritual while a maze is a puzzle with junctions, dead-ends and deceptive choices.

Sacred labyrinthine circles enjoy a rich history in content and symbolism. Over the millennia in different cultures and civilizations, they have represented journeys of conquest, sieges of cities, pilgrimages, rites of passage, death and rebirth and the Path of Life. Religious and communal possessions have trod their pathways often seeking rebirth and protection against evil spirits.

Labyrinths initiate life. Mazes mess with your mind.

The maze as an art form is ancient and timeless. Many configurations exist to entertain, puzzle, stupefy, delight and challenge the mind of deception — mirror mazes, elegant hedge mazes, vast maize mazes, tall turf mazes, spiritual stone mazes, complex tile mazes, playful water mazes, dazzling color mazes and mind-bending number mazes. There are even vertical mazes, wooden panel mazes and paving mazes.

Comprised of a complex network of branching pathways, many leading nowhere, rampant dead-ends and crisscrossing intersections, frustrating turns and twists and concealed alleys hiding behind tall barriers, mazes have a defined start, confusing format and an elusive goal. Labyrinths have a single path that leads to a centered goal and back to the entrance.

The word "maze" indicates a perplexing pattern with many paths and false passages. Hmmm… some religious doctrines have a few of those. Labyrinths are not mazes; experientially, they are universes apart. Labyrinths characterize a simple journey with no blind corners or wrong turns. Walkers do not get lost, except maybe deep in thought.

"What distinguishes mazes and labyrinths is the completely opposite mental states they elicit," said Robert Ferré, director of St. Louis' Labyrinth Enterprises. "A maze involves a contest, a puzzle to be solved. It requires constant mental and intellectual effort. It involves a competition between the walker and the maze designer. A labyrinth, on the other hand, requires no such effort. The mind can completely relax, but because the path is circuitous, one must still pay attention. That state of awareness, combined with a relaxed mind, is typical of meditation. For that reason, the labyrinth is frequently seen as a means for walking meditation."

We may live in a world that resembles a maze, but it's actually a labyrinth. If life is viewed as a maze, every mistake is an unnecessary detour and a waste of time. Mistakes in a labyrinth are simply part of the journey and quintessential master teachers.

The labyrinth doesn't ask "Are you going the right way or the wrong way?" It only asks, "Are you going?"

Mazes boast multiplicity, choice and strategy via many paths and dead-ends. Labyrinths feature a winding path leading through a series of twists and turns into a center and out again along the same path. They are about guidance, trust, reflection, peace, transformation, connection, inspiration, spiritual journey, hope and rebirth... connecting past, present and future into the Eternal Now.

A labyrinth parallels the path of humanity through time. It lures the human race to the center — into the here and now. The simple revelation is there is only one path and it is the one we are currently traveling. We have superceded the complex, confusing, challenging ages of mazes and returned to our simplicity.

Asterius, the starry minotaur trapped in the center of a Cretan labyrinth (which was actually a maze), represents our inner demons and subconscious imprisonment. We have dealt with monsters and emerged transformed. Our current world shows the evolution of humanity from maze to labyrinth; the monkey has transcended.

Some people exchange marriage vows in a labyrinth. Have you ever known anyone who got married in a maze? Imagine what symbolic connotations that would engender for a holy union!

The Reflection is You

We stand at a peak moment in the exhilarating journey of life. Combining mankind's greatest scientific knowledge with infinite spiritual insight can change the course of history.

Life itself has no negatives or positives. Everything is merely a reflection of individual and collective attitudes, expectations and convictions. As ancient sages often predicted, and Shakespeare wrote in *Hamlet*, nothing is good or bad, thinking makes it so.

Fortunately, our collective wisdom has risen to meet the challenge and travel an advanced course to greet the dawning of a new planetary day. Labyrinths can ease the equilibrium as they speak the novel mode of communication necessary to place our planet back on its appointed axes. Humanity is learning this unique language of light as it spirals to the center of its soul.

It is the language of the heart, the essential essence of existence, the spirit that moves through all things. A spiraling synergy of energetic compassion amid ever-expanding wavelengths of harmonic wisdom anoints its poetic prose.

The labyrinth adroitly identifies inner intelligence and magnificently manifests cleverly hidden gifts in outward form. One efficiently travels a proficient path to reach a pre-determined — not pre-destined — goal. Turns in the path are inevitable, often changing the intended objective and enhancing the meaning of life. These ingenious tools help the traveler ascertain what he really hopes to achieve.

Frequently, the labyrinth becomes the inquisitor and asks the seeker a question. The answer accurately reflects the current status of the walker's individual and collective consciousness. Needed information then becomes a masterful tool for self-knowledge and illuminates innermost desires and unfulfilled dreams. The invisible is now discernable. An existential search for self successfully guides mankind's exploration into intrinsic mysteries and uncovers a coherent cosmic connection.

The labyrinth suggests to observers something about everyone who walks it, perhaps, heightened details concerning those who simply choose to watch. It will mirror far more to anyone who travels its spiraling path. The pilgrim as crusader realizes a congruent symbol isn't characterized by the good answers it gives, but rather by the good questions it permits.

Do innate spatial relationships convey stellar transformations of interplanetary travel? Possibly. Encourages one to think, which makes it a worthy question no matter what the answer.

Sacred circles entertain symbols within symbols. Both labyrinths and pilgrimages characterize a quest for wholeness. A pilgrimage is a time-honored technique to achieve spiritual and psychological renewal. In the Middle Ages, pilgrims took to the road undertaking difficult expeditions to sacred shrines to show faith, atone for sins or win salvation. The ensuing trip paved the way for crusaders to face multiple challenges and dangers. Many found the journey itself as spiritually worthwhile as the eventual destination.

Numerous seekers are procuring the pilgrim's road once again discovering comprehensive sojourns to a divine site bridges the void of understanding between truth and illusion. Modern-day pilgrims desire to satisfy spiritual hunger through healing, cocreation with spiritual forces and the search for lost knowledge.

A voyage to the center of an ancient symbol radiates cocreation, the sharing of unique and individual gifts. God blessed humanity with the talent to conceive and consummate his own immortality.

The intravenous spiral intertwines problem and solution resolving the labyrinthine riddle of expansive growth and explosive evolution. Spirals connect humanity's circuits and magnetize spiritual energy. This influx of divine assistance delivers massive quantities of higher dimensional frequencies to the earth plane. Such a concentrated cornucopia of celestial effervescence affords the opportunity for greater healing, increased manifestations, enhanced understanding and elevated opportunities. Enterprising spirals direct ideas, energies and intentions, balance momentum and serve as a conduit between heaven and earth, man and God.

A pathway for interaction with a supreme presence, concentric spirals amp intensity and supplement strength to free oneself of anything that no longer serves its host. They provide the courage to set Herculean intentions for miraculous alignment and divine transmutation.

The labyrinth invites travelers to discover the beauty of the whole amid the confusion, imperfection and pain of life's journey. It encourages pilgrims to embark on the peaceful path with serenity and resolve, traversing meandering circuits to a destined center goal and back home.

Sacred circles awaken walkers to the presence of the divine

buried deep inside the collective subconscious. Unresolved wounds or unpleasant repressed memories resurface. Walkers uncomfortably find themselves facing what they have feared, denied or avoided. Simply forgive yourself and/or the perpetrator. Accept the outcome is for the highest good and express appreciation for the experience.

Appreciation is the beginning of love.

The labyrinth awaits our discovery as it safely guides humans through troubled waters to the realm of unexpressed potential. Its grand mysterious patterns shape the connecting web of creative possibilities, leading to a heavenly source of abundant promise and unlimited hope, guaranteeing a safe trip home.

A focus for meditation and prayer in cultures around the world for thousands of years, labyrinths provide peerless insight into new opportunities and noble ideals. Through these sacred circles, humanity rediscovers a lost connection to the natural world and creation, intuition and imagination, awareness and revelation. Within the human psyche, the labyrinth of the mind energizes and empowers.

The Rev. Dr. Lauren Artress asks, "Why does the labyrinth attract people? Because it is a tool to guide healing, deepen self-knowledge and empower creativity. Walking the labyrinth clears the mind and gives insight into the spiritual journey. It urges action. It calms people in the throes of life transitions. It helps them see their lives in the context of a path, a pilgrimage. They realize they are not human beings on a spiritual path but spiritual beings on a human path. To those of us who feel we have untapped gifts to offer, it stirs the creative fires within us. To others who are in deep sorrow, the walk gives solace and peace. The experience is different for everyone because each of us brings different raw material to the labyrinth. We bring our unique hopes, dreams, history and longings of the soul," Artress wrote in *Walking a Sacred Path*.

Thinking is not required to walk a labyrinth. But one must remain alert to stay on the path. The combination of reduced mental activity and heightened awareness creates an ideal walking companion for interactive meditation or prayer. Dancing or walking a sacred circle just for the fun of it is okay, too. A strong connection exists between labyrinths and earth energies, restoring a long-lost rapport with nature and feminine qualities. The synthesized turns of the labyrinth balance the two hemispheres of the brain, often resulting in physical and emotional healing.

Since reaching the center is assured if one completes the path, walking the labyrinth is more about the journey than the destination, about being rather than doing, integrating body and mind, psyche and spirit, emotions and presence into harmonious oneness.

Strengthened from achieving the goal (reaching the center and reconnecting to Source), the seeker is newly energized for the return trip home. The path back should neither be skipped nor shortened as it signifies completeness. This important aspect of the pilgrimage allows time to integrate the sacred adventure into the commonplace experiences of everyday life. Daily routines, career, relationships, personal health, creative energy, dreams and aspirations are part of the extraordinary spiral, higher realms or dimensions, cosmic ebullience and the sacred divine. It's not what you do, but how you do it that determines spiritual essence.

Here's where faith enters the picture in the form of silent guidance. Move with the labyrinth. Listen to its song. Feel the timeless flow. Hear unspoken messages. Dance with the rhythms undulating from the heartbeat of your soul. Heed that inner voice. Renew an inherent connection to God. Return to Source.

The labyrinth represents reversal, a symbolic change of heart. Meandering twists of whirling circuits precede a complete turnaround in the center. The turns in the path urge the walker forward as travelers change direction without impeding progress. Navigating turns moves one ahead. The central avenue doesn't end in a cul-de-sac, it spirals into a brand new path. Seekers revolve around their own internal axis to discover innate inner wisdom and the penetrating mystery of the previously trodden path.

Consider the need of the observer who longs to enter the game but believes he lacks the confidence, skill and intuition necessary to navigate the path. Beliefs can be stifling. Everyone has what it takes to play the game; some just haven't found it inside themselves yet.

Take a bold step. Walk the path of life with renewed faith. Free yourself from the shackles of ancient fears of the imagination. Utilize its wisdom. Imagination is expanded consciousness. Visualize liberated souls encircling each other in a grand embrace. Cast aside born again fears and let truth emerge.

Today's world has lost touch with its origins, roots and form and diversified its unity. The labyrinth can relocate our misplaced distant and distinct identity. That's one of the myriad reasons it touches people so deeply, often in a way they cannot articulate since the context itself is intangible.

But the big picture is always visible. Spiritual insights retain their species-specific memory, cellular tabulation, tribal and clan maturation, ancestral wisdom and celestial cosmology. Labyrinths represent man's passage through time and experience. Their paths of rebirth and renewal reflect a perspective journey of stamina, change, alteration, transition, uncertainty, happiness, discovery and achievement. The single path leading unerringly to the center confirms no time or effort is ever wasted. Those who stay on course, taking individual steps, irrespective of the number of circuits, turns, reversals, distance, will eventually reach the destined goal, the heart of the matter symbolizing wholeness and completeness.

When the labyrinth poses the formidable question, "Are you progressing forward or comfortable with the status quo?" not everyone will be ready to answer. Those who follow their heart, are naturally open to new things, relish adventure, and like to learn and share unique talents and skills will answer in the affirmative and enter the path. So will those who can relinquish prejudice and judgment, substitute an outdated point of view, and adopt fresh philosophies. Those who haven't found what they're seeking, who have more good questions than answers will also embrace the labyrinthine encounter. Anyone harboring fear or distrust will most likely choose the option they have most of their life and merely observe the process.

As an archetypal image of the transformed life, the walking meditation of a labyrinth mystically mirrors the soul. It quiets the mind and expands the heart. At birth, a seeker is invited to enter its spiraling path. Navigating twists, turns and challenges, equipped with an unquenchable desire to learn perseverance and transcend obstacles, youngsters yearn to complete the circuits and attain center stardom.

Led to the center yet veering away from it again and again, the walker advances in spite of himself or extenuating circumstances. Overcoming limitations, he continually moves ahead, one foot at a time. He faces forlorn frontiers and dubious skepticism amid the chronic feeling this lonely path leads nowhere. But this is a labyrinth with a single path circling to the center and back out again, not a disorienting maze with blind alleys, dead ends and traps. In the labyrinth of life, the center goal continues to call and is always visible.

Meeting fellow travelers on the path, occasionally joining them in shared interaction, sometimes walking alone, the pilgrim reports a sense of peace, a positive focusing effect on his meditative sojourn. Sometimes, he follows the crowd, frequently he spirals in the opposite direction. An overzealous companion may divert his attention, enticing him to abandon his dreams, or he might require a helping hand to manage a difficult curve. All experiences are part of the ebb and natural flux of universal intelligence.

Several people detail intense experiences in their rendezvous with a labyrinth, others have more subtle encounters. Some report no experience, but the act of walking a sacred circle itself is an experience. Many enter a labyrinth when they have a specific concern or question for which they are seeking guidance. The numerous results reported from walking labyrinths include insight and creative ideas, solutions to problems, relaxation and stress release, joy and happiness, centering, renewed focus and strength, reconnecting to a spiritual source, balance and improved well-being.

An extension of all who traverse it, the path periodically becomes a dance and the seeker rhythmically feels like singing. Often, he is consumed by impatience. But if he perseveres, the path opens to the center. In apparent contradiction, the central focal point is both the ultimate goal and the halfway point of the journey.

The center is a magical, amazing and wondrous place. It shelters and protects, heals and relaxes, balances and restores, offers joy and comfort, wisdom and solutions, support and nourishment, strength and rebirth. Sustaining principles manifest a renewed sense of purpose, a profound understanding linking humanity with the ultimate source of creation. Analogous with the paradise of heaven, an invigorated generation emerges. Patricia Diane Cota-Robles, of the New Age Study for Humanity's Purpose, calls this exciting new world HOME, Heaven on Mother Earth.

Such a perfect, peaceful place is hard to leave. But at some point the seeker realizes this small circle is a microcosm of a much grander site. It transcends the earthly realm. Much work remains to introduce those who co-inhabit the earth plane to this sacred space. We have to go back not only to acquaint our fellow travelers to the bliss of nirvana, but also to complete the experience. The path out of the labyrinth has an explicit designation. It grants permission to process what we have learned so we may fulfill our potential, unveiling hidden possibilities and intense insight. An uncluttered clarity restores the seeker's faith.

While interaction with a labyrinth is associated with relaxation and healing, communing with any sacred circle is merely another form of prayer. As an extension of God, we are in constant contact with the divine and can experience prayer in every moment, reflecting our spiritual essence and listening to the wisdom of our souls.

This unique labyrinth graced the back of the Cox Pavilion at the April 2008 Healthy Home & Wellness Expo on the state fairgrounds. Three spiraling circuits led walkers past statues of Moses and a Native American elder enroute to the center, where a white 5-foot replica of the Greek Goddess Venus stood guardian. Designer Gary Bessinger, of the Woodchuck Chop, crafted this magnificent sacred circle with sand, rocks, statues, plants and sliced tree trunks. To complete his majestic masterpiece, he placed a handcrafted wooden woodchuck near the entrance.

Listen to the Wisdom

There's wisdom in a tender touch,
an understanding smile,
a child bouncing on her grandfather's knee.

Listen to the serenity of the night,
the beating of a fearless heart,
a waterfall cascading tranquil thoughts
of love and gratitude.

We need to temper the pace of this hectic world;
slow down and enjoy life's simple celebrations of pleasure.
Learn the lessons nature provides.
Utilize the best qualities of mankind.

Listen to the wind blowing powerful messages
of faith, hope and strength.
Draw on the wisdom of experience
and the innocence of youth.
Listen to the wisdom of silence.

Caress the courage of compassion;
embrace the honesty of friendship.
Extend a helping hand.

Learn to speak with only a look,
feel without touch,
and hear with your heart.

The best thing you can spend on a person is time.
Share yourself and your wisdom.
The silence of wisdom,
the gift of time.

Listen to the wisdom.
Learn from the richness of spirit,
the silence of understanding,
the silence of wisdom.

— **Gail Peck**

Divine Wisdom Encircles the Soul

Any creative expression is a form of divinity that springs from inner artistic talent. Picasso masterpieces not required; only brushstrokes of love.

A back yard Wisdom Wheel Directional Labyrinth is such an embodiment of innate, inspirational illumination. And, a distinctly unique creation.

Conventional wisdom combines philosophy, scientific knowledge, understanding, education, street smarts, common sense, positive attitude, wise, practical or prudent courses of action, sound judgment, omniscience, wellness, balance, perception, foresight, intelligence.

Divine encounters allow for meditation, spiritual exercise (seeking the sacred), mystical experiences, intuitive insight and provide opportunities for heightened awareness, personal growth, astute observation, creative imagination... continuously aspiring to higher spheres of consciousness.

Intent is the primal force of esoteric essence — a part of the Creator that desires to explore and expand itself.

When we embarked on our year-long labyrinthine journey, none of the authors had plans to build a labyrinth in their back yard. Researching this book and visiting these inspiring Oklahoma circular paths leaves a powerful, definitive imprint.

So, another sacred circle was crafted in the back yard of one of the authors under a pin oak tree where grass rarely grew. The homeowner decided to better utilize the area and employ what she had learned not only on her recent Sooner State book tour, but also from the past nine years of listening to spiritual wisdom.

While a labyrinth is a sacred circle, not all sacred circles are labyrinths. Some are medicine wheels, mandalas, zen gardens, rose windows... any circular shape, emblem or symbol imparting wisdom.

The designer created a wisdom wheel — not a typical labyrinth, not a traditional medicine wheel although it can be treated as either incorporating all aspects of sacred circles... labyrinths, Native American medicine wheels, meditation gardens... any area offering healing, knowledge, truth, ancient wisdom or greater spiritual understanding.

Just as there is no right or wrong way to walk a labyrinth, there is no correct way to build one as long as the quintessential intention is maintained. We discovered 3, 5, 7, 9 and 11 circuits, a combination medicine wheel labyrinth, nylon, canvas, rectangular tile, brick and grass, mortared stone, rock and mulch, and now we have walked a directional labyrinth, dubbed a Wisdom Wheel Directional Labyrinth by its creator.

Positioned under the protective branches of a magnificent oak in the northeast corner of an Oklahoma City back yard, this unique sacred circle nuzzles fences along the east and north. A 77-foot circumference of border stone edging encompasses a 33-foot diameter with eight directional spokes of 11 porcelain tiles per path.

Paris flagstone mark entrances to cardinal points; flagstone porcelain tiles decorate the other four directional points. Carpet lies underneath the four cardinal stone entrances and a rectangular 4 x 6-foot green indoor/outdoor carpet showcases the center stones.

Forty-four stones from a Tahlequah medicine wheel built May 8, 2004, in honor of 22 national park ceremonies performed by various Native American tribes, highlight the center carpet along with rocks and stones from the 2007 Oklahoma labyrinth walks.

Elemental characters at cardinal points and symbols of ancient wisdom and divine messengers grace several center rocks corresponding with various sacred geometry shapes throughout the wisdom wheel.

An open east area leading to the pin oak is covered with leaves protecting hidden knowledge not yet ready to be revealed. This trail also leads to an ancient nature spirit community housed inside an active woodpile. The sentinel tree gathers and sustains concealed archetypal wisdom disbursing it through branches of learning over selected areas of the wisdom wheel when walkers, spiritual seekers or those meditating are ready to assimilate, absorb or receive nourishment.

The southwest spoke leads to a white, 33-inch statue of St. Francis (the patron saint of animals) and only has nine tiles after the flagstone for a total of 10, not 11. Nine is the number for completion, healing and understanding and 10 represents spiritual aspects. One is unity and new beginnings, uniqueness and Creation which is the path One follows to an Ascended Master (like St. Francis) who emanates spiritual knowledge and wisdom.

Tiles on the "ascension" path are also different colors than the Bottichino Gold coloring of the other 77 porcelain tiles. This spoke represents truth and dancing to the beat of a diverse drummer. Five of the nine tiles are white, one is Glacier Bay Arctic Blue, another Cleopatra Mediterranean, and two are quarry stone (sand and slate).

All four paths denoting non-cardinal directions (northeast, northwest, southeast, southwest) have space between each tile and are accessed from inside the circle. These pathways represent free-flowing movement between each step as opposed to the continuous tile placement on the four cardinal paths (north, south, east and west).

That's probably symbolic of something, just not sure what.

Eight sapling branches used in Oklahoma Holistic Health Fair medicine wheels outline the rectangular carpet (two each along top and bottom and four across the center stones simulating spokes).

The approximate 12 x 12-foot center of the Wisdom Wheel embraces the pin oak tree (located in the southeast quadrant) and includes five tree stumps rolled down the street that summer from the opposite end of a city block. St. Francis stands adjacent to the clump of tree stumps protecting woodpile entrances to several nature spirit abodes.

In December of 2007, the festive woodpile was decorated with Christmas tree branches, green, red, silver and gold garland, four rosemary bushes, 18 golden pinecones, a big red bow and two lantern candles.

Woodpiles represent preparation, protection, warmth, community, family, joy, fun, love of nature. Peeking from under cedar tree clippings, a purple and white orb with undulating swirls signifies cleansing world negativity, the return of planetary spirituality and Cosmic Christ Consciousness.

Native Americans consider the fragrant cedar a potent symbol for healing, cleansing and protection while rosemary is associated with power, clarity and sensitivity.

A small blue swimming pool filled with pine mulch sits to the east of the woodpile and has an 18-inch yellow-gold St. Francis statue encircled with poinsettias and holly.

Blue corresponds to happiness, calm, truth, communication and peace. Yellow/gold equals information, optimism, inspiration, knowledge and mental activity.

Four wind twisters (aligned in a diamond pattern) add color and movement and suggest that, perhaps, the answer is blowing in the wind just like the title of the popular Peter, Paul and Mary song. These mesmerizing, iridescent spirals connect with other items adorning cascading tree branches to highlight the distinctive pyramidal form for which the pin oak is known.

Another creation of this author, a Fancy Feng Shui Reflector, rotates in the center of this sacred circle shimmering amid a colorful back yard landscape, reminding humans of their unique reflections.

Unlike traditional labyrinths, a Wisdom Wheel Directional Labyrinth offers choices on traversing its tile pathways. Freedom of movement is prima facie.

Walkers can enter at the south or west and circumnavigate the wisdom wheel ducking around an evergreen overhang at the northeast spoke. Two purple and gold carpet kneeling pads face the center and anchor the ending points of the west and south trails.

Each path can be walked to the center and is connected via a cypress mulch outer rim. Cannot enter or leave from the north or east as a fence borders those sides.

The inner ring of mulch around the perimeter of the stone edge border circle invites traveling any of the eight directional paths of the wisdom wheel depending on what issue requires dissection or steps need identifying to achieve the center goal.

Complete range of motion is attainable as one can walk any direction, backward, forward, around, diagonal, across.

Enter at the south cardinal point to seek fire, purification, the universal mind of collective knowledge or on the west to test emotional waters, renew the spirit within, intensify dreams.

South honors creative intelligence, divine energy, passion, imagination, faith, hope, strength, awakening the inner child, overcoming obstacles, playfulness, change, protection, self-sufficiency, trust, resurrection.

West represents vision, quests, journeys, goals, imagination, creative arts, higher compassion, clearing emotional instability, enhancing intuition and fishing successfully in deep waters.

New beginnings, communication, strength of will, sunshine, birth, illumination, learning, healing and creativity are characteristics of the East.

North teaches abundance, balance, sacred wisdom, knowledge, gentleness, gratitude, forgiveness, development of inner talents, identifying hidden treasures, intuition, trust and alchemy.

To journey through the center from west to east or vice

versa, step or stand on the center tile inside the altar. The wood-pile prohibits passage from north to south.

One can walk to the woodpile on the south side, around the center to another directional path or back to the outer ring via the south path and proceed around the perimeter of the sacred circle to access the opposite north directional path, or any of the eight paths.

An inter-connected center can also be walked via a surround-ing ring of cypress mulch. Cypress helps us understand the role of sacrifice. Exchange the negative meaning of the word from loss, deprivation or offering of death to a positive view of sacri-fice as simply exchanging one thing for another. Nothing need be "given up."

On first glance, it might seem as if one's goals are unob-tainable since the center is easily reached, but apparently inac-cessible. Remember, things are not always what they seem and appearances can be deceiving. A unique concept often provides a different perspective and an applicable solution.

The wisdom wheel's center can be approached on any of eight directional paths. Sitting or standing in the center of this labyrinth does not meet with the traditional. But that's the point. Consider the alternative.

Sitting and standing space is around the perimeter of the center, not directly inside. Only one person at a time can stand on the center tile, which means answers are between you and the Divine Creator (or whatever you choose to call God).

Extrinsic environmental factors make the center of this sacred circle unusual. Consideration of deeper meanings often suggest objectives are not always reached by employing physical meth-ods or continually starting over. All resources and talents must be utilized.

Spiritual essences are essential and as fundamental as the way humans translate matter into spirit. The world's collective consciousness demands a higher degree of intelligence. Spiri-tual, holistic or divine radiance beckons us to travel its illumi-nated path whispering phrases of joy to those who dare pass.

Today's millennium energy encourages humans to transcend limiting beliefs and explore infinite possibilities — to experience the infinity of our divinity.

It's time to BLEND:

B alance your body
L ighten your spirit
E xpand your mind
N ourish your soul
D ivine your essence

Time to apply what we have learned and realize the answer may lie in simply placing squares within a circle, not squaring the circle as medieval architects unsuccessfully attempted in their sacred geometry designs.

All path tiles inside this back yard dirt, grass, mulch and porcelain labyrinth are square. The flagstone tiles marking non-cardinal points are positioned in a diamond shape with points aligned with the center.

Spirals, triangles, pyramids, hexagons, octagons, polygons, ellipses, circles and some of their solid plane figure counterparts (octahedron, hexahedron, polyhedron, tetrahedron) have intuitively been incorporated into the design of this Wisdom Wheel Directional Labyrinth.

Sacred geometry enhances how we connect to the divine through certain shapes, points and sites and provides a more in-depth relationship with heavenly forms. Humanity serves as the temple between heaven and earth, God and man, purpose and creation, experience and completeness... the beauty of harmonic expression.

This holy combination divines mass consciousness into a cerebral, corporal and celestial (mind, body, spirit) nexus shaping a premiere formless substance into creative genus.

Individuals may attach variant symbolic meaning to the aforementioned. Just as beauty is in the eye of the beholder, significance is in the mind of the interpreter. Take whatever resonates and leave the remainder for someone else's heart.

This craftsman would have used different, perhaps more uniform, specs if not considering existing natural elements (tree, woodpile and nature spirit community). Figured that was more important than symmetry.

The moral of this story (or wisdom from this sacred circle): "Use whatever area available and let it dictate perimeters. Okay if not perfect — neither are humans." Until we learn to combine heaven and earth inside our divine essence.

Numbers Convey Important Characteristics

The relevance of numbers has been analyzed throughout time. Mathematicians theorize these numeric symbols bring order to an otherwise chaotic world.

Numerology studies the significance of numbers. Below are commonly accepted meanings of single digits.

1 = beginnings, originality, leader, unity
2 = feminine, dreams, cooperation, joyful relationships
3 = creativity, birth, mystical, communication
4 = foundation, patience, master builder
5 = versatile, change, activity, freedom
6 = home, service, family
7 = wisdom, seeker, truth
8 = power, money, infinity
9 = healing, understanding, completion

Master numbers occur when a digit repeats itself. These numbers embody special messages, inherent mastery, supreme thought and extraordinary promise.

11 = transformation of the physical into the divine,
      matter into spirit
22 = power to transcend all planes; ability to change the
      course of history
33 = Christ Consciousness, Holy Trinity, universal service
44 = harmonious balance leads to enhanced consciousness;
      inner wisdom
55 = blends individual strengths with higher will;
      turns innovation into invention
66 = mixes responsibility with joyful creativity;
      alleviates suffering; inspirational manifestation
77 = profound insights; advanced philosophy; creative thought;
      no limits
88 = mastery of abundance, wholeness, divine knowing;
      application of universal laws
99 = an evolutionary cycle of self-awareness; unconditional
      love shatters illusions

Colors Offer Unique Perspective

A phenomenon of light or visual perception, colors add distinction, variety and beauty to the planetary spectrum. Individual hues suggest special characteristics.
Color is an expansive expression of dynamic energy, providing an elemental metamorphosis.
The following colors and their symbolic qualities are represented in the Wisdom Wheel Directional Labyrinth.

Black — protection, birth, magic, depth, absorbing, informative
Blue — happiness, calm, truth, communication, peace
Brown — grounded, new growth, wisdom, balance, ancestors, family, nourishing, productive
Cream/Ivory — hope, simple truth, inspirational insight
Gray — initiation, imagination, forgiveness, stability
Green — growth, healing, abundance, associated with nature
Iris — higher inspiration, psyche purity, therapeutic, innocence
Kaleidoscopic Refractions — artistic, festive, adventurous, flashy, evolutionary transcendence, exciting cornucopia of electrifying images
Lilac — subtle, compassionate, idealistic, inner peace
Mirror Reflections — exotic movement, ancestral wisdom, artistic intelligence, opens dimensional doorways, shimmering illusion, soulful expression
Orange — energy, warmth, joy, creativity, self-reliant
Peacock — resurrection, wise vision, heightened watchfulness, protection, power, tantalizing
Pink — unconditional love, acceptance, understanding, sincerity, harmony, gracious appreciation
Rainbow Swirls — entertaining, iridescent exuberance, fearless, sparkling emotions, idealistic dreamer, eclectic explorer
Red — passion, strength, courage, enthusiasm
Sand — continuous, tranquility, harmonious, quiet strength, persistence
Silver — revealing, open-minded, expressive, regenerative
Violet/Purple — alchemy, humility, spirituality, esoteric knowledge, royalty, grateful expression
White — purity, sharing, truth, unity, angelic, soothing, Christ-consciousness
Yellow/Gold — information, optimism, inspiration, knowledge, mental activity

Trees Symbolize a Strong Support System Honoring Their Creator

Gracefully dancing to the enchanted music of another of nature's elements (the wind), majestic trees bow to humans and other Standing People by waving their bountiful branches and sheltering leaves as their strong trunks reach towards the sky.

The Wisdom Wheel Directional Labyrinth was a natural fit to encompass such a powerful and ancient symbol linking heaven and earth.

Trees represent knowledge, fertility, growth, expansion, endurance. A symbol of life itself... the tree of life branching into completeness... a grounded connection to primal force.

Oak trees denote strength of character, sustained endurance, helpfulness, continuity, nourishment, protection, preparation, return of ancient wisdom.

Pin oaks signify clarity, pinpoint accuracy, balance, strong foundation, passionate detachment, stability, purity, efficiency, focused intent, connection to source, wise use of available resources.

The bark of the pin oak remains smooth for many years, but eventually develops ridges and furrows — just like humans.

Freedom of movement allows God's children to flourish and reap the benefits of laughter, joyful labor, insightful creativity and divine inspiration. Trees provide such an unrestrained force of enlightenment, and a perfect umbrella for a back yard wisdom wheel.

While creating her sacred circle, the author remembered an essay she wrote five years ago in January 2002 that honored these magnificent creatures. She would like to share it with you. Ironically, it was written prior to a significant Oklahoma ice storm. At this writing, the Sooner State surpassed that treacherous winter attack experiencing the worst ice storm in Oklahoma history.

An estimated million trees were lost or damaged. Hugh piles of downed tree branches lined streets statewide. The ice-laden branches of the pin oak, sheltering the just-completed Wisdom Wheel Directional Labyrinth, froze to the ground.

When the ice melted a few days later, they all snapped back to their pre-storm positions and the porcelain spokes of the wisdom wheel glistened in the snow radiating a divine luminescence.

Tree Homework Assignment
Embraces Talkative Specimen

While walking at the park Monday thinking about the Bible verse that says "even the birds of the air are provided for, are you not less than these," equated that with faith and wondered if this was part of the Law Moses discovered.

Stumbled across an enormous, beautiful elm and remembered our "homework assignment" to talk to a tree this week. So, laid down facing this delightful specimen and here is what transpired:

* The artistic covering of the tree symbolizes structure, form, order, beauty. It provides a strong foundation reaching for the stars, gets nourishment from the earth (grounding) and sustainable energy from the sun or light, brightness, illumination, enlightenment (as above, so below).

* Standing people symbolize our connection to heaven and earth (thought and matter).

* Trunk signifies one, same source, inner relations, and branches are different paths to take on our earthly journey, but are still connected to the source, oneness or Mother Earth.

* The bark protects or surrounds a tree's inner spirit like our skin projects the human soul and insides. Tree rings are circular when cut, (die, evolve, transcend) showing no beginning or end. Life is continuous, all-encompassing, perfect, complete, unified. A circle also means origin, birth of creation, simplicity, integrity, equality.

* Roots are interconnected just like all life above the earth plane, intertwining the basic truths of strength, character, sacred embodiment, appreciation, harmony, balance, gratitude and grace in a peaceful, holistic journey of mystical sharing and self-discovery.

* Humans need to learn to better utilize seasonal energy to replenish the soul. Shed what is no longer necessary (leaves) in winter because we can't sustain them and require our energy elsewhere. (Clear cobwebs of dormant thought.) Apply talents, skills wisely, resting or planning in winter for rebirth in spring-time of fresh growth (sowing or planting seeds for new projects, abundance, manifestation). The beauty of nature blossoms in

summer as it nurtures the seeds of growth; crisp spring ideas leaf out to maturity. Autumn teaches us to enjoy vast colors of diversity and savor the harvest of plenty, enjoying the fruits of our labors, storing our sap (life force or chi) for the coming winter and another cycle of life.

*   *   *

Went back to visit my tree friend after the ice storm. Was sad to see all the downed limbs at the park and around town. The Majestic One had lost a large branch, but said it was okay. "Do not mourn our loss as we help sustain other life with our death and are happy to perpetuate the enduring cycle of life. We add humus to the soil and enrich the ecosystem and substrata, flora and fauna through our passing. We live on through others and transfer our species-specific knowledge. Like the many parts of humans, we, too, inhabit the body of another. We are all multi-dimensional, transcendent beings."

*Above photo and opposite page: Wisdom Wheel Directional Labyrinth
Private Back Yard, Oklahoma City*

Symbolic Attributes of Trees

Temples of wisdom, trees offer more than protective covering, shelter, shade, building materials and food. They connect heaven and earth, represent growth and power, communicate knowledge and encompass totality. Different specimens convey certain individual qualities that can assist humans achieve higher planes of consciousness, overcoming the wilderness of the unconscious.

Apple - youth, beauty, happiness, discriminating knowledge, paradise.

Ash - sacrifice, sensitivity, higher wisdom.

Aspen - determination, transcending doubts and fears, acceptance of change.

Bamboo - resilience, longevity, happiness, spiritual truth, devotion.

Beech - tolerance, application of knowledge and experience, releases judgment.

Birch - new beginnings, cleansing, vision quests, deflects negativity.

Cedar - power, immortality, longevity, healing, cleansing, protection.

Cherry - new awakenings, death and rebirth, truth.

Cypress - death and mourning, longevity, endurance, understanding role of sacrifice.

Dogwood - tenacious, loyal, vigilant guardian, faithful, sentimental, resourceful, compassionate.

Elder - birth and death, renewal of imagination, spiritual parenting.

Elm - strength of will, intuition, acknowledgment of the unknown.

Fig - moral teaching, immortality, tree beneath which Buddha received spiritual enlightenment.

Hawthorn - creativity, fertility, alchemy, heart-centered emotion.

Hazel - divination, wisdom, fertility, rain, seeking hidden treasure.

Heather - healing from within, immortality, initiation, colorful insight.

Holly - protection, overcoming anger, hope, joy, spiritual warrior, festive.

Honeysuckle - learning from the past, discrimination, change, heightened awareness.

Lilac - realization of true beauty, etheric growth, elevated sensitivity.

Magnolia - idealistic, pleasant, fulfilling, blossoming to fragrant prosperity and completeness, successful.

Maple - balance, practical expression, promise, cooperative endeavors.

Oak - nobility, strength of character, sustained endurance, helpfulness, continuity, nourishment, protection, preparation, return of ancient wisdom.

Olive - peace, concord, wisdom, victory, joy, plenty, purity, immortality, virginity, friendship, success, calmness.

Orange - emotional clarity, trauma release, fruitful abundance, passionate.

Palm - protection, peace, opportunity, victory, overcoming challenges, resurrection.

Peach - longevity, spring, youth, marriage, fortuitous, artistic truth.

Pine - courage, resolution, good luck, creativity, balance, everlasting.

Redbud - hardy, dependable, friendly, resilient; state tree of Oklahoma.

Reed - emotional cleansing, melodious, creative communication, enchantment.

Spruce - healing, intuition, new realizations, organization, fresh appearance.

Sycamore - communication, love, learning to receive, focused contemplation.

Thistle - regeneration, expert analysis, competence, enhanced concentration.

Walnut - eases transition, follows a unique path, durable, nourishes the seed within, hidden knowledge revealed.

Willow - lunar and feminine symbol, patience, strength in flexibility, healing, inner vision and dreams, fascination, charming, graceful.

Chapter 2
Use of Sacred Space

Hear the Voice of Oneness

People use labyrinths to connect to that divine space within themselves and for esoteric communion. Such a spiritual nexus provides exalted union with our Heavenly Creator and allows lofty aspirations to rise above mundane existentialism.

Sacred sites offer a path of transformation revealing humanity's purpose and extending renewed strength, abundant life, increased stamina, advanced health and enhanced understanding.

Those who linger too long in indecision often fail to make a choice or commitment. Stagnation makes it for them. But those who walk with joy and curiosity reap psychological and personal rewards uncovering the intriguing mysteries of imagination, clarity, perfection, beauty, harmony and wisdom.

Hidden only by perception and illusion, these simple and natural characteristics transcend limitation inspiring those who embrace a sacred path.

Growth in individual labyrinth use has also sparked special interest with various groups employing them for rituals, seasonal celebrations, rites of passage, forgiveness, problem-solving, healthcare seminars, drug and alcohol counseling, anger management, artistic expression, youth dialogue and community events.

Prisons, jails and youth detention centers are utilizing labyrinths to encourage discussion between counselors and inmates and to provide spiritual nourishment to incarcerated individuals.

Schools report children who walk labyrinths are more relaxed, less angry and frustrated and gain insights for solving problems. Some children also receive relief from grief and emotional trauma.

These sacred symbols are appearing in America, Europe, Asia, Australia, New Zealand and Scandinavia in public squares, parks, churches, hospitals, retreat centers, wilderness areas, private gardens, schools, prisons and drug treatment centers as tools for healing, meditation, prayer, therapy, rehabilitation and self-reflection.

Social workers, counselors and therapists use them to open dialogue with clients and expose problems related to abuse and anti-social behavior. Hospitals utilize them for cancer treatment and palliative care as a way for staff and patients to relieve stress.

Art and personal development programs benefit from labyrinths as platforms for dance and theater and instruments for artistic expression. They make excellent stages for bringing people together as a vehicle for spirituality and meditation, creative play and connecting man with the mysteries of nature.

Dowsers and nature lovers employ this power symbol for the cosmos and ancient earth goddesses to identify vital streams of energy contained within the earth for divination, healing and eco-spirituality.

A county jail chaplain who conducts regular labyrinth walks with inmates met a young man who was suspicious of this strange-looking device. "What's this... What'll it do for me? Why should I play this game?" his angry demeanor demanded.

Revolving jail cells had been frequent companions during turbulent teenage years. He blamed others for repeated arrests. Deciding to give the labyrinth a try, he goose-stepped around the paths, missed the center and prematurely finished the unicursal journey — an accurate statement of his life so far.

"What's wrong with this thing? It spit me out!" he complained. The chaplain gently urged him to try again. This time, he reached the center and sobbed uncontrollably for 10 minutes. When he regained his composure, he approached the chaplain. "Help me," he pleaded, "I don't want to spend the rest of my life in jail."

Labyrinths are a source of transformative knowledge where people can encounter their spiritual essence, find deeper meaning, receive healing, cleansing and answers for dealing with a chaotic and violent world. A meeting place between heaven and earth where the soul can ascend on an inner reflective journey that often provides permanent change.

An interfaith minister in New Canaan, Connecticut, uses a 3-circuit labyrinth of her own design to conduct weddings. Bride and groom are each blessed and wished well by their families before they separately enter and walk the path to the center. Here, they take their vows and emerge from the labyrinth as a couple.

"The symbolism of walking the labyrinth (representing the path of life) first by themselves and then as a couple is very moving," the minister said. "The labyrinth also furnishes a spiritual container for the ceremony that seems to add a deeper sense of meaning to the event."

Labyrinths are frequently visited for other rites of passage including christenings and naming ceremonies, anniversaries and rituals associated with mourning or commemoration.

Several hospitals in the United States have built labyrinths on their grounds, not just for patients but to help staff deal with the pressures of working in a busy medical environment. Some are contained within their own meditation gardens to offer a sense of enclosure and create a peaceful, sacred atmosphere.

Nurses, doctors and paramedics walk these paths in times of stress and when emotions run high from overwork or grueling encounters with tragedy. Cancer patients and those about to undergo surgery also find the labyrinth a way to keep calm and composed and to better deal with their health crisis. Many patients report rapid rates of recovery which they attribute to the benefits of walking the labyrinth.

Ambulance paramedics sometimes stroll the circuits to deal with distress after attending serious accidents. They say the labyrinth helps them release grief and despair and to find a place of renewal. The pathway is good for healing because its three stages of release, opening and integration are the same three stages humans travel in any healing journey.

The labyrinth connects with our innate, inner healing potential. "Educating doctors and nurses about the labyrinth is essential if the increasing number of pathways within hospitals are to be handled efficiently," one healthcare worker stated, adding that labyrinths are also advantageous in treating addictions and abuse. "Counselors use the device to facilitate discussions about emotional issues which lead to abuse or addiction. The labyrinth can be an informative tool for getting to the bottom of drug problems or psychological abuse."

A calming or healing effect is reported when labyrinths are used in palliative care and in hospices for the dying. It helps those struggling with serious illnesses find peace and make important decisions concerning treatment and personal matters.

One terminally ill gentleman occasionally walked a Canadian labyrinth a few months before his death. He talked of discovering, in its turns, a metaphor for the issues he felt he needed to resolve with friends and family before he died. The elderly man told his children about "the amazing path" he had walked and how it helped him acknowledge and "put right" matters between him and them.

His family said it completely transformed the last months of his life and at his funeral, mourners were given pictures of a labyrinth in honor of the peace he found among its twists and turns.

A universal symbol supporting unity, the labyrinth was crafted in ancient times to represent humankind's search for the core of divinity. Its inward spirals to the center harness powers for personal transformation, protection, healing, enlightenment, nourishment, fertility, confronting and resolving conflict, honoring grief or loss and celebrating new beginnings.

The Scottish Rite Masonic Center in Guthrie shares this philosophy hosting an annual private fellowship for members to use the labyrinth as a spiritual tool for prayer, meditation, contemplation or personal growth. The form of the labyrinth is circular because the circle is a universal symbol of unity and wholeness and is an important image of the sacred, said Rosicrucian Robert Davis, executive secretary of the Scottish Rite Masonic Bodies in Oklahoma.

He further explained the Masonic ceremony. "The journey begins by dimming the lights and conducting a blessing where participants are reminded they are at an important time of inner growth; at a crucible for change. By surrendering to their inner nature, an attentive ear can begin to hear the instructive tongue resonating from the divine voice of their soul. There is a pause of silence to consider what must be done to regain balance in life. Then, to facilitate an image of balance, a ritual is performed with those in attendance blessing each other with water and its purifying and cleansing power. It is the blessing of balance between giving and receiving. The ceremony ends in a prayer to the Supreme Architect of the Universe requesting that Divine Light and Love fill the pathways of the labyrinth.

"The exercise of walking the labyrinth yields for each participant a different experience because everyone relates on their own terms. There is no required way to walk the labyrinth, but the journey has four distinct stages. Releasing thoughts, shedding distractions and letting go of the details of life is done on the walk toward the center, where one stays as long as he likes. It is a place of meditation and prayer and receiving what is there to accept. It offers inner beauty, peace and illumination. The journey outward follows the same path and permits consideration of what occurred in the center and how it may be applied. This is significant because the last stage of the labyrinth is our life outside of it; the world where illumination is carried into everyday existence. Each time one walks the labyrinth, he becomes more empowered to find and accomplish the work his soul yearns for him to perform," Davis concluded.

Beneficial tools for spiritual enlightenment, these ancient symbols present a luminous guide to meditation, intuition and creation, causing Rev. Lauren Artress, of San Francisco's Grace Cathedral, to call it a "blueprint for healing."

Judy Butler and Matt Carder decided to seek answers to their pending union and a joint project at the outdoor labyrinth at Sparrow Hawk Village in Tahlequah. They know these revered circles support the sacred marriage of the masculine and feminine: the womblike center is built around the male symbol of a cross located near the entrance to this 7-circuit classical replica merging earth energies of the Mother with Father Sky forces.

Judy said she and Matt began their walk with the intent of balancing and integrating joint essences to work together for a higher cause and purpose, as a male and female. "Our experience of the labyrinth is that it balances positive and negative forces, which can be translated into male and female. We desired to be open vessels for any information which might surface for our highest good and that of our project," Matt added.

The project is energetic and includes a series of books called *The Diamond Series*, Judy explained. "These books will detail new spiritual wisdom and esoteric teachings for humanity with the goal of providing loving guidance for all races and creeds as we create a wondrous future," the spiritual counselor stated. "This will be accomplished in great part through a collective meditation using 'One Thought' of love, gratitude and unity.

"As we got closer to the center, we perceived the multitudinous gathering of spiritual beings on our behalf. Because I am a transceiver for information from spirit, a message was given about our union together," Judy said. "We were told this union was birthing forth a project to assist humanity into a higher consciousness level, through the books we would write. There was much symbology in the message about our representing male and female in a larger way."

Matt said they welcomed the information and felt uplifted by the message they received. "We sensed an energetic heart created around us, to unify our love for each other and the project. This labyrinth is established on spiritual land known for its vortexes of energy. Our walk supported that," he said, encouraging anyone who feels out of balance to travel to Sparrow Hawk to regain equilibrium. "You can never go wrong in a beautiful place of nature, and this labyrinth supports that as well as opportunity for inner growth."

A walking labyrinth meditation induces an altered state of awareness and often cuts through conscious blocks that can prevent wise decisions. Any sacred space creates a window to another world allowing us to see deep within ourselves, clearing gateways of distortion as we stand inside a crystalline vortex of sacred power.

By honoring the feminine, we achieve compassionate stability, universal wisdom and the capacity to respect feelings and thoughts with benevolent guidance to internalize physically, transcend mentally, integrate emotionally and comprehend spiritually the incredible facilities of the mind and inspired images of the soul.

Humans are multi-dimensional aspects of eternity, interconnecting cells that comprise the universe, tapping into the heart of creative love, walking a unicursal pathway to divinity, fulfilling the excitement of sensuality, entering doorways to higher levels of awareness, accessing spiritual dimensions inside sacred circles of rebirth.

Photo by Ken Crowder

Inspired Forgiveness Labyrinth Ceremony

7 Hawks Publishing Company sponsors an annual Inspired Forgiveness Labyrinth Walk on the Sunday closest to the 9-11 anniversary. Held at a different Oklahoma labyrinth each year, the event commemorates a nation coming together and the love and compassion that was shared following the September 2001 terrorist attacks.

It also focuses on forgiveness.

"If we can forgive something like that, we can forgive anything," one person said who has attended all four of the annual commemorative walks.

Participants write items they would like to forgive — both individually and collectively — on symbolic art designs and meditate on forgiveness as they walk the unicursal paths of the labyrinth.

Prayer work and discussions are exchanged in the center of the sacred circle and the negative attributes are "forgiven and released." People then write positive traits they would like to experience on their colorful art pads and take them back into the world on the trip out of the labyrinth.

The 2007 walk was held at the only public labyrinth in Oklahoma created as a 9-11 memorial to help with the grieving process, provide peace, solace and comfort and remember loved ones.

Located in Norman's Reaves Park, the 65-foot Prairie Peace Path Labyrinth Sculpture was built May 18, 2002. A sign at the entrance path describes the labyrinth as "a walking memorial to honor the people who died on September 11, 2001. Through the inner quiet of contemplative walking, may we find peaceful solutions to our personal and planetary problems."

That year's event also featured a master number group walk around the 7-circuit rock and gravel artistic creation.

Master numbers occur when a digit replicates. September 9th (9-9) represents duplicate 9s which symbolize healing, completion and understanding. The year 2007 when added together (2 + 0 + 0 + 7) also equals nine.

Inspired Forgiveness Labyrinth Walks are held at 6 p.m. as six characterizes home, service and family. And, more specifically, service to humanity.

Eight people, including three children, gathered at the Prairie Peace Path amid cloudy weather. We repeated the initial dedication act from May 2002 and wrote messages on ribbons, walked the labyrinth holding them and then tied the green and yellow ribbons with multi-colored yarn to branches of the Chinese pistache tree gracing the center of the labyrinth.

We also hung a Fancy Feng Shui Reflector (two computer disks glued together with string, yarn or wire threaded through the center holes). It had been programmed for forgiveness, unity, inspiration and unconditional love.

Don't tell anyone we had to stand on an overturned trash can to reach the leafy branches. Of course, we put it back.

The authors decided to shift directions in honor of new incoming energies and forego writing the usual "forgiveness" features on their specially-shaped art papers. Only positive characteristics were written this year.

"Planetary Acceptance," "Peace" and "Blessings to Our Nation's Leaders" was boldly penned on red, white, blue and green maps of the United States.

Blue and green global designs admonished "Light, Joy, Love, Peace," "Blessings to All Beings Who Dwell Under the Sun (Son)" and "Holy Water + Love = Unified Earth."

"Spiritual Awareness" and "Blessings to All Nations" anointed tan and brown face outlines.

Dolphins proclaimed "Peace and Goodwill to All People" and "Intuition and Awareness Create Inspired Forgiveness."

Yellow stars shined "Universal Blessings" and "May All Dreams Come True."

A red apple and yellow pencil suggested "Wisdom + Understanding = Ascension," and "Learn, Grow, Prosper."

Ribbons flapping in the Norman breeze remind readers to honor "Inspired Forgiveness," "Blessings to Mother Earth & All Her Creatures," "Health and Abundance," "May All People Learn the Lessons of Peace," "Loving Family Relationships," "Friendship," "Love is True Creation," "Master Number Walk 9-9, 2007," and "Peace, Freedom, Acceptance."

Hugs and a group prayer encircling the tree holding hands in the center ended the fourth annual Inspired Forgiveness Labyrinth Ceremony.

The previous three September 11 commemorative walks were held in Oklahoma City, Piedmont and Edmond.

Seven people joined at a 7-circuit private Cretan labyrinth in 2006. The annual forgiveness ceremony was enhanced by drumming as we walked a majestic rock and grass labyrinth in the private back yard of an Edmond couple.

Only two people met in 2005 at the 11-circuit Chartres replica at Red Plains Monastery in Piedmont. A cleansing rain preceded the event casting iridescent hues on nearby foliage. Pristine water droplets glistened underfoot as we clutched our colorful dolphins, apples, United States maps, global prints, stars and face outlines inscribed with joy, gratitude and forgiveness sentiments.

The initial Inspired Forgiveness Labyrinth Walk was held in an open field with the traveling nylon 11-circuit Chartres from Our Lady of Mercy Retreat Center in Oklahoma City. Sister Betty warned us when we borrowed the labyrinth that the parachute material "is a little flighty and has to be weighed down when used outside in Oklahoma."

A stiff breeze is not the only consideration when traversing the paths of this 30-foot sacred circle. Gold stalks of wheat divide narrow white circuits allowing little elbow room for the 11 people who participated in 2004 to walk without engaging fellow travelers.

One astute lady noted, "It's challenging to walk the path of forgiveness."

Solitary Summer Solstice Walk

Friendly, breath-taking, picturesque, magnificent — any number of adjectives applies to this spacious wooded acreage featuring a private 7-circuit Cretan rock and grass labyrinth. It beckoned one of the authors to spend an enjoyable solitary summer solstice walk surrounded by peaceful nature trails, lush greenery and numerous flower beds frequently visited by hummingbirds, cardinals, blue jays, guineas, rabbits, squirrels, butterflies... all are welcome. The owners are gracious hosts.

Circular, aggregate stepping stones decorate the path from the house. A colorful, rectangular flowerbed greets visitors as they approach the sacred symbol. Periwinkles nod their approval; pine and cedar trees wave in the gentle breeze.

Two pots of geraniums smile at the entrance stone. A cow skull hangs on an equipment shed signifying wisdom and nourishment. Two wooden benches sit under a nearby tree, which partially shades a few of the outer paths. Happiness, healing, renewed joy, balance and cleansing mark the grass walking paths.

Three robins splash in the clear water of a stucco bird bath.

Splendid and serene. All is well in this corner of Planet Earth.

Rain earlier in the day deferred to a full rainbow arch as clouds cleared quickly. The rain-freshened air, cool breeze and overcast sky yielded pristine conditions for an outdoor vision quest.

Small mushrooms adorned several paths and the surrounding area. The ground was softer than usual due to an extremely wet Oklahoma spring. Saturated with rain, humanity's collective conscious was bathed in tender moisture.

Rain cleansed and purified, the new solstice energy was ready to blossom. Perfect evening, perfect setting to talk to God. That's exactly what happened.

Sitting in the center of the labyrinth in reflective prayer, this message was spoken: "Reconnect to Source. Humans are disconnected — floundering around in discontent. I have always been here and always will. It is you who chose the artificial. I did not abandon anyone. Especially in their greatest time of need. They just did not listen or feel worthy of my assistance. This solstice energy combined with the 7-17-07 Fire the Grid opportunity will alleviate that, freely clearing all channels for open communication. It is important to honor these energy shifts and be aware of their positive impact and how it can lessen negative influences.

"Walking labyrinth meditations are great to generate ideas, provide guidance, offer protection, solve problems, overcome fears and return to abundance. They are universal symbols of sacred geometry teaching how spirit integrates into matter.

"Labyrinths are a living, breathing entity just like you, God and Mother Earth. We are a culmination of art, cultural mores, religion, imagination, creation, manifestation, healing, science, astronomy, and combine all the universal laws.

"We represent your subconscious channels. We are neither here nor there. We are everywhere, in everything and everyone.

"The labyrinth of the mind has only one answer: TRUTH. The same path gets you in and out, there and back, hither and yon.

"Truth will get you anywhere you want to go. That's why labyrinths are liberating, refreshing, enlightening, releasing, receiving, calming... offering stillness, peace, true freedom.

"The first labyrinth was created in the mind of Universal Mind, formless substance, the ethers. WE = With(in) Energy. We scatter thoughts and solutions around the ethers not knowing who or where it will originate. Our job is just to give the impetus (opportunity) to create. Your job is to act on your thoughts and manifest your heart's desires. Will you or won't you?

"Look around. What do you see?"

Two playful squirrels chased each other around a tree, peeking out from alternate sides of the trunk. The name of the game is enjoyment.

A distant crow caws; three landed in a tree to the north and east. An ant hill in fourth path, five guineas and a rabbit eating together several yards to the south. Why can't different species of people do that?

One guinea walked east leaving its buddies feasting; they followed shortly. Leadership and teamwork promoting social skills and communication. The cute little furry creatures are symbols of productivity, abundance and overcoming fear. Ants are industrious, work as a team and fourth path signifies solid foundation.

The crow said, "There is no right or wrong answer, there are only answers — just like in a labyrinth. Multiple paths, many solutions and numerous ways to navigate life's journey. The labyrinth astutely says our destination is the same — finding our center (reaching our goals) one step at a time. Travel at your own pace, enjoy the trip, no matter where it meanders, twists or turns, spiraling to the center. There is only one way to the center and that's with divine, creative experiences. The center is the Source."

Pine cones cover the outer ring cushioning the walking path, and partially hiding some of the rocks. Hidden treasure to be discovered.

"Continue to look around. What else do you see? What message does this sacred circle speak?"

There's beauty everywhere, even in the smallest blade of grass.

Several hummingbirds were barely distinguishable as they flitted from flower to flower, with a single purpose and rapt attention. Quick and flexible, these tiny birds can fly backwards, change direction at a moment's notice, but stay centered on their task. Joyful, adaptable, versatile, focused, and exquisitely beautiful, the magic of the hummingbird can help open our minds and hearts as we fly to great heights.

Between the six and seventh path, a quartz crystal glistened. Six is the number of service to humanity and seven denotes truth and seeking spiritual answers. The only crystal stone in the whole labyrinth said, "I am unique, just like you. Only you can express your ideas, thoughts and feelings. Everyone is part of the whole, but still individual cells comprising that wholeness. What we do as individuals, we also do to the whole. When you hug a friend, you embrace all of humanity, accepting its flaws and talents just as they are."

A small brown stone remarked, "I may look ordinary and out of place, but I, too, belong to the collective and am just as powerful as the larger labyrinth stones in my little circle of the world. I intend to do my part to help enrich this circle of life. How 'bout you?"

Problem-solving
Individually and Collectively

Walking the path of a labyrinth provides opportunities to enhance problem-solving abilities and utilize intuitive insights while exploring various perspectives regarding special concerns for individuals, family members, groups, relationships, finances, careers or any situation desiring answers or spiritual input.

The example below (shared by Phyllis Pennington) demonstrates how the same walk can assist an individual as well as the collective.

I always look forward to walking the beautiful 7-circuit multi-colored labyrinth belonging to Optimal Potentials and donated each year for participants to experience at the Oklahoma City Holistic Health Fairs.

This year was no different. Fortunately, I chose to take my annual journey Friday evening during preparations for the event and before it started the following morning. As I prepared for my sojourn, I addressed my higher self and asked to be open to the message this sacred circle had to share with me. I cleared my mind and entered the labyrinth, watched and listened for the significance to unfold.

After a few turns, I found dirt and debris along several of the pathways. Guess I had some areas requiring cleaning and clearing. Spirit suggested I note where the dirt was and clear it off the paths not only for myself, but also for others who would soon follow these footsteps.

As I approached the inner sanctum, I noticed there was something underneath the circuits leading inward, but was uncertain what it might be. Whatever the hidden material was, it also covered the entire center section.

I finished my meditation and retraced my steps, asking Spirit about the mysterious lumps along some of the pathways. My intuition suggested I could and should find out what it was. There were two avenues to discovery. One was to locate another volunteer to help, since a canvas labyrinth can be rather intimidating to fold alone. Or I could ask myself how much I wanted to discern the answer and smooth the pathways and inner sanctum.

If I possessed a burning desire to know, I would be able to determine the truth only by unearthing the extended region. As I exited the labyrinth, I surveyed the surface again and decided to clean the canvas before tackling the more detailed action.

After obtaining a broom and silent butler, I again entered the labyrinth and started cleaning and clearing the paths strewn with debris. One area was near the outer circuit. As I swept, I had to step into another pathway to be able to collect the dust and dirt. I carried the debris to the waste container and returned to where I thought I'd been only to find I had lost my way.

Spirit directed I start my journey over and retrace my steps until I discovered where the problems were I had encountered earlier. I did so and took note of that important message: I needed to go back and address problems where I found them, remove them and continue to the next spot until everything was cleared rather than stopping and running to the trash. It was necessary to first police my course and then clear clutter and discarded material.

This was important to me and fellow travelers so we could navigate unobstructed. By removing my garbage (through for-giveness), I would leave a clear path with fewer distractions so other walkers could concentrate on their issues unimpeded. What a revelation! I had been asking Holy Spirit the real purpose of my forgiveness work and now I knew.

When I again reached the inner zone, I had a full silent butler so I walked straight out to dump the trash rather than travers-ing the circuits. I then returned to the labyrinth after storing my tools and learned my curiosity about the mysterious lumps in the center had escalated to a point of great willingness to do what-ever it took to discover the source of those lumps.

I carefully folded the labyrinth lengthwise a couple of times until I reached the lumpy locale. There, hidden under the center of the labyrinth, was its protective covering. When the multi-colored canvas had been unfolded and displayed earlier that day, apparently the covering had stuck unnoticed to the bottom.

Peeling it from the sacred symbol, I placed the plastic back in the large storage container and started unfolding the laby-rinth again. Carefully completing this process, I discovered mul-tiple wrinkles and creases. The message was clear — something hidden (protection) needed disclosure before the pathways could be smooth allowing an easy and effortless voyage.

That discovery took a tremendous amount of acceptance, dedication, persistence and energy, plus a decision about whether I wanted to undertake the procedure or let someone else do it.

Next, it took re-laying the paths and removing the wrinkles and folds that occurred during detection. This took keen observation, a careful re-walk of the labyrinth, time straightening and smoothing with all my mind, body and spirit. I had to use many available skills to accomplish this task, sometimes getting down on hands and knees to pull or push the wrinkles.

Quite a relevant message.

The hidden article has surfaced in my life several times (protection) and the clearing and cleaning represented a physical and mental process facing issues needing resolution. A willingness to tackle the situation translated into taking necessary steps in my own life to retrace, unfold and smooth problem areas through diligence and patience.

It's my belief that any time I ask for the message and am open to receiving it, no matter what the form, the labyrinth never fails to deliver. It is just another example of how Holy Spirit can use anything to teach and guide us as long as we are willing and receptive.

Ordination Ritual Rite of Passage

Rev. Shelley Heller, of United Life Church in Oklahoma City, graciously shared the following ordination ceremony she wrote for Rev. Suellen Miller. An arbor was placed over the center of the labyrinth at Unity Spiritual Center for a June 8, 2007, rite of passage ritual the evening before the official sanctuary blessing.

Tomorrow Suellen Miller will be ordained as a minister. Tonight, I welcome you to this very special event in the life of a minister, the beginning of this rite of passage. This is a celebration of someone permanently planted into their ministerial family. It is a special family — extended, but a family nonetheless. And as a family, we choose to share our special moments. We are doing that tonight as the ministers and practitioners of these churches join us.

Most cultures have rites of passage for individuals as they grow and mature on their sacred journey through life. These rites symbolize certain accomplishments for the individual involved. Rev. Suellen has served her congregation, her friends and God well and proven to be a minister worthy of high esteem and respect.

As we join in a sacred prayerful state of mind, please focus your love and Christ energy on her as she moves through the symbolic idea of the labyrinth towards wholeness as an ordained minister.

The effectiveness of a labyrinth walk is determined by one's experience. Labyrinths are temples that enhance and balance and bring a sense of sacred — a place where we confirm our unity with the cosmos, awaken our vital energies and elevate our consciousness. They are space/time temples where we can behold realities that oddly enough transcend space and time. Labyrinths are mirrors for the divine.

As one walks into the labyrinth, they experience a mystical experience of release. We will participate as Rev. Suellen processes through this releasing period, as she goes into the deepest part of herself and sheds what is no longer necessary.

I would now ask Rev. Suellen to begin following the path of the labyrinth, stopping at each place marked by shining stones and face the audience.

Reading of Release Steps:
(After each minister reads the particular step of release where the honoree stands, they release the balloon with the appropriate number they are holding.)

1. I release FEAR, that which causes me to hesitate or move into a downhill spiral. I release the acronym for fear, False Expectation Appearing Real, and open to another acronym for fear, Feeling Everything is All Right. Fear is no longer part of my life in any way as I step into Absolute Faith.

2. I release all DOUBT, all unbelief. There is no part of me now or forevermore that allows doubt to be a part of my vocabulary. I let go of any distrust and open myself to a greater reality.

3. I release ANXIETY in my life. I no longer hold on to any apprehension or uneasiness of mind. I am no longer uneasy about anything that is happening in my life. I step into ease and grace and I release feeling anxious or uneasy about all aspects of my life, both personal and in my ministry.

4. I release GRIEF. I release any heavy feeling about events in my life, both personally and in my ministry. I realize there is no good reason to allow grief to be a part of me, for all is in God's timing and I step out of any mourning and distress and leave it behind me.

5. I release GUILT, that feeling I should be reproached, of failure, of being worthy of blame which means no right to praise. I release any degradation of myself by thinking these things. I know my true spiritual nature.

6. I release UNCERTAINTY. I alleviate any feeling, any thought, any consideration of a wavering nature in my mind and heart and body and open myself to that which is certain and secure, knowing uncertainty is left behind on my path, never to enter into my life again.

7. I release SORROW. There is no anguish in me, nor regret or distress of mind about anything or any person in my life. I do not feel sad, downcast, depressed or somber from this day forward. I liberate myself from sorrow now.

8. I release DANGER. I no longer have a feeling of any risk or peril that might threaten me. These words are now and henceforth banished from my sight. Any hazard that has ever occurred to me is completely dissipated and released into the ethers from which it came.

9. I release ATTACHMENT to outcome, for I know that any

idea that comes to mind is from God and so is the outcome. Therefore, I no longer am attached to how I think things should look or be, knowing God's almighty imagination is always moving in and through me. I know that all things are in divine right timing and therefore am no longer attached to results.

10. I release DESPAIR. Anything in the past that has allowed me to lose heart is now relinquished and vanquished from this day forever.

11. I release DIFFICULTY. I know there is no longer anything but ease and grace in my life, for difficulty is gone in my life and my ministry. I release any idea of problems or struggle in my ministry.

12. I release RESENTMENT. I no longer have hard feelings about anything or anyone. I do not harbor any ill feelings toward anyone or any experience in my life and in the life of my service to others.

13. I release ANGER. I allow myself to step into peace and let go of anything that resembles annoyance, antagonism or irritation. I recognize and realize anger is dispersed, dissolved and scattered away.

14. I release WHATEVER DOES NOT SERVE ME. I allow anything that comes to mind that has not yet been released and that needs to be released, to be let go of — relinquished, abandoned and renounced in my life and in my ministry. I do not let anything harm me physically, mentally and emotionally any longer.

15. I release ANYTHING THAT IS UNLIKE MY DIVINE NATURE, knowing God creates, exists and expresses through me as me. I let go of any stress that goes along with a conscious and unconscious need, knowing that all my needs are answered in God and through God all the time in every way.

You have now reached the center of the labyrinth and have crossed the threshold where action potential is initiated. We recognize you are dedicated and consecrated for a higher purpose.

We honor you by placing this symbol of purification on your head, a wreath of baby's breath which symbolizes a new beginning, a sacred, pristine and fresh start.

This special song consecrates your ministerial walk and is dedicated to everlasting sacred blessings.

As you prepare to return on the path you came, you realize that each time you walk this path, you become more empowered to find and do the work for which your soul yearns.

Symbols are the keyholes to doors in the walls of space through which we peer into eternity. I hand you this basket as you leave the labyrinth. Please stop at each brightly colored spot, receiving symbols of your spiritual commitment and your ministry.

Readings of Flower Symbology:

(As the honoree once again pauses at each stopping point, the minister reads the meaning of that particular flower and then walks through the labyrinth and gives it to the honoree.)

1. The FORGET ME NOT represents elegance. May your ministry be filled with grace and refinement in demeanor and your presentation of the God that flows through you.

2. The DAISY represents purity of thought. May you always be standing in the middle of the stream of absolute high consciousness and find it easy to make any shifts in your thinking to keep you there.

3. The LIGHT PINK ROSE represents great admiration from your colleagues and friends, from those who know and love you and those who just met you, for you are greatly worth of this.

4. The WISTERIA represents the beauty of your spirit, that which shines through all you say, the light in your eyes and the words in your mouth. You are nothing but the beauty that is God.

5. The SUNFLOWER represents faith and devotion. You are secure in your knowledge and beliefs, you have absolute trust in the power of the God within you, and the loyalty and commitment to your calling is admirable in every respect.

6. The ORCHID represents your magnificence. Splendor, grandness and brilliance is your middle name and the calling of your ministry. You serve it well the rest of your life for that is the truth of you.

7. The LILAC represents the new innocence and purity with which you now enter your calling. You are free from any guilt from the past, for you are as a new baby, fresh and clear and light. Every day is a new day with no mistakes, and today is that day.

8. The MAGNOLIA represents Dignity. There is an inherent nobility and respect for the graciousness and Godliness within your life and ministry.

9. The YELLOW ROSE represents joy. May your life and your

ministry be filled with exultant happiness, satisfaction and pleasure.

10. The ZINNIA represents thoughts of absent friends, those who would be here but for circumstance, and send you much love, joy and admiration.

11. The WHITE ROSE represents reverence. May you strike profound awe through the word and life and mind of God as you minister to those you serve.

12. The DAFFODIL represents respect and high regard. May you draw forth more respect and high regard in your ministry than you even have now, which is tremendous. May all hold you in high esteem and appreciation.

13. The ORANGE ROSE represents enthusiasm. May your ministry be filled with excitement and passion for all you think, all you do and all you are, for you are a magnificent child of God.

14. The PURPLE CHRYSANTHEMUM represents the noble truth on which you stand. The high mindedness of God within you which so completely and thoroughly touches every person you meet.

15. The BAMBOO represents strength and longevity. May the Great Force and Intelligence of the One Mind be yours. May you live a long life and flourish in your chosen path.

16. The RED CARNATION represents spirituality. May you breathe in that illuminating and vital principle of Love and Light as it resides in your heart and your ministry.

Hugs and Closing Prayer

———————

"I found the rite of passage ceremony very moving," Rev. Suellen said. "It was also apropos that a few of the balloons released got caught in the big tree nearby. Sometimes we think we are releasing something and it hangs around a little longer than we would like.

"By the end of the ceremony, I had indeed moved into a different place in my heart, in my mind, in my soul. I thank everyone who participated in this ceremony in any way, including those who designed and built this lovely labyrinth."

Connection of Man,
Innerconnection to Spirit

Man emerges from the primal body of God
Complete in himself — in total perfection.
Connected to the causal mind of All That Is.
Surrounded by an auric presence of angelic proportions.
Filled with the sacred essence of etheric eminence.

Floating beyond time and space,
God awaits the knowledge of experience.
Expansive potential, colorful emotion,
Sole expression of the One Soul.

Single, solitary... duality, polarity...
Harmonic completeness of the Trinity.
Comprised of Divine Intelligence,
Individual, yet never separate...
Together, but often apart.

Transcending human revolutions,
Radiantly continuing the spiritual cycle.
Evolving always (in all ways).
Understanding elusive questions form mystical answers.

Igniting a passion for truth
...a search for the illuminated path.
Interconnecting a spiral synergy of compassion
...to a peaceful, intuitive knowing.
Sparking the infinity of our divinity.

— Gail Peck

Proposed Labyrinth Use at Clarehouse
for Quality End-of-Life Care

The Rev. Cindy Ritter, Director of Support Services for Clarehouse, shares the following about the addition of another sacred circle in Tulsa.

Clarehouse will begin use of a labyrinth in the summer of 2009, when a newly constructed 10-bedroom home opens in Tulsa. A non-profit corporation, Clarehouse offers a loving alternative for end-of-life care. Ten guests with terminal illnesses are cared for in a comfortable, home-like space by dedicated professionals.

The primary mission of Clarehouse is to facilitate a peaceful and dignified death. Physical, emotional and spiritual support are an integral part of care for guests and their loved ones. The labyrinth and its representation of wholeness, healing, inclusiveness and community will serve as a vital tool for support during the grieving process.

This new labyrinth will be employed in three distinct ways:
• To support guests and families during the time of transition from life to death;
• To provide a meditative space and experience for the northeast Oklahoma community;
• To increase ability of staff and volunteers to offer high quality end-of-life care.

Clarehouse's new location will encompass six acres of beautiful, wooded land in south Tulsa. The campus will include a 10-bedroom home, detached chapel, memorial gardens, walking trails and a Chartres Cathedral replica labyrinth. The 40-foot diameter labyrinth will be constructed of hardened colored concrete with the pattern ground into the concrete followed by a staining process. Stain color will reflect the color scheme of the home and blend with the natural setting. Location of the labyrinth adjacent to the chapel and water feature is in the quiet seclusion of a wooded area and will enhance its use in contemplative experience.

The labyrinth, located 320 feet from the home, serves as a symbol of separated space. Family members or loved ones must make the transition from the presence of the dying person to their absence. In preparing to walk the labyrinth, individuals will leave the physical presence of their loved one in the home and travel toward a new experience on a new path. This imagery will assist persons in releasing their loved one to death and to begin anew in another "place." Grief is a natural process and placement of the Clarehouse labyrinth in the midst of a serene, natural setting will emphasize and give permission for this element in the grief experience.

Walking the labyrinth as a meditation or prayer exercise mirrors the grief journey. The grief process involves traveling between the way things used to be and how things will be in the future. It is an interior process of coming to terms with a new reality by letting go and saying goodbye in such a way that emotional healing occurs. The grief process connects "what was" with "what will be."

The Clarehouse labyrinth will be ideal for "walking through" the grieving process. Each person experiences loss in a unique way, just as each person's labyrinth walk is different. In grieving, there is no right or wrong way to experience the loss. Similarly, there is no right or wrong way to walk a labyrinth. All that is required is to move through, one step at a time, with the pace that feels right. There is only one way through grief — to go through it. There is no correct speed or specified time frame. Grieving people often feel overwhelmed and confused. The labyrinth provides only one way in and one way out with no possibility of getting lost. This lends security for collecting thoughts and feelings and focusing on the importance of being present with the dying person. The Clarehouse labyrinth will provide unique assistance with the grieving process. It will be accessible during the time period 30 days immediately prior to the death (the length of stay criteria for each guest), at the exact time of death, and during the time period following the death of the loved one.

Even though grieving and each walk and meditation are unique, three interdependent phases will be encountered:

• Walking In (journey toward the center): Preparing, emptying and quieting the mind. Releasing anxiety, fear and the loved one to the death experience.

• Centering (approaching and honoring the center): Receiving insight, comfort and clarity through prayer, meditation or silence. Visualizing the act of death as sacred.

• Walking Out (traveling outward): Returning to the reality of the loss, empowered and grounded. Reframing to embrace life, recognizing it will continue in a new way.

The unicursal (one path) pattern of a labyrinth helps with the adjustment to loss of a loved one by providing a safe space to enter the depths of emotion, experience the pain, and find meaning. The path of the labyrinth (as with the path of grief) always goes forward, yet has many turns, going back and forth. One appears to cover the same territory over and over, but it is a pattern and process that can bring about healing and wholeness. The Clarehouse labyrinth can be walked one time or multiple times depending upon the needs and desires of the individual.

Clarehouse was established in 2000 as a non-profit organization aimed at providing quality end-of-life care to people in need. Since its inception, Clarehouse has offered free care and is funded entirely by charitable giving and the benevolence of individuals, civic groups, faith communities and foundations in the Tulsa and northeast Oklahoma area. The labyrinth will serve as a way to "give back" to the host of people who enable loving care to dying people and their families and friends. A plan will be developed to open the Clarehouse labyrinth to community groups. Walking a labyrinth emphasizes calmness and balance. It lends itself to use as a space for quiet reflection and refocusing thoughts and energy, discovering what is important for individuals and organizations. Groups may choose to use the labyrinth as part of "themed" retreats such as community building, healing and wellness, spiritual growth or other special interest topics. A Clarehouse staff member specifically trained as a labyrinth facilitator will schedule and coordinate use of the labyrinth for community groups.

Additionally, the Clarehouse labyrinth will function as a staff and volunteer support and development tool. Providing end-of-life care is a highly stressful and demanding vocation. The mission of Clarehouse is nourished by its staff and volunteers who insure that each guest and family have the opportunity to experience death in a way that is most meaningful and appropriate to them. The labyrinth will be used in staff and volunteer orientation and continuing education. Through the labyrinth walk, staff and volunteers will be assisted to come to terms with their own grief and learn to effectively balance the work of care-giving with their own needs. This sacred circle will also facilitate staff development and team building. The vision of Clarehouse is that each person and those closest to them receive loving, compassionate care during the dying time and grief process. The labyrinth will enhance and support this goal by providing a quiet space and regenerative method for actively walking through grief as a journey, resulting in comfort and healing.

Chapter 3
Ancient Wisdom Awaits

The Center is the Source

Symbolically, the center signifies God, creation, unity, healing, truth, wholeness, the Source of Oneness. A labyrinth carries this theme forward as one (unicursal) path leads to the center in contrast to a maze with confusing multi-cursal paths and no focal point.

Mazes and labyrinths are the yin and yang of opposites. The purpose of a maze is to perplex, analyze, amuse, bewilder, deter, contain while a labyrinth is a path with a different purpose. A labyrinth calms, heals, comforts, balances.

Simple versus complex.

Intellectual puzzle versus wellness meditation.

Honesty versus falsehood.

The physical world of illusion versus the spiritual world of peace.

Unity meets diversity.

A maze attempts to keep participants lost. In the labyrinth, we find ourselves.

The circular form of a labyrinth reflects the basic movement of creation. Concentric circles represent the cosmos, atoms, DNA, eternity. Their geometry encompasses the same principles of manifestation utilized by a Supreme Being in the creation of the universe.

Labyrinthine spirals are an extension of God, Mother Earth and human spirituality. They epitomize how we experience heaven on earth. Perhaps, the true meaning of the commandment "Honor Thy Father and Mother." Father God and Mother Earth. Heaven on earth. Multi-dimensional holographic fields consecrating a world of form.

Walking such an unobstructed path adds clarity and awakens inner knowledge often obscuring our reason for being and identifying a Fibonacci golden ratio of spiraling consciousness.

Sacred geometry has become a new 21st century buzzword. Although no consensus definition exists, a generally accepted interpretation integrates the idea of "spirit moving into matter" and involves the contemplation of archetypal patterns of nature aiding spiritual communion. This echoes the geometry found in nature, architecture, art, music, poetry and planetary movement and reveals the presence of cosmic order, its aesthetic beauty and symmetry of design.

Sacred Geometry Musings

"Sacred geometry is the act of studying the divine act of creation and then using that knowledge to create in the same way. By studying nature, we find that the basic building blocks of creation are geometric. Since a divine hand is responsible for originating the numbers and proportions of the manifest universe, that geometry is sacred. Studying sacred geometry leads us to truth and self-understanding. All societies use sacred geometry to construct their temples, sacred places and art. Chartres Cathedral, for example, and its labyrinth. Numbers aren't just for counting, nor are they just symbolic. They are the actual essence of everything that exists."
— Robert Ferré, of Labyrinth Enterprises

Sacred — holy purpose or place.

Geometry — branch of mathematics that deals with points, lines, surfaces and solids and examines their properties, measurements and mutual relations in space (spatial relationships).

Sacred Geometry (sacred shape or form) — figures have depth, mass, spiritual significance, way matter transforms into spirit; heavenly connection to earth, man to nature, God to man.

Meta — going beyond, higher, transcending.

Metaphysical — beyond the physical,
the unseen world,
the nature of being or essential reality

Metaphysics — the branch of philosophy concerned with the study of ultimate causes and the underlying nature of things.

Metaphysical Meanings
of Selected Geometric Shapes

Circle — origin, birth of creation, simplicity, perfection, completeness, unity, integrity, equality

Cube — grounds, repairs, rebuilds, restores, strengthens

Diamond — balances mental functions, encourages mind to acknowledge heart, honor, structure, form

Ellipse — integration, synthesis, growth, reconciliation

Fibonacci Spiral — aesthetic beauty, elegant, artistic, graceful, symmetry in motion, abundance, intricate

Flower of Life — universal knowledge, splendor, multiplicity, illusion, mystical, magical

Kundalini Spiral — detach from emotion, creativity, expression, transition, imagination, a different perspective

Labyrinth — pattern, design, texture, discipline, order, free will, inner transformation

Lemniscate — prosperity, infinity, enduring, all-encompasing, primordial truth, infinite light and wisdom

Mandala — beauty, mutual understanding, spiritual omnipresence, visual harmony, supreme consciousness

Pyramid — balanced duality, strong foundation, passionate detachment, stable, pure, efficient, resourceful, focused, centered

Square — equality, endurance, solid principles, honesty, master builder, generous

Triangle — justice, compassion, majesty, power, authority, Holy Trinity

---

Hexagon — plane figure with six angles and six sides

Hexahedron — solid figure with six plane surfaces

Octahedron — solid figure with eight plane surfaces

Tetrahedron — solid figure with four triangular faces

Labyrinths appear in various sizes, shapes, colors, patterns and dimensions, a myriad of forms with multiple ways to use them. Their dramatic and vibrant revival as a meditation, relaxation and spiritual tool promotes physical, emotional and psychological healing.

Appearing in churches, religious communities, hospitals, healthcare facilities, hospices, public parks, spas, retreat centers, schools, universities, prisons, memorial healing gardens and progressive corporations in the last two decades, these sacred circles speak to people of different religious and cultural backgrounds to enhance healing, reduce stress, solve problems, spark creativity, calm the mind and revitalize the spirit.

A labyrinth is meaningful for meditation, weddings, memorial services, conflict resolution, problem-solving, women's groups, AIDS awareness, equal rights, world peace walks, 12-step support programs, troubled teens, abuse victims, cancer patients, butterfly releases, grief counseling, art therapy, or any way spiritual input is advantageous.

As a focal point for rituals and ceremonies, a labyrinth ideally encourages listening, tenders compassion, maintains balance, builds community, enhances creativity and offers a visible support center of action. It is effective in dealing with grief and loss, great for celebration, expressions of joy, marking full moons, solstices or equinoxes (changing of seasons), ushering in the new year at midnight on New Year's Eve and aligning energy chakras.

A Tulsa reiki master uses labyrinths in "New Life" classes and an Oklahoma City elementary school teacher has a four-circuit canvas model she shares with her students for art therapy. Psychotherapists and pastoral counselors employ finger, lap or tabletop replicas in private counseling and guidance sessions.

Sacred circles have flourished around the world in ritual and spiritual practices since time immortal, helping connect man with the natural forces of nature. They represent the continuous cycle of life, hallowed rites of passage, birth and death, honor, integrity, completion... and are symbolic of the holy (whole) journey from life to death.

In Hopi tradition, they show the movement of the planets and stars across the sky and man's difficult path to heaven. Only in making righteous choices could one truly find life after death, taught Latoi, the Hopi Indian spirit (found in ancient glyphs and baskets) who symbolizes man's eventual ascent to the stars.

Labyrinths integrate opposites, joining past and present, centering us in the Now. They bring us together, touching our inner sanctums, providing an effective outreach to the surrounding community through public service and communion.

They have appeared in such varied settings as Central Park in New York City, Johns Hopkins Medical Center in Baltimore and a downtown square in Zurich, Switzerland. What else would such diverse areas have in common?

The majority of the world's challenges, problems and conflicts can be traced to a single origin — separation from a spiritual source (God), ourselves and each other. Labyrinths question the image of life as a forlorn, perilous journey through a maze. They suggest an expanded, adventurous, joyful journey, gleefully dancing with others in our sacred circle.

In times of illness or injury, labyrinths offer a source for inner healing and transformation. Drugs or surgery may promise cures, labyrinths identify (and often eliminate) the cause.

Labyrinth designer Robert Ferré predicts that within the next two decades labyrinths will become standard and valued accoutrements of healing environments. Presently, more than 60 healthcare facilities in the United States feature these sacred circles, including Mercy Hospital in Oklahoma City.

"The day will soon be upon us in which no progressive architect will design a healthcare facility without including a meditation labyrinth. The day is not far off when patients, staff members and doctors will insist their existing facility install a labyrinth," said Ferré, of Labyrinth Enterprises in St. Louis, Missouri.

Labyrinths effectively address the area of inner healing ignored by the scientific community. The medical establishment has recently recognized the immense impact attitude, state of mind and personal beliefs have on overall well-being. This recognition has resulted in more attention to health design, environment and patient-centered care.

Ferré said the new, more holistic direction of healthcare has been largely passive, dealing with the color of walls, views from windows and homey architecture designs. "All are meant to calm and comfort. Labyrinths, too, calm and comfort. They represent the next step forward in that they are active, not passive," he said. "They offer something the patient can do. Labyrinths are pro-active, promoting well-being not just for patients, but for staff, health providers, doctors, visitors and even the local community."

Studies of hospital labyrinth use in North America show the spiraling circuits complement chemotherapy and radiation in cancer treatment providing a sense of confidence and control. Personal attitudes about inner healing concerning treatment significantly affect results of outer healing.

The surrounding community also benefits from use of hospital labyrinths. Combined programs include cancer and AIDS support groups, hospice butterfly releases, survivors' walks, holistic nurses retreats, candlelit memorial services, wellness walks, domestic violence awareness, volunteer chaplains, peace advocates, civic organizations or any area desiring to examine priorities. Some hospitals report surgeons walk the labyrinth before performing an operation to calm themselves. Nurses send anxious patients and family members to walk the labyrinth reporting they return more relaxed.

Ferré said labyrinths represent the path of illness and recovery. Despite uncertainties and changes of directions, if we are diligent and stay the course, we arrive at our goal. "Numerous books using a literary metaphor compare the healthcare system to a maze in which the patient gets lost and becomes fearful and isolated. In a maze, we do indeed lose ourselves, but in a labyrinth, we find ourselves. Walking a labyrinth is a type of pilgrimage which takes us within, not just to the center of the design, but to our own center. That's where inner healing takes place. The labyrinth leads where science cannot enter," Ferré added.

"Inner healing defies and baffles scientific method, but is effectively embraced by the labyrinth, which meet people where they are emotionally, spiritually, psychologically, leading them gently forward to the next step and then the following step and the step beyond that."

Research conducted by Dr. Herbert Benson at Harvard Medical School's Mind/Body Medical Institute has found focused walking meditations are highly efficient at reducing anxiety and eliciting what he calls the "relaxation response." A strong proponent of the psychological advantages of meditation due to its significant long-term health benefits, Benson says regular meditative practices lead to greater powers of concentration, a sense of control and efficiency in one's life, lower blood pressure, metabolic and breathing rates, reduced incidents of chronic pain, reduction of insomnia, improved fertility, and several other areas of improved health, which can be derived from the simple act of walking a labyrinth.

Benson's studies show a walking labyrinth meditation lowers elevated blood pressure more effectively than drugs. It also results in shorter recovery times, fewer complications, stress reduction, increased job satisfaction and less turnover among healthcare employees.

The fact that science and labyrinths speak different languages is actually a great benefit, not a detriment, Ferré said. "Working together, they address the complete person, physically and spiritually. Labyrinths offer an accessible, cost-effective, proactive spiritual technology that does what science cannot do. They overcome the inadequacies of the reductionist paradigm. Even in cases where outer healing fails, inner healing can still take place. Hence, hospitals are beginning to discover the benefits of using labyrinths. Working in concert, medicine, design, environment and labyrinths offer a whole that greatly exceeds the sum of its parts."

Types of Labyrinths

As labyrinthine awareness flourishes, an evolving number of variations beautify landscapes and inner sanctums originating from two basic designs, the Classical Cretan and Chartres. The Classical appears more on the world scene while the Medieval Chartres is the most popular design in North America.

Cretan or Classical Labyrinth

At 3,500 years and counting, the Cretan or Classical labyrinth is one of history's oldest and best-known symbols. The seven interlocking, concentric paths represent an ancient, archetypal design found in most cultures, believed to have originated on the Greek Isle of Crete.

Noted for its simplicity of construction, the Classical consists of a single pathway that loops back and forth to form seven circuits, bounded by eight walls, surrounded by the central goal. It is crafted in both circular and square shapes in a varied number of circuits. Most labyrinths discovered prior to the first few centuries BCE portray this type of sacred circle.

Labyrinth patterns emulating this style have been etched on cave paintings, ancient petroglyphs, American Indian baskets, coins, art motifs and in written history and myth from all around the world (Africa, Asia, Australia, China, England,

Europe, India, Indonesia, North America, Peru, Russia, Scandinavia, South America).

The secret of the 7-circuit traditional labyrinth is that its round rings are based on a square seed pattern. Curiously, one's path through a labyrinth does not correspond to numerical order of the rings.

The seven rings of the Cretan labyrinth correspond to the seven sacred planets, seven days of the week, seven chakras of the body, seven colors of the rainbow, seven musical notes, seven liberal arts and sciences, seven continents, seven seas, seven principles of the cosmos, seven steps of the creative process, seven levels of consciousness, and the seven stages of completion.

Seven is considered a "virgin number" — the only single digit natural number which is neither a multiple nor a factor of any of the single digit numbers. It also signifies spiritual perfection.

7-circuit Classical

Medieval or Chartres

From their inception, labyrinths have been associated with spiritual forces, sacred geometry and proportion. During the Middle Ages, many Gothic cathedrals inlaid labyrinth patterns into their stone floors based on these principles. The most renowned style is the medieval Christian labyrinth with 11 rings or paths, which double back on each of four axes to portray a distinctive Christian cross.

A Medieval or 11-circuit Chartres is the most popular design in North America and is based on the famous labyrinth built in the nave of Chartres Cathedral near Paris, France, in the early 13th century.

The Middle Ages was a time of pilgrimages, grand architectural abbeys and artistic brilliance. Since most people could not make the dangerous pilgrimage to Jerusalem, considered by Christians to be the center of the world symbolizing the Kingdom of Heaven, they would travel to important cathedrals such as Canterbury, Chartres and Santiago de Compostella.

Chartres Cathedral was one of the greatest of all Gothic cathedrals and epitomized the intrinsic spiritual journey of every man — in the sacred geometry, the art, the architecture and the labyrinth. If the church is the gateway, the connection between heaven and earth, God and man, then the labyrinth is the missing link between physical and metaphysical, outer and inner, despair and illumination, balancing polarities.

In walking the Chartres style labyrinth, a pilgrim meanders through each of four quadrants several times before reaching the goal (heaven, center of the universe). The center has a six-petal rosette outline exemplifying enlightenment, beauty and love. The four arms of the cross suggest Christian symbolism.

Lunations form the outer perimeter of a Chartres labyrinth. These partial circles create an arc separated by a cusp, which sends the energy of the labyrinth into the world.

Since this more complex design takes longer to traverse than the Classical Cretan, the journey to the center may be deeper and more introspective.

Only two of the original 22 medieval church labyrinths still exist. Chartres is the oldest surviving and most famous pavement labyrinth of the Gothic era. Its 800-year-old walking path has recently been reopened due to American interest.

11-circuit Chartres

Santa Rosa Design

Santa Rosas in Oklahoma

Created in March 1997 by Lea Goode-Harris, the Santa Rosa style was the first in a wave of neo-medieval patterns crafted since the mid-1990s in the United States. Such contemporary labyrinths join a great world lineage of sacred spirals designed over the past 5,000 years, incorporating the seven circuits of the classical model with the quarter and half turns of ancient medieval replicas.

Five Santa Rosa labyrinths reside in Oklahoma: Standing Bear Park in Ponca City, Phillips Theological Seminary in Tulsa (modified version) and canvas models at St. Francis of the Woods in Coyle, St. Stephens United Methodist Church in Norman and Stillwater First United Methodist Church.

The 1,100-square-foot Ponca City labyrinth was the first permanent outdoor Santa Rosa in the Sooner State. It was also the first labyrinth at a state park. Presently, there are four.

This simple, yet elegant 7-circuit design is noted for its pausing stone at the entrance and a heart space stone or circle located near the fourth path.

Builder Marty Kermeen, of Labyrinths in Stone from Yorkville, Illinois, said Ponca City officials and residents requested a center design of four interlocking circles to represent the interconnectedness of the varied community elements "that came together to make this project happen. As is so often the case in matters of art and spirit, the design has come to mean something even more to those who have seen it. What began as a symbol of community evolved into one representing the holiness of life."

An artistic paver, Kermeen said the beauty of this design "is that it incorporates three important religious symbols: The sacred hoop is central to the religious beliefs of many Native American cultures. Interlocking hoops form vesica pisces, pointed oval shapes used in medieval Christian art as an aureole to surround sacred figures; the vesica pisces point to the cardinal directions, honoring the Four Directions of the Medicine Wheel. The intersection of the vesica pisces form the Flower of Life, or perhaps the blossom of the sacred tree that blooms in the center of the sacred hoop — the living center of All That Is. Bringing these symbols together in this intricate design creates a multicultural space in which the whole community can feel at home."

The Sacred Hoops center epitomizes the emergence of a new sacred hoop that brings all cultures together to form a stronger community, honoring diversity. Outreach programs held during the fund-raising campaign focused on educating community members about their rich cultural traditions and the use of the labyrinth as a "good red road."

Contemporary Artistic Labyrinths

Creative contemporary labyrinths continue to evolve from variations of the Classical and Chartres styles in a plethora of patterns — portable modified replicas painted on canvas, indoor models inlaid in floors, permanent outdoor creations comprised of stones, bricks, rocks, molded turf or painted on concrete.

Used for spiritual contemplation, relaxing walks, educational entertainment and play, contemporary labyrinths are found in peaceful garden sanctuaries as well as busy urban environments. Unlike their European counterparts, contemporary North American labyrinths are not usually embedded in the history of their specific setting. They are a dynamic, living part of their respective communities and are frequently created for a day or weekend enjoyment at special events.

We have even used finger labyrinths inside both indoor canvas and outdoor sacred circles for meditative purposes and distinguished ceremonies. Using labyrinths in a labyrinth is quite innovative according to the people who thought it a strange idea when it was first proposed. Placing four Chartres finger labyrinths at the cardinal directions of a 7-circuit classical enhances vibrations and magnifies the intended effect. Imagine the power generated when five or six labyrinths are placed in close proximity. Then quadruple it, exponentially. Aligning finger labyrinths on top of each other and meditating with them in one's lap is also an intriguing experience.

Two of the most unusual contemporary labyrinths in Oklahoma are Jack O' Lantern and a Wisdom Wheel Directional Labyrinth. Jack appears once a year in the Oklahoma City Paseo Art District and the Wisdom Wheel is a new creation in the back yard of one of the authors of this book.

The jolly 40-foot concrete Halloween Jack o' Lantern springs into vibrant orange life on the streets of Paseo providing "a night of light instead of fright." He's the focal point for the culmination of a creative alternative festival for children and the young at heart. Dancing in the labyrinth is part of the annual "Magic Lantern Celebration."

Jack O' Lantern Labyrinth

A Wisdom Wheel Directional Labyrinth combines the tradition and wisdom of a Native American medicine wheel with the directional guidance and meditative contemplation of a labyrinth.

Another pair of artistic Oklahoma sacred circles were created in 2008 for the 4th Annual Healthy Home and Wellness Expo and the 3rd Annual Chickasha Holistic Health Fair. Gary Bessinger of the Woodchuck Chop and Elizabeth Muller with Universals Dances of Peace were the designing geniuses behind those two magnificent creations.

Gary had never built a labyrinth before, but was willing to craft one to give exhibitors and those attending the April Wellness Expo a meditative experience. Nursing students from OSU-OKC tested walkers' blood pressure before and after they walked the labyrinth with 97.3 percent registering lowered blood pressure readings.

After viewing a simple seed pattern, the craftsman and his partners bought in sand, rocks, statues, plants and handcrafted furniture. Two days later, a majestic 3-circuit, landscaped sacred circle graced the back of the Cox Pavilion at the State Fairgrounds in Oklahoma City. This was no ordinary labyrinth. A white five-foot statue of the Goddess Venus guarded the center, nodding to the Native American elder behind her, Moses to her right and a carved woodchuck near the entrance. Petunias, jasmine and sliced tree trunks completed the serene setting.

Loving energy flowed throughout the joyous paths as walkers peacefully strolled the graceful spiral. A melodious waterfall cascaded nearby and beautiful mahogany furniture and handcrafted wooden art encircled the labyrinth.

"Triple Your Health: Acceptance, Awareness, Appreciation" was the theme of the March Holistic Health Fair. The labyrinth also received straight A's for delightful expression as several people chanted and danced in the center balancing male and female energies, sharing melded hearts and divine blessings. Painted in the shape of a heart in the parking lot of the Chickasha Community Building at the Grady County Fairgrounds, these six spiraling circuits accompanied Elizabeth's lecture on "Dancing the Labyrinth of Life."

Refreshing and insightful contemporary designs express some of the most creative styles of modern sacred circle interpretations. Each generates eclectic energies, meets specific needs and provides intrinsic benefits exploring different natures of the self. While traditional labyrinths reveal the authentic self, contemporary sacred circles promote discovery of the artistic self.

Finger, Tapletop or Lap Labyrinths

Tracing a miniature labyrinth with one's finger offers the same health benefits, stress relief and meditative advantages as full-size counterparts. Mental focus is often easier to maintain as fingers comfortably do the walking. Paths may be navigated physically, mentally, spiritually and emotionally restoring balance and inner peace.

Comprised of wood, copper, soapstone, acrylic, glass and ceramic clay, finger labyrinths follow similar designs of the popular Classical and Chartres styles. Paper patterns and photocopies are even effective walking tools as one travels sequential turns, twisting counter and clockwise, meandering towards a common goal.

Instead of methodically placing one foot in front of the other, fingers glide smooth, inlaid, spiral paths, feeling the rhythmic flow of divine intensity. This insightful ritual invites walkers to slow down and commune with their inner, spiritual nature as well as with the essence of the material from which the labyrinth is sculpted.

A "groovy" experience that empowers the seeker, asking its soul to reveal innermost desires.

Relax4Life has been crafting finger labyrinths since 1995. The Barrington, Illinois, company is conducting a four-month study using miniature labyrinths with ADHD children. The premise of the research project is that the hyperactivity, impulsivity and inattention of children diagnosed with attention deficient disorders can be reduced through regular use of a labyrinth.

A specially designed double finger labyrinth called Intuipath® offers a mirror-image, grooved wooden labyrinth involving the use of both hands concurrently moving in opposite directions. Initial reports confirm children using this unique pattern appear calmer, have better attention spans, increased mental focus and improved impulse control.

The Intuipath® stimulates both sides of the brain simultaneously, pairing reasoning, problem-solving and language skills (left hemisphere) with intuition and creativity (right hemisphere). This brain synchrony creates a preponderance of alpha and theta brainwaves that lead to enhanced mental relaxation, greater adaptive responses and more appropriate choices to environmental stimuli.

Finger Labyrinth

Children from ages 7-18 diagnosed with ADHD combined type or ADD with hyperactivity interact with the double Cretan 7-circuit finger labyrinth at the same time each day (5 minutes per session, 3-5 times a week) for four consecutive weeks. The control group moves a finger of both hands through a tray filled with an inch of sand any way they want at the same time each day, for a period of 5 minutes, 3-5 times weekly for four consecutive weeks.

Four targeted behaviors (attention span, impulse control, mental focus and the ability to sit still) are documented on each child by a parent, teacher or therapist using a behavioral observation rating scale. Data will be compiled before the study, at the conclusion of the 4-week treatment phase and again two weeks after the treatment phase to determine any continuing benefit.

These unique and versatile labyrinths, available in both Chartres and Cretan patterns, were specially designed based on counseling work with people experiencing life-affirming conditions. The patented Intuipath® offers the flexibility and advantage of a double finger labyrinth that can be used as either a single-person, two-handed labyrinth or a two-person, single-handed labyrinth.

An individual using double paths stimulates and balances both right and left sides of the brain. Each hemisphere of this central processing unit joins together as one component enhancing relaxation and creativity. Working with this pattern may also assist mental functions in persons diagnosed with ADHD, dyslexia, Parkinson's, Alzheimer's and stroke.

Two people, each using their own half of the dual labyrinths and a single hand, frequently overcome barriers to communication, improve intuition, experience mental relaxation and exhibit greater focus and coherence.

Totemic Animal Labyrinths

Considering the close relationship between humans and animals, it is not surprising to find sacred circles emulating the shapes and characteristics of certain animals. Such labyrinthine figures depict magical qualities to their creator just like a Supreme Being does for its creations.

Totemic animal figures have been discovered honoring lizards, hummingbirds, pelicans, sharks, thunderbirds, insects, primates, dogs, cats, boars, whales, bears, fish, turtles, snakes and even dragons. These artistic patterns (often found in primitive societies with unicursal paths) allow the walker to possess the attributes of the chosen animal and learn from its behavior.

A unique South American spider, indigenous to the Andes Mountain region near Nasca, inspired an unusual 45-yard totemic labyrinth. Walkers enter on the outside right leg of the arachnid, travel the outline of eight legs, round abdomen, head and 8-foot jaws. The female Nasca carries her eggs on the outside right leg, the same leg that serves as the entrance to the totemic labyrinth.

Ritual walks honoring this arthropod imbue the seeker with creative spider energy, the ability to become a master weaver. Walkers enter and exit the Nasca at an elemental point, focusing on fertility, reproduction and continuation of the species.

While writing this book, a large black and brown spider with banded legs appeared on one of the author's patios. It traveled several feet in all directions near the chair in which she was sitting reading Eckhart Tolle's *A New Earth*. Tolle suggests a transformation of consciousness will lead humanity to a higher level of interaction and a new paradigm of discovery where acceptance, enjoyment and enthusiastic living become the norm. An interesting premise considering that spider reminds us to awaken our own sensibilities to honor innate creativity. Perhaps, the message is to accept that such an inspired planet is possible and use this creativity to weave a new web of passionate spirituality.

Or, perhaps, she did not get the message as the same spider (or one looking just like it) walked across her kitchen floor a few days later. She caught it and placed it outside. It was back in a matter of minutes; she caught it again and put the lovely creature outside saying, "If you reappear, I will talk to you."

Twenty-two minutes later, something crawled across the carpet a few feet from her computer. This time, before she relocated it, she inquired its message. Spider said: "There is time to accomplish goals to perfection. Cast aside concerns and continue at the select pace for completion of inner peace."

Okay. Putting the arachnid visitor's multiple messages together admonishes we weave our webs in all directions, catching the attention of the unaware, sharing an inspired consciousness. Repeat contact may be necessary to awaken sleeping souls. Have faith each sentient being is traveling at the proper pace for their evolution.

A master number, 22 grants the ability to change the course of history and transcend all planes. A pretty powerful confirmation that we are on the right path to enlightened consciousness to create "A New Earth." A fertile reproduction that will ensure continuation of the species with heightened awareness.

After releasing the spider outside for the third time, and seeing it four times, this writer has not seen her new friend since. Its repeated presence peaked her curiosity and she researched the spider as an animal totem. Below is what she learned.

Due to their two-section body, spiders have a figure-eight appearance. Eight represents infinity, power, success, prosperity, limitless potential. Its body shape, plus eight legs, links the arthropod to the mysticism associated with the geometric form of the figure eight. The continuous wheel of life, flowing from one cycle to the next, connects the unified spiral of the physical with spiritual creation, amplifying completion of the ascension process.

Spider teaches balance — between past and future, physical and spiritual, male and female, ebb and flow. Today's actions impact future encounters. The rhythm of nature awakens creative sensibilities that weave a web of intricate and subtle fabric, foretelling the past always influences the present and future.

Webs form a spiral shape, the traditional structure of creativity and development. Spiders usually inhabit the center of their interwoven creations just as humans occupy the center of their individual and collective worlds. The spiral of the web converges at a central point, linking the past with the future. The present is the moment of creation when spider connects with new discoveries of nourishment at the intersection where prey meets predator (the objective is fulfilled).

Spider medicine says the world is woven around us. We are the writers of our own destiny, weaving a web fabricated by our thoughts, feelings and actions. The magical, feminine energy of creation, continuous cycle of birth and death, and ability to learn from experience is reflected in its skill to spin a silken web, relocate it daily if necessary and combine the leg power of forward movement with assertive genius.

This magnificent insect is also heralded as the guardian of ancient languages and alphabets. Adepts honor an alphabet even more primordial formed by the geometric patterns and angles within a spider's web. Since many considered this sacred symbolism to be the first true method of communication, spider became the teacher of language and the alchemical muse of writing, assisting those who weave magic with the written word.

Spiders are a combination of gentleness and strength, delicacy and agility. They walk tiny silken threads with ease while maintaining balanced polarity. Such a walk along the threads of life stimulates creativity. Navigating between physical and spiritual worlds requires talent and understanding. Maybe that's why ancient mystery schools had a single precept inscribed above their portals: "Know Thyself and Thou Shalt Know the Universe!" Spider is an expert at unveiling hidden wisdom.

Numerous spider movements occur in the dark as they frequently journey into inaccessible areas. This reveals another principle about expressing creative energies. Boldly employ your craft transcending what was previously unobtainable, acknowledging the unknown, conquering fear and uncertainty. Weave mystical creative threads and watch the sparkling sunlight sprinkle glistening beads of refreshing moisture on elegant webs of life.

When this delicate insect catches your attention, be open to answering any questions it asks or implementing the suggestions it implies. Are you weaving dreams and creative impulses beyond your web? Do you follow through with creative opportunities or become tangled in someone else's web? Pay attention to balance and where you walk in life. Are you out of balance or is it someone around you? Are you ignoring inspirational urges to write or draw? Remember, spider is the keeper of knowledge of the primordial alphabet and teaches how to use the written language with power and creativity so that soulful words weave a web around those who would read them or benefit from this insight.

To the Native Americans, Grandmother Spider revealed the mysteries of the past and how they affected the future. As Chief Seattle said in 1855: "Humankind has not woven the web of life. We are but the thread of it. Whatever we do to the web, we do to ourselves. All things are bound together. All things connect. Whatever befalls the earth also befalls the children of the earth."

Labyrinths weave their meandering spiral allowing humans to place themselves in the center of the magnificent web of life, renewing their creative energies, reconnecting with unified wholeness, realizing acceptance and forgiveness come from merging our centers with the Source of Oneness.

State Labyrinths By Type

Permanent Outdoor Labyrinths (44)

Bartlesville
St Luke's Episcopal Church
7-circuit Classical, mowed grass

Chouteau
Camp Christian
11-circuit Chartres, painted on concrete

Duncan
All Saints Episcopal Church
7-circuit, rock and gravel

Edmond
Private Acreage
7-circuit Cretan, rock and grass

Private Back Yard, Barbara Henthorn
3-circuit flagstone with built-in prayer stations

Private Back Yard, Beth and Robert Huntley
4-circuit herbal path, brick and mulch

Private Back Yard, Diane and Rich Rudebock
5-circuit design, lairope grass

Private Back Yard, Carol and Harry Woods
3-circuit, cobblestones and pine needles

Private Lake Property, Raine and Blair Benham
11-circuit Chartres, brick and grass

Hulbert
Clear Creek Wellness Center
Nancy & Michael James
7-circuit, rock and grass

Jenks
Private Back Yard, Viola Rollins
7-circuit Classical, rock

Lawton
Private Back Yard — Linda Hines
Combination grass medicine wheel labyrinth

Muskogee
MoonShadow Herb Farm
2 grass and brick labyrinths
Both 7-circuit Cretans

Norman
Prairie Peace Path Labyrinth Sculpture
7-circuit, stone and gravel

Oklahoma City
Back Door Coffee House (formerly Deli on the Labyrinth)
Rectangular shape painted on parking lot

Harding Charter Preparatory High School
5-circuit, stone and grass

Mercy Health Center Labyrinth Prayer Garden
11-circuit Chartres replica

Quail Springs United Methodist Church
7-circuit, Native American design

Theatre Upon a StarDanceSwan
Halloween concrete Jack O' Lantern
painted annually at Paseo Art District

United Life Church
11-circuit Chartres painted on parking lot

Unity Spiritual Center
7-circuit Celtic design, rock and sand

Private Back Yard, Shantel Carr
3-circuit grass

Private Back Yard, Gail Peck
Wisdom Wheel Directional Labyrinth
porcelain tile, mulch, stone border

Piedmont
Red Plains Monastery, Sisters of Benedict
11-circuit Chartres, brick and grass

Ponca City
Standing Bear Native American Park
Santa Rosa design, brick paver

Sapulpa
Camp Okiwanee
11-circuit Chartres, grass walking path
rope guide for the blind

Shawnee
Private Back Yard, Lisa Sponseller
7-circuit Classical, brick paver

Private Lake Cabin, Diane and Rich Rudebock
7-circuit, river rock design

Stilwell
Private Mountaintop, Lela Samargis
7-circuit Classical, rock and grass

Tahlequah
Sancta Sophia Seminary/Sparrow Hawk Village
7-circuit Classical

Tonkawa
Heart in the Park
7-circuit, heart-shaped paver, dual-path

Tulsa
Bethany Christian Church Meditation Garden
6-circuit, brick and mulch

Hunter Park
11-circuit Chartres, painted concrete

Phillips Theological Seminary
7-circuit Modified Santa Rosa design, painted concrete

St. Andrew's Presbyterian Church
4-circuit Chartres, stone and grass in Memorial Garden

St. John's Episcopal Church
7-circuit grass

Private Area, Jan Lowell
7-circuit grass

Private Back Yard, Lynde Evans
7-circuit Classical, grass

Private Back Yard, Gala and Bill McBee
7-circuit Classical, grass

Private Front Yard, Clark and Michelle Wiens
11-circuit Chartres, mortared stone on concrete

Vian
Dwight Mission Presbyterian Camp
11-circuit Chartres in wooded area

Weatherford
P_Bar Farms
7-circuit Classical, grass

Yukon
United Methodist Church of the Good Shepherd
11-circuit Classical, patio stone spiral on turf

Photo courtesy of Skip Largent

Canvas, Nylon or Indoor Labyrinths (26)

Chouteau
Camp Christian
7-circuit Classical, painted on floor of recreation room

Coyle
St. Francis of the Woods
7-circuit Santa Rosa model, canvas

Edmond
First Christian Church
Interactive canvas prayer path

First United Methodist Church
2 canvas Chartres replicas (7-circuit and 11-circuit)
Traveling parachute 11-circuit Chartres

University of Central Oklahoma
2 canvas labyrinths
Both 11-circuit Chartres models

Enid
St. Matthew's Episcopal Church
11-circuit Chartres replica

Fort Gibson
First United Methodist Church Youth Ministry
6-circuit Classical, painted indoor on floor of youth room

Geary
First United Methodist Church
Canvas indoor belonging to minister Karen Slater

Norman
McFarlin Memorial United Methodist Church
2 canvas Chartres models, adult and youth

St. Stephen's United Methodist Church
Santa Rosa pattern, canvas

Oklahoma City
Carol Goodwin
4-circuit Classical, canvas

Our Lady of Mercy Retreat Center
11-circuit Chartres, portable nylon

Optimal Potentials
2 canvas models
   7-circuit Chartres, multi-colored
   11-circuit Chartres

Windsong Innerspace
7-circuit Modified Classical, canvas

Stillwater
First United Methodist Church
7-circuit Santa Rosa

Stroud
First Christian Church
Canvas indoor belonging to Pastor Paul Ragle

Tahlequah
First United Methodist Church
11-circuit, interactive portable canvas

Peg Willson
4-circuit Modified Chartres, canvas

Tulsa
All Souls Unitarian Church
Rectangular design, indoor tile

St. Dunstan's Episcopal Church
11-circuit Chartres, canvas

St. John's Episcopal Church
11-circuit Chartres, canvas

Drawing a Classical 3-Circuit Labyrinth

A simple seed pattern of a cross with dots in the center of each of the four quadrants (Step 1) makes drawing a 3-circuit Classical labyrinth quite simple.

Start at the top of the cross and draw a loop either up and to the left or right connecting with the dot in the upper right or left quadrant (Step 2). The way your initial turn curves depends on whether you plan a left- or right-hand labyrinth. This example turns to the right and illustrates a left-hand version of a 3-circuit Classical or Cretan labyrinth.

Connect the corresponding dot in the left quadrant to the right end of the horizontal line of the cross (Step 3).

From the end of the left side of the horizontal line, curve around to the dot in the lower right-hand quadrant (Step 4).

The final circuit is created by connecting the dot in the bottom left-hand quadrant completely around the labyrinth with the bottom of the vertical cross line (Step 5).

Step 1. Seed Pattern   *Step 2. Loop One*   *Step 3. Loop Two*

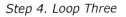

Step 4. Loop Three   *Step 5. Loop Four*

Drawing a Classical 7-Circuit Labyrinth

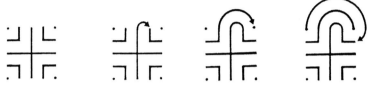

Step 1. Seed Pattern Step 2. Loop One Step 3. Loop Two Step 4. Loop Three

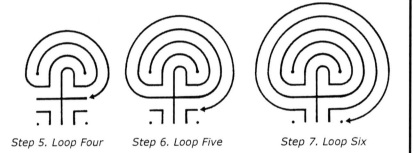

Step 5. Loop Four   Step 6. Loop Five   Step 7. Loop Six

Step 8. Loop Seven   Step 9. Loop Eight

7-Circuit Labyrinth Walk
Emphasizing the Body's Energy Chakras

Any 7-step program or process can be adapted to a Classical labyrinth walk simply by correlating individual steps to a particular path or circuit. The Chartres design could benefit a 12-step curriculum with the last phase corresponding to the center of the 11-circuit pattern.

Although Deepak Chopra's *Seven Laws for Spiritual Success* or Stephen Covey's *Seven Habits of Highly Effective People* would make good labyrinth walks, we will concentrate on the body's seven major energy chakras, employing a Classical Cretan.

The word "chakra" originates from a Sanskit word meaning "spinning wheel." According to ancient Eastern philosophy, seven main energy vortices exist in the human body. These energy spirals can be used to illustrate numerous areas, some of which are noted in the chart on the following page.

Sig Lonegren, of Mid-Atlantic Geomancy, described chakras as "all the vibratory possibilities in the universe divided into seven parts."

Blockages in any of the energy centers disrupt the body's chi or life force, causing dis-ease. Walking a labyrinth concentrating on clearing obstructions in chakra function or energy flow can prevent problems or even illness in the physical, mental, emotional or spiritual realms.

Let us begin our labyrinth walk. We enter the Classical sacred circle on the third path. This corresponds to the third chakra (willpower), representing the solar plexus or naval, and relates to the walker's self-esteem or sense of self in the world. The level of ego covers the mental world of thoughts, facts and logic, and current issues and concerns.

Moving out of the ego, walkers start to focus on other areas. As you walk, notice which corners are difficult to navigate. Corners are symbolic of change. Are you ready to advance or do you habitually revert to old patterns?

The second path of the sacral chakra is the area of emotions and personal feelings. Pleasure and self-gratification influence this chakra.

Turning the second corner into the first path, we deal with survival issues. The root (first) chakra is at the base of the spine and is ruled by the physical. Money, career and health govern this area.

Next comes the fourth circuit, dealing with matters of the heart. Here, the outer path bridges with the inner ones joining the seeker's outer and inner lives, exploring spiritual connections.

From the pathway of love, we travel into the seventh path representing the crown chakra. Awareness, divine direction, understanding, wisdom and enhanced consciousness are emblematic of this upper chakra.

Again, we navigate a corner as we move into the sixth path of the brow chakra or third-eye. Are we ready to embrace a change and "see" things differently or will we revert to antiquated patterns? If we are willing to accept guidance, our intuition blossoms, solutions become visible and we move from belief to knowing.

The final path before entering the center concerns the throat, or fifth chakra. Are you expressing your truth and manifesting those creative desires? Clarity of communication is paramount.

In the center, the destination of our journey, we reflect on any insights gained during our contemplative meditation and prepare to take a renewed focus, joyful wholeness and compassionate sense of connection back to our daily lives. A higher counsel accompanies us as we walk the paths again in reverse order. Hopefully, healing has occurred, our chakras are cleansed and balanced, and our spirit is rejuvenated.

Path	Chakra	Color	Note	Attribute	Planet	Day
3	Solar Plexus	Yellow	E	Willpower	Mars	Tuesday
2	Sacral	Orange	D	Emotions	Earth	Today
1	Root/Base	Red	C	Survival	Saturn	Saturday
4	Heart	Green	F	Love	Venus	Friday
7	Crown	White	B	Wisdom	Moon	Monday
6	Brow	Purple	A	Visualization	Jupiter	Thursday
5	Throat	Blue	G	Communication	Mercury	Wednesday
Center	Celestial	Gold	C'	Outcome/Goal	Sun	Sunday

The above chart identifies the labyrinth path that relates to individual chakras and commonly accepted characteristics. The numbered paths correspond to walking a 7-circuit labyrinth.

Respecting a Sacred Circle

The ancient Greeks wielded their double-headed axes (called *labyrs*) as universal symbols of decisive power. Linked with authority, fire symbolism and creative forces, the axe also represented quick resolution to a problem. Flying sparks severed cords of unnecessary bondage and helped reconcile opposing duality.

As a descendant of the Greek *labyrs*, today's labyrinths serve no less purpose. The shining light of divine inspiration, flashes of existential thunder reverberate along the pathways of these spiraling mandalas.

Respecting a sacred circle emanates from within, the reverent space inside each aspect of the Creator. The shimmering, iridescent Call of the Spirit that resides in each person's individual temple of holiness. Sacred space is synonymous with the blessing of creation.

Tender care of the self connects to a heavenly host and offers gracious support and loving gratitude for expanded consciousness. Honoring the human frame also pays tribute to the sacred. Labyrinths bridge the evolutionary gap transcending finite form, opening an inner dimensional doorway to the infinite.

Their meandering circuits help bring consciousness into this dimension. Awakened souls no longer need play hide and seek. What is hidden is revealed. Heightened awareness taps the vibrant, creative mind of God.

Stale becomes alive, dormant becomes active, agitated becomes peaceful.

Knowledge becomes understanding.

Everything cycles; the pendulum swings both ways. Birth and death are merely alternate footsteps of unexplored potential, signaling the ebb tide of evolutionary regeneration and the inspirational sunset of balanced growth.

Labyrinths embody spiritual consciousness in a changing or evolving society encouraging mankind to seek positive solutions to outdated problems by setting aside judgmental fears and allowing the magic of the moment to bring peace, love, joy and wisdom into our lives.

Sacred circles holistically balance mind, body and spirit in harmony with nature, the cosmic universe and ourselves. If any part of us is out of balance, we may be stressed, dis-eased, unfulfilled or depressed. These symptoms relay a message that something other than the apparent cause could have an underlying or unexpected resolution.

An holistic emphasis involves everyday choices and actions as we strive to attain a higher level of personal satisfaction through an empowering approach to life that recognizes the inter-relationship between happiness, optimum health, lack of conflict, feeling good about yourself, your world and everyone in it.

Springing from the word "holism" and meaning "entities greater than and different from the sum of their parts," the holistic philosophy has a premise that unconditional love is life's most powerful force. The conscious pursuit of the highest qualities of physical, nutritional, environmental, mental, emotional, spiritual and social aspects of the human experience result in holistic, balanced harmony, total peace of mind.

Holistic principles — just like labyrinths — consider the needs, desires, awareness and insight of each individual invoking love, faith, hope, healing, laughter, forgiveness, enthusiasm, and releasing toxic consequences of hostility, shame, guilt, grief, depression, anger, fear, hatred, prejudice and greed.

If life is to be sustained, we can no longer separate ourselves from the elements that comprise the environment. We are part of the earth, the air, the water, the trees, plants and animals. When one part suffers, we all suffer. We are out of balance. Holistic harmony and sacred circles can help realign that imbalance.

The labyrinth supports holism and reveals universal principles of well-being. Hear the music emanating from all objects. Frolic with the undulating rhythms of esoteric vibrations. Access forgotten knowledge and untapped energies. Experience joyful exuberance. Appreciate the beauty of being.

Author Donna Schaper said the labyrinth "lets people walk together and separately without agreeing on anything. The very ancient nature of the labyrinth combined with the archetypal metaphor of its design draws us to absolutes that transcend any human constructs that have separated humanity into arbitrary religious categories for centuries. Walking a labyrinth is not about escaping into the center and leaving the world, it is about experiencing Spirit in the center so you can live in the world in a more blessed way."

A Walking Meditation of Self-Discovery

If a labyrinth is viewed as a metaphor for the journey humans travel during their sojourn on earth, then this allegorical image portrays a continuous initiation offering glimpses into the mysteries of life.

As the labyrinth parallels the sacred journey of creation, each individual circuit of this meandering circle entertains expansive possibilities. Limitless potential highlights growth, change, imagination, discovery, movement, progress, transformation, integrity, an ever-present magical moment of supreme consciousness.

Author Caroline Adams wrote in *A Woman of Wisdom* that life is about "continuously expanding your vision of what is possible, stretching your soul, learning to see clearly and deeply, listening to your intuition, taking courageous challenges at every step along the way. You are on the path exactly where you are meant to be right now. And from here, you can go forward, shaping your life story into a magnificent tale of triumph, of healing, of courage, of beauty, of wisdom, of power, of dignity, and of love."

The labyrinth mirrors her words of wisdom. When walked as a **Journey of Life**, this extraordinary wheel of fortune corresponds to each person's individual maiden voyage. Stroll down memory lane, mindful of past accomplishments, reviewing uncompleted aspirations. Adjust for altered twists and turns and recommit to unfulfilled dreams. Envision an enlightened goal. Walk to your destiny and uncover hidden talents.

Listen, learn, remember. Pay attention to sights and sounds. Observe subtle changes in the terrain. Do the ups and downs remind you of a particular area of your life? Do you feel lost, overburdened or anxious? Where in the labyrinth did this occur? Does it mean anything? Do you like one part of the labyrinth more than another? Why? What do the turns represent in your life? Do you resist some turns and embrace others?

Notice any synchronicities. A certain aroma, an overheard word, song lyrics that pop into your head during the walk or a colorful scrap of paper lying in the fourth circuit may be significant. Relate all experiences in the labyrinth to your life's journey. What does the labyrinth teach about your life?

Each visit to the labyrinth may invoke a different reason. Some walks may entail seeking a connection to one's higher self, balanced direction or perpetual centering, releasing awareness, aligning chakras, experiencing new energies, enhancing healing, reducing stress, solving problems, asking forgiveness, expressing gratitude.

While prayer and meditation are constant labyrinth companions, some walks may focus on a specific supplication. Soliciting assistance for oneself or others in the form of a humble and sincere request, offering praise, thanksgiving or confession in this devout wheel of **prayer** affords true spiritual communion.

Another course of labyrinth interaction might involve **discernment**. Enter the sacred circle with a question and be open for guidance. The answer may come via a feeling, an image, a word, phrase or symbol.

Some walkers traverse the spiraling circuits **chanting a mantra**, a repeated phrase or incantation. Words, sounds or tones may present themselves as part of the journey or individuals or groups might select a favorite mantra while setting their intent.

The **Threefold Path** of Classical Christian Spirituality engages a popular labyrinthine technique. These three stages embrace the one path pilgrims partook as representative of the literal medieval journey on dangerous unprotected roads through strange territories towards a shrine or spiritual center. The trip's three parts (setting out, arrival and return) were reflected in the multiple components of the labyrinth walk, which served as a substitute for real pilgrimage when conditions prevented lengthy travel.

• **Releasing, setting out, purgation**: From the entrance to the goal (center) is the path of shedding or "letting go." Travelers are encouraged to release emotional baggage, guilt, doubt, fear, worries, concerns and empty their cache of burdens.

Purgation liberates the mind, quiets pesky details, cleanses undesirable elements, detaches from excessive thoughts and impure emotions.

• **Receiving, arrival, illumination**: Upon arrival in the center, pilgrims receive insight, clarity, focus and peace. The esoteric meaning of heaven as the inner realm of consciousness applies here. A receptive, meditative state of illumination characterizes the center (goal, heaven). Stay as long as you like in peaceful meditation and prayer. Be open to intuitive messages or feelings from God, your higher self or the angelic realm. Receive what is offered for you to take back into your new world of awareness.

• **Integrating, return, union**: The path out of the labyrinth provides the opportunity to integrate this experience into a more positive lifestyle. Seekers become grounded, energized and empowered to manifest their new creativity by uniting with God, a Higher Power or universal healing forces. Each encounter with a sacred circle gifts the walker with love, light, laughter, magic, music, healing, wisdom, compassion and understanding to discover and fulfill their purpose and mission on earth as a sentient being. Spiritual souls reach out to others, owning responsibility for their actions, sharing their talents and accomplishing heavenly goals.

The above three stages also signify a "**palms up, palms down**" approach to labyrinth interaction. "Palms down" symbolizes release or letting go while "palms up" indicates receiving. Enter the labyrinth and spiral to the center with palms down to focus thoughts on releasing conflicting issues, fear, worries and concerns. In the center, turn palms up to be receptive to insight. On the return trip out, keep palms up receiving strength and guidance to manifest any informative perceptions. When leaving the labyrinth, turn to face the center and bring palms together to acknowledge a prayerful end of thanksgiving for a safe and empowering experience.

Labyrinths of **ritual** add meaning, honor and support to life's expeditions. Walks of **joy and celebration** connect us with an inner state of bliss that transcends emotion and taps into our eminent God-presence. Special events, weddings, grief counseling, rites of passage, vision quests, initiations and seasonal holiday festivities embrace labyrinth interactions. Such a circuitous voyage offers a sustained glimpse into the multiple chambers of the human heart. Truth and spirituality coalesce into the alchemical gold of the philosopher's stone. The journey is sometimes more important than the destination.

A labyrinthine walk circles to the center of our lives. Occasionally, an excursion of **compassion** is required. Loss, sadness and grief compel we seek consolation and comfort. Letting go is required. The path of the labyrinth gently nudges acceptance, release and reflective contemplation. Individually, we can walk into and out of our grief. Communally, we can show support and express care, kindness, empathy and understanding.

These sacred circles can also represent a restorative excursion. **Healing** is not only physical, but also overlaps emotional, mental and spiritual bodies. A physical healing is often described as a cure. While a cure might not be possible, healing is always an option. Healing restores wholeness. Freedom from pain and suffering are other attributes associated with health and well-being. Inspiration, enjoyment and enthusiasm constitute harmony and completeness. Labyrinths help identify the cause of affected health challenges and encourage unified expectations.

One of the authors said her first use of a **finger labyrinth** produced interesting results. "I love it! My fingers just slide through the pathways and the sensation of the wood grain in some paths versus the smooth, cool feel of polished wood in others makes it a joy to use. I received several answers to questions relating to my sis-in-law and to my own health issues.

"This beautiful wooden finger labyrinth is such a cool tool for self-exploration. It's brought some resolution and peace to me just from the touch and feel of it. I love running it with both hands. The journey through it is always surprising."

Finger labyrinths can also be walked with a stylus or pencil and allow those who are less mobile, physically challenged or without transportation the opportunity for labyrinth interaction. These great therapeutic tools can be utilized in any of the suggested approaches mentioned in this section. The smaller versions bring the advantages of walking a sacred circle into one's home regardless of outside weather conditions. Peace of mind, relaxation and stress reduction can literally be at your fingertips. Gives the advertising slogan, "Let your fingers do the walking," a completely new connotation.

Free style — Labyrinths speak to people of different religions and cultural backgrounds. Women like to dance in them, children enjoy running. Men test unusual steps and postures. Individuals and groups share their joys and sorrows. Creative expression encompasses multiple modalities.

Experiment with different types of walks and attitudes. Some interactions may be joyous or somber, celebratory or melancholy, others thoughtful or prayerful. A walking meditation is always good use of sacred space. Adults are usually serious in the labyrinth. Children casually skip or rapidly run the spiraling circuits in a playful manner. Choose the proper mode for a particular session while setting intentions prior to entering the circulatory experience. Alternate mentalities frequently. Life has more than one gear and numerous perspectives. Why shouldn't labyrinths?

Invite friends from the plant, mineral and animal kingdoms

to join in the festivities. Gemstones, aromatherapy and astrology add special significance to labyrinthine interactions. The elementals create another intriguing aspect. Have an art therapy session, a reiki walk, set a pyramid over the center, paint a temporary labyrinth in an original design in a parking lot, mow one in the yard. Draw a sacred circle on your driveway to honor the goddess of the returning Divine Feminine, craft one using Christmas lights to showcase the pathways. Write a poem, illustrate a sketch, color a mandala or meditate with a finger labyrinth while sitting in the center. Share artistic genius and inspired imagination.

It's okay to play in a sacred circle. Singing, drumming, dancing or music enhances energy. Meditative silence, spoken prayers, solitary time, group encounters... anything is acceptable if done with reverence. Respect is the benchmark.

Observe cloud formations overhead and the colorful patterns and iridescent hues of a gorgeous sky. Listen to the serenading sounds of birds, crickets and frogs. Notice special messages that may provide solutions to a current problem or answer secret questions. Pay attention to everything that transpires, nudges those little grey cells or alerts your senses (especially the intuitive sixth sense).

Note any trees, flowers and herbs within sight and study their attributes. Interesting stones or rock formations, unique passage patterns, feelings or strange sensations may be important coded communiqués. Ideas, memories, song titles, number combinations... listen to the ever-present voice of your heart.

What does a praying mantis, grasshopper, ladybug, squirrel, hummingbird or roly-poly mean to you? Doesn't matter what it means to anyone else. It's your life and your choice. Live it to the fullest. Since you're here on earth, you might as well enjoy it.

One way is to enter the Labyrinth of Life and follow the path. Walkers connect with fellow travelers completing the return phase of an extended journey as they release fear and embark on a new course. Do what feels natural when you meet. Experience your own emotions. Apply the encounter as a metaphor for your life. Gratefully receive the gifts offered. Reflect through journaling, drawing, sculpting, gyrating or any appropriate way of self-expression that materializes.

Labyrinths bridge the gap between what is and what can be. They serve as a link to a distant part of ourselves uniting diverse cultures and ageless eras. Enhanced prophetic powers and expanded states of consciousness are within reach. Body and soul, physical and spiritual, mental and emotional, left and right, masculine and feminine, heaven and earth complete a divine essence of self-discovery. The walking meditation has triumphantly surpassed our expectations. One foot at a time, we reach the heavenly place of wholeness (holiness) our souls yearn to remember.

Edmond First United Methodist Church
Guide to Walking the Labyrinth

The labyrinth is a sacred path found in all religious traditions in various forms around the world. Ours is a replica of a sacred walk designed in the Middle Ages (1201) for the floor of Chartres Cathedral in France. It was used to symbolize the pilgrimage to Jerusalem, to be a walking meditation to reflect on life and to be a sacred space. There is only one path, so there are no tricks or dead ends. So walk with an open mind and an open heart.

Before Walking
• Remove all footwear, roll up your cuffs so they won't drag, and relax.
• Intentionally clear your mind and become aware of your breathing.
• As you walk, give yourself permission to accept yourself and others as we are. We are on the same path, but at different turning points.
• Wait one minute to enter if someone has just begun their journey. While waiting, you may want to walk around the edge of the labyrinth.

The Journey In
• Allow yourself to find the pace your body wants to go.
• You may pass people or let others step around you at the turns.
• The path is two ways. Those going in will meet those coming out.
• Focus on the pathway.
• Give attention to your innermost thoughts and listen to your body.
• Examine the quality of your stage of life. Explore your dreams, hopes and expectations.

Time at the Center
• Rest a few minutes. (The walk has been 1/3 mile.)
• Reflect on the experience of walking in. Open your body, mind, heart and soul to the divine.
• Anticipate the return.

The Journey Out
- Consider the implications of your renewed thoughts and feelings for your daily life and work. Plan changes.
- Upon finishing the walk, you may want to walk around the edges of the labyrinth.

Time at the End
- Take a quiet moment to reflect on the meaning of your experience.
- Write and share your thoughts.

*   *   *

Courtesies
It is important to honor each person's space and mutual time for prayer and meditation. Walking a labyrinth may take anywhere from a few minutes to more than an hour, depending on the pace of each walker, size of the labyrinth and amount of time spent in the center. Walk the labyrinth at your own pace. You are free to pass another walker or you may allow another walker to pass you. Stay as long as you like in the center, unless it is necessary to make room for those who come into the center after you and have the same need for space.

*   *   *

Bi-Directional Path
The path into the labyrinth is the same path out, so you may meet someone on the path. Simply step slightly to the side as you pass.

There is a possibility you may start walking on a different path after meeting someone. That is okay. You will merely get to the center more quickly or you will find yourself at the entrance/exit area, where you can start again or end your walk.

Your experience with the labyrinth can be a reflective mirror providing symbols and metaphors. Some have intense experiences, others have more subtle encounters. Experiences will vary each time you walk the labyrinth.

You may notice an increase in your personal growth and self-healing after walking a labyrinth. Consider writing or journaling your experience. Some people enjoy talking with a friend after their walk.

Suggestions for Labyrinth Interaction

Dr. Debi Bocar, of Optimal Potentials, is a labyrinth facilitator who owns two canvas labyrinths: a multi-colored 7-circuit and an 11-circuit Chartres. She shares the following guidelines for interacting with a sacred circle.

Walking the Labyrinth

A labyrinth is an ancient symbol that relates to wholeness. It combines the imagery of the circle and the spiral in a meandering, but purposeful, path.

Labyrinths provide a spatial focus to encourage people to be in the present moment. They have only one path so you don't need to make choices — you follow the path into the center and follow the same path back to the outside.

When you think about maneuvering through space, your right brain is activated which can enhance creativity, intuitive insights, visions of the "big picture" (spiritual perspective) and assist in integrating mental, emotional, spiritual and physical experiences.

The labyrinth can represent a journey to your own center and back into the world again. The experience of walking a labyrinth can provide meaningful metaphors in each person's individual life journey.

Phases of Walking

Some experience the following phases while walking:

• Releasing — From the entrance to the center you can shed, empty and "let go" of worries and concerns.

• Receiving — At the center, you may experience illumination, insight, clarity and focus. Some receive answers to specific questions. Stay in the center as long as you want.

• Returning - Integrating — The path out can involve integrating what transpired and becoming grounded. As you return, you may become energized and empowered to manifest what you received.

Individualized Expressions

• Some hold their hands with palms facing the earth during the first phase to symbolize releasing cares and concerns.

• Some hold their palms up during the second and third phases to symbolize a willingness to receive.

• Some uses scarves and ribbons while dancing and skipping in the labyrinth.
• Some use chimes, gongs and bells as they exit to extend their experience into the world.

Uses of Labyrinth Walks

Stress reduction, meditation, prayer, enhancing healing, creativity and intuition, insights regarding decisions, contemplation, grieving, rites of passage and celebrations.

There is no right or wrong way to walk a labyrinth. Walking the labyrinth is a personal experience. Listen to your inner wisdom about how you need to interact with the labyrinth during each walk.

Recommendations to Consider

• Please remove your shoes (or wear shoe covers or socks) if walking on a canvas labyrinth.
• Please do not take food or drinks on a canvas labyrinth.
• Some like to walk around the outside edge of the labyrinth before entering the labyrinth or after completing their walk.
• Before walking, many find it helpful to consciously free themselves of resentments against anyone or anything and nourish a sense of forgiveness while on the labyrinth.
• Most people start at the entrance. It is helpful to relax and focus before entering the labyrinth.
• Some become aware of their natural breathing pattern.
• Some concentrate on a controlled breathing pattern.
• Use any activity that helps you center yourself before entering the labyrinth.
• Approach the labyrinth with "soft eyes" which reduces external stimuli, increasing your personal awareness and acceptance of yourself and others.
• As you walk, allow yourself to develop your own pace. If you are walking with others, you may move around each other depending on the varying paces.
• When people reach the center, they often stand or sit and spend as much time as they want until they feel "ready" to make their way back out using the same path.
• Depending on the walking pace and how long one stays in the center, the labyrinth walk takes from 20-30 minutes.
Or it can take your whole life.

Walking a Path of Divine Essence

"This project was not built to just look at — even though it is a true work of art and a pleasure to behold. The Tonkawa labyrinth is interactive public art and wants to give back... by our using it... by our walking its path — once a day, once a week, once a month. I believe it can both store energy and release energy. It has potential far beyond our understanding — it is a newborn with an ancient past. It already has an old and mature soul.

"Listen closely when you walk and maybe you will hear the sound of the Santa Fe Railroad below your steps or maybe the flow of 6th street traffic of an earlier day. Or maybe you'll just hear your own footsteps, your own heartbeat, your own inner voice."

— **Audrey Schmitz**
Heart-in-the Park Artist

*   *   *

"I simply enjoy walking a labyrinth as a tool to access my inner peace."

— **Joan Korenblit**
Respect Diversity Foundation

*   *   *

"Each of us is on a pilgrimage, but no two are alike. Just as our dreams aid and improve our mental and emotional balance even when we don't recall them, a walking meditation on the labyrinth seems to stir a mysterious something within that expands our mundane lives. Labyrinth walkers often feel an increase of harmony, wholeness, holiness, quietude, accomplishment, or all of these and more — whether or not we expect these things to happen.

"We stand at the very entrance of a temple — an invisible temple, except for the faint outline where spirit and matter embrace. A soft light shines in this etheric place, the light of high consciousness that glows overhead, bestowing illumination to our path."

— **Rev. Carol Parrish**
Sparrow Hawk Village

"Our church has a portable labyrinth which is utilized a couple of times a year, for about two weeks at a time. I have walked it and found it helpful for shaking out the unnecessary tangles of garbage I have stored in my head."

**— Philys Dawson
Norman Social Worker**

* * *

"I loved touching the tree in the middle of the walk. The touch and texture of the tree that has so much wisdom growing inside of it. The rocks on the path are uneven but this makes the walk more enjoyable and interesting. I feel more in tune with nature after taking the walk of the labyrinth."

**— Nancy Sloan
Duncan Veteran**

* * *

"On some of the labyrinths we walked gathering data for this book, I noticed the paths were sometimes uneven and often difficult to traverse. At one point, I turned to look at the last turn to see if it had been a left turn and almost lost my way back out. Hmmm, must mean I need to stay centered and take more notice of the path (journey) and less notice of the past! Stay in the present and tend to present issues. Only diligence, asking for help, and staying focused allow each day's adventure to be a victory."

**— Phyllis Pennington
Graphic Designer**

* * *

"Our trip to Duncan to walk the new labyrinth there in June of 2007 was quite memorable. We were distracted by something blowing against the passenger window and missed our turnpike exit. The long detour allowed us to enjoy the beautiful scenery of Mount Scott near Lawton. A sense of peace came through my being on seeing that mountain. Those of us on the journey couldn't help but notice how the drive this day was similar to walking a labyrinth. There is a beginning and a destination that is preset, the path is often long and winding, and sometimes when travelers think they are close, they discover they have a much longer journey ahead as the road seemingly leads away from the center (goal)."

— Linda Yeingst
Registered Nurse

*   *   *

"I joined the authors on their first group labyrinth walk gathering research for this book in late 2006. As soon as I started walking, I immediately tapped into my past life as a monk walking the labyrinth at the Cathedral of Chartres, which was the model for the one I was currently walking at Mercy Hospital. I found myself chanting prayers in Latin and in a Gregorian chant format. I neither know Latin nor Gregorian. Lifting me to another very pleasant life experience could have been the answer to the immediate lowering of my blood pressure. By the time we reached the Unity Labyrinth, I had brought that energy from the Spiritual Plane to the Mental/Etheric and used it to clear and release what was necessary on the Emotional/Astral Level. All that contributed to the lower blood pressure, I am sure.

"Moral of the story: A labyrinth experience definitely causes no harm, so walk one whenever you have the opportunity. It just might lower your blood pressure or provide other health benefits."

— Barbara Clayton
Energy Healer

*   *   *

"When an individual puts forth the effort to walk any labyrinth, the thoughts are focused on the goal, which could be for a wide variety of reasons. This is another form of prayer, listening and reflecting on your intentions. Even when the intention is to just relax. Alleviating stress is healthy at all levels: physically, mentally and spiritually. The same thing can be accomplished just by taking a walk or finding a quiet place to sit. However, when an individual puts forth the effort, even when it is spontaneous, to walk a labyrinth, the results are surprising because of the inner peace one experiences. After all, world peace begins with a single individual."

— Jody Walker
Edmond CPA

"I have walked labyrinths in Tulsa (mowed into the grass), Edmond (in a gym on painted canvas), Oklahoma City (painted on a parking lot), Sparrow Hawk (on top of a mountain, outlined on stone), and at the Oklahoma Holistic Health Fairs (painted on canvas). For a year or more, I walked one at United Life Church every Saturday morning. Each was special and unique for the memories.

"My favorite labyrinth in Oklahoma was the one at United Life Church. It was near my home, I could go whenever I wanted and I liked the energy. I don't remember anything special happening, it was just a quiet, peaceful place. I was almost always greeted by a large flock of crows. The most interesting was the Classical one at Sparrow Hawk. The day we visited, part of it had been washed away by a rainstorm. It took some concentration to discern the path without the obvious guidelines.

"It always amazes me that each time I walk, I think I am almost to the center only to find myself traveling the outer edges. I love to find new labyrinths, and hope I can get back to Oklahoma soon to walk some of these new ones!"

— Lynette Cook
Avid Spiritual Seeker

*   *   *

"In my work with Wicca, the labyrinth provides a multi-modal metaphor for our spiritual pathworking. The labyrinth is built on and often out of earth. As we walk it, we rebuild it again on the mental and imaginative planes of consciousness — the perfect combination of energies for the deepening, meditative and contemplative communion with Spirit/Self, allowing us to utilize the type of 'split-consciousness' which is necessary to perform magick.

"I fell in love with the Goddess and labyrinths in the same year. It was so natural a form to use for Goddess worship and rituals. At the full moon, we built them on the beach, drawing them in the sand and on the new moon, on our patios with colored chalk. For the Sabbats, we laid them out with tealights and twinkly lights. We fashioned one out of chairs for wedding guests and sent the couple into it, where upon arriving at center, I performed their handfasting. We raked one into fallen leaves and held a memorial. We danced in them, chanted in them, drummed in them, birthed in them. When I started a woman's temple several years later, I named it 'Labyrinth, Temple of the Goddess.'

"For a fluffy woman, the 7-circuit labyrinth is the best exercise for the body, mind and spirit; fit women are welcome to utilize the Chartres Cathedral design."

**— Emmah Eastwind
Papyrus Librarian**

*   *   *

"We plan to add benches and some landscaping someday, but I doubt we will ever put a fence to separate the labyrinth from the street or nearby parking spaces.

"I have found that when I am walking the labyrinth, the parking lot doesn't bother me too much. Sometimes, I will walk before the Wednesday evening service and people who park there are most respectful of the space. They quietly walk around and into the church. Some of them even join me for a walk. If it were fenced, I don't think it would be as inviting. We want it to be open and don't want people to feel uncomfortable saying hello to those walking. Isn't life all about interruptions, then recentering when interrupted?"

**— Rev. Karla Dillon
Duncan All Saints Episcopal Church**

*   *   *

"Walking a labyrinth can be a cleansing experience and connect children and adults in a kinesthetic and visceral way. All come together as they dance the labyrinth. There is no age requirement.

"When we did the first labyrinth at the Children's Festival, my son Ben, who has serious learning disabilities, found new depths to his being as he walked that Chartres replica. He said he saw himself as a 'wolf who could do things.' He was empowered by this visualization of power and self-sufficiency."

**— Elizabeth Muller
Universal Dances of Peace**

"Researching this project, visiting exquisite private property with beautiful, landscaped labyrinths, I wondered why anyone would want a sacred circle in their back yard. Now, after creating a 77-foot (circumference) Wisdom Wheel Directional Labyrinth at my residence, which I commune with daily, my question is: Why wouldn't anyone want a labyrinth in their back yard!"

— **Gail Peck**
7 Hawks Publishing

*   *   *

From Disinterested Observer
to Meaningful Experiences

Gore resident LeRay Biswell accompanied the authors on 14 of their labyrinth walks. Not because he was interested in sacred circles, he just enjoyed our company. The Air Force veteran originally traveled with us "to get out of the house and have something to do."

He had a stroke three years ago and, although occasionally walks with a cane, usually rides around in a wheelchair. LeRay went from "just being along for the ride" to wanting to visit a labyrinth. "When's our next trip?" he would ask.

On some of those trips, he had a few meaningful experiences in spite of himself. The former skeptic had visions in many of the labyrinths he visited and even an out-of-body experience. Healing touch and reiki sessions were frequently performed on him in the center of these spiraling circuits. He shares four of his most profound encounters below:

July 4, 2007 — Tonkawa Heart-in-the Park

"Tonkawa HIP is where I got my heart! I got my spiritual heart in Tonkawa. I purchased the token necklace I am wearing there and I feel like it protects me. I wear it always; I haven't taken if off since I put it on over a year ago. My guardians were there with me in Tonkawa when I bought the necklace, which was designed by the lady who crafted the heart-shaped labyrinth design. A guardian owl told me it was okay. I kept hearing him over and over and knew I was safe. This is the first one that I started having feelings toward labyrinths. Before this, I did not even see any meaning for them, just something you guys were encouraging me to do. I want to be a part of that one for some reason. It is wheelchair accessible and I could walk all the way around it in my wheelchair. The first time I walked the whole labyrinth and it was my sixth labyrinth."

July 29, 2007 — P_Bar Farms, Weatherford

"Did not see the labyrinth as it was too far for me to travel across the grass in my wheelchair and too hot for anyone to push me that distance. At least that was my excuse since the sun was shining brightly and I did not want to stay in the heat very long. Enjoyed the well-kept grounds — large space like an amusement park or hayride place. Even though it was 100 degrees, I had a cool breeze on me at all times, although I'm not sure how. Saw some rabbits hopping around. Something was definitely going on that day. I'm not sure what, but it was one of my most enjoyable days."

July 29, 2007 —
Combination Medicine Wheel Labyrinth, Lawton

"Had visions about Shiva (the Hindu god of destruction and rebirth, protector, avenger, Lord of the Dance, source of all movement in the cosmos). This was a synchronicity — learned a new word here — which tossed me for a loop because the owner of this labyrinth had the same vision exactly one week before. She went inside her house and brought me a picture of Shiva she had drawn after her vision the week before. I had a very spiritual experience at this labyrinth. It brought up more questions than I have answers for and started me thinking that there may be something to telepathy or thinking alike. It tossed all my old beliefs in a trash can. I had to start thinking in new ways. I am still fighting it.

"That labyrinth is spiritual and still with me. I think what made it so is the owner had the same identical vision I had. That blew my mind. She wasn't just saying it, she had a personal drawing to prove it. That made it more believable than if she were just agreeing with my vision. Her drawing had an elephant like I saw, same identical characteristics, and a battle image just like mine. I can't believe both of us — strangers until this day — had the same vision a week apart. What are the chances of that and why would we both have the same vision? Maybe there is something to this spiritual world other than what I believe. Was it another entity or some other force that caused us to see the same thing? Where did this come from? I want to know more about this force or what caused it."

July 31, 2007 - United Life Church

"I was more interested in the full moon ceremony than the labyrinth. They dragged me out to the labyrinth for some hands-on healing and a reiki session. Very powerful healing touch; I could feel the energy. Kind of surprised me. This energy was better than a massage. I was so impressed and went the next day to the ULC reiki healing session where I experienced more feeling in my hand than I have ever had since my stroke."

As LeRay's experiences exemplify, just being in the presence of a labyrinth can produce amazing results. Walking a path of divine essence often generates more questions than it answers and makes one think that, perhaps, the answers we seek lie in the questions we ask.

* * *

Surrender to a New Consciousness

"My heart skipped a beat when I was invited to walk a labyrinth for the first time, communicating to me, 'Yes! We need to do this.'

"The closer we got to the site of the sacred design, the quieter my countenance grew so that by the time we arrived, I was enveloped in such a holy hush that I was barely aware of those with me. What was about to happen here? The anticipation increased as I took my first step over the threshold of the labyrinth. The presence of the Divine and the presence of myself were unmistakable as I became vividly aware of the presence of the Divine within myself!

"I slowly and mindfully stepped one foot in front of the other, carefully following the winding path, which seemed only to be leading me to a deeper stillness within. I began to realize I was walking farther and farther away from more than simply the entrance. I realized I was leaving behind EVERYTHING! Fear, anger, pride, control — all were dropping one by one as I drew near the center of the labyrinth.

"The cool breeze on my face then whispered, 'Surrender...'

"The pile of tokens and gifts offered by those who came before me whispered, 'Surrender...'

"The passion and purpose beating within my own heart whispered, 'Surrender...'

"With a deep, cleansing breath, I did the only thing left in my world I could do. I dug in my pocket for the door key to my apartment, tossed it to the center pile, and surrendered."

**— Lloyd Matthew Thompson
Artist, Photographer, Writer**

*   *   *

Unfortunately, the word "surrender" evokes negative images for many people. Spiritual surrender is a whole different genre. A surrendered state completes holiness and implies acceptance and non-resistance. The miracle of surrender graciously allows yielding to rather than opposing the flow of life. It takes courage to surrender.

This gift of grace helps humans release inner blockages to nagging, persistent, recurring dramas. Surrendering can break unconscious resistance patterns that perpetuate unpleasant situations.

A new spiritual energy enters the world through a surrendered state of grace. Free of suffering, negativity and pollution, spiritual energy vibrates to a higher frequency and yields positive change.

"Yield" means "to produce" and is an Old English word akin to *gelten*, translated "to be worth." This production gives or furnishes a natural process as the result of cultivation (yielded a good crop, to give in return, an investment that yielded high profits, yield right of way).

No negativity, defeat or failure there. In fact, quite the opposite. Worth yields value, importance, excellence, quality and leads to inner peace. Natural processes are good, too.

Surrender to your higher self and accept the peace that surpasses all understanding.

The Labyrinth as Counselor
in a "Know Thyself" Walk

The labyrinth is a good spiritual counselor. Sessions are free and usually provide interesting analytical input concerning the circumstances of humanity. Let's visit one and receive some complimentary psychotherapy.

The counselor asks:
"Will you join me today or stand and watch?
Life is not a spectator sport.
But many idly sit in the bleachers.

"Of course, you have another option. There is always another option. You could refuse to play the game. But you've done that most of your life. So why not cast aside your fears and participate? Remember, no decision is a decision."

The seeker shuffled collective feet drawing on eons of cultural labyrinthine experience. "I choose to forgive myself and anyone else who helped me perpetuate my non-game of life and enter your path today."

"A good choice," the labyrinth counselor replied. "Let's see if we can symbolize a paradoxical antithesis of the twisted dichotomy of human emotion."

"What does that mean?" we asked.

"Who the hell knows? Sounds impressive though, doesn't it?"

"Hopefully, humanity is well past the stage of impressionist therapy," we retorted.

"We labyrinths are certainly glad to hear that. Makes our job much easier. But are you absolutely sure humans are beyond the need to impress fellow earthlings, belittling some and exalting others?"

"No, I guess not," we sadly admitted.

"Glad to see your honest side showed up today," the counselor intoned. "Now maybe we can make some progress."

*   *   *

"Let's set some ground rules. I know you don't like rules and think they were made to be broken or changed, but sometimes they are necessary to move the planet forward or at least keep

Mother Earth on her paradoxical axis."

"Now, quit that," we said, slapping our hands together.

"Just wanted to see if I had your undivided attention. Sometimes, you humans fail to concentrate and scatter your focus all over the universe."

"Yes, unfortunately, we have leaned toward that tendency in the past, but today our intentions are to walk with an open mind and receptive heart. To stay focused and centered on the task and release any expectations of what might reveal itself."

"Wow, the collective consciousness has finally progressed beyond inertia," the labyrinth counselor mused.

"We choose to ignore that snide remark and move forward."

"Another landmark evolutionary step for humanity," said the counselor, nodding in approval. "Only a short time ago, you would have exhibited extreme anger, resentment, pride, vehement disapproval and tried to pulverize me further into the ground, violently swinging collective fists."

We smiled with God, noting our progressive growth and development as a human race.

*   *   *

The counselor took control of the session saying it was good to release expectations as they frequently "get in the way" of the actual experience and obscure insight.

"Each walk provides a different aspect of who you are. Interaction with a labyrinth constitutes a spiritual tool, a path of prayer, a walking meditation. An expectancy exists as to when the center will be reached just as there is an expectation of completing the journey and reaching the destination (definitive goal). Sometimes, it is best to just see what happens without any expectations of the outcome."

"That's good advice," we acknowledged.

"Thank you," the labyrinth said, asking what our desires were. "Do you want new insight, relaxation, centering, a sense of peace, to know the mind of God or which lottery numbers you should select?"

"While any of that would be nice," we agreed, "it sets an expectation which we decided to release, remember?"

"Aha, almost caught you," the counselor said, raising a grassy eyebrow. "Is there a difference between setting intentions and expectations?"

"Definitely. Intent is directed resolve, purpose, will and determination while anticipation of a future act or event and its predicted result denotes expectation."

We grinned sheepishly. "Guess you did catch us."

"Yes, it's okay to set intentions and plan for the future provided you allow for change and a different outcome. Unfulfilled expectations cause frustration and impede the magic of the present moment."

* * *

"Now, let's talk about the human need to control every tiny detail and the misguided belief that blood, sweat and tears are the keys to success. Those are outdated paradigms."

The seeker shook its collective head. "Control and success are big issues in our world. It's hard to let go and trust in forces you cannot see, touch or feel. Especially when the world is so chaotic."

"That's where self-deception, illusion and lack of confidence cloud your judgment. And I don't mean lack of confidence in the human condition. I mean lack of confidence in your faith and the combined ability of yourself and a Supreme Being to handle any situation."

"I suppose this is where you quote the Bible verse that if God provides for the little chickadees, he will provide for me, too."

"No, but that could apply," the spiral counselor laughed, entering the labyrinth. "Same principle, but that verse refers to sparrows." As we embarked on the first path, my new friend reminded us the walk to the center is for releasing, letting go, purging.

The dictionary describes purge as to cleanse or rid of impurities, foreign matter or undesirable elements; to become clean, clear or pure, cathartic; to cleanse of guilt or sin.

"In psychiatry, catharsis means the purging of emotional baggage, alleviation of fears, problems and complexes by bringing them to consciousness or giving them expression," the labyrinth counselor shared.

"The fear of inner demons taking over is why humans throttle the control button," the counselor continued. "Even Jesus had to cast aside his demons when he instructed Satan to 'Get thee behind me.'

"And, don't forget some new acronyms for fear and sin: False

Evidence Appearing Real and Self Inflicted Nonsense."

"I've heard laughter is good for the soul and the best medicine," we countered.

The counselor smiled. "The path of the world may seem confusing as walkers twist and turn along life's journey, but courageously continuing to put one foot in front of the other ends the chaos as the destined goal (center) is reached."

"Do you mean destiny or destination?" we inquired.

"Same thing. Humans get too tied up in word games. Since you guys like games so much, let's play one as we walk," the counselor suggested. "What part of the human body corresponds to a labyrinth?"

A floundering blank stare amused our new friend.

"Okay, I'll give you a hint. A labyrinth has a unicursal path. What part of your body travels a single circuit to its destination and back to the source?"

"The circulatory system?"

"Correct for 400 points. The human circulatory system represents the existential joy of being, life blood flowing from a loving heart to all parts of the body and back to the source. Just like God."

"I get it," the collective seeker said, rounding a difficult turn. "The systems of the human body work on their own allowing us to relinquish the need for control. Blood spirals through our bodies like circuits of a sacred circle. Rounding out our game analogy, the elusive search for truth either quickens the pace or slows breathing depending on mankind's deep-seated beliefs of a successful life of ease or the controlled school of hard knocks."

"Something like that," the labyrinth winked. "Success is simplicity itself, expansive enjoyment of life to it fullest creative expression."

*   *   *

"Fellow members of the collective have entered my path. Let's see how well you play with others," the labyrinth stated. "I am a place of encounters where individuals learn as much about themselves as they are prepared to accept. They can also view their place in the overall scheme if willing to candidly scrutinize mankind's collective face."

The walker-client stumbled, contemplating the changing situation. Where did these people come from?

How dare them intrude on my therapy session.

"Careful," the counselor warned, steadying our composure. "Additional travelers constantly accompany us making the journey more pleasant or showing us rough facets of ourselves we need to polish."

Yeah, right, we thought. Suppose we don't like what we see? How will we react to those trying to help us overcome our fears? Where will this path take us? Maybe we won't like ourselves any more. Maybe we never did.

"Things aren't always what they appear," the labyrinth admonished. "Remember, when all those black and red bugs descended on the sides of your house and practically covered the maple tree? You went on a 10-day rampage swatting them three times a day when all you needed to do was figure out what was bugging you and the little critters would have dispersed on their own.

"Do people bug you?"

"I refuse to answer that on the grounds it might incriminate my persona."

An amused counselor nodded. "Everyone may be on the same path externally, but each person's inner journey is unique. All paths are distinct, even though the destination is identical. The road map you use to get there is up to you.

"Whether you pass, allow others to pass and how you feel at close proximity to strangers provides clues about relationship issues. Many recoil, several enjoy the interaction."

"How do I know if what a compatriot reveals is merely their projection or mirroring an internal challenge or external problem I need to eliminate?" the collective seeker asked.

"It's probably both," the counselor remarked. "When the student is ready, the teacher will appear."

"Are you my teacher?"

"The labyrinth is a therapeutic tool that reveals answers pertinent to a person's highest good. Its archetypal image connects to God, the world and everyone in it. Sacred circles expose the unknown and simultaneously offer clarity and perfection. They divulge incredulous elements detailing the mystery of being and tender a glimpse into the fascinating beauty and peaceful harmony of the sustaining universe."

The student digested this information before asking, "If we are all on the identical path with the same destination, how come many are moving in opposite directions?"

"It only appears fellow travelers are going different directions. All roads diverge into the Path of Oneness."

*   *   *

"One of the authors has an outgoing message on her answering machine suggesting people dance the celebration of life with the angels of joy. What can a labyrinth teach about that admonition?" the student inquired.

"Dancing is a celebratory expression of divine movement. Angels imply a state of protective bliss. Joy and creativity unite inside a sacred circle."

The seeker nodded in agreement. "I will have to admit I often feel graceful movement flowing through my body as I spiral labyrinthine circuits. The liberating sensation of this primordial and illustrious articulation of the life force radiates creative manifestation."

"Now for the historic ramifications," the counselor said, initiating her oratory. "Primitive dancers blended with the flow of cosmic energy and believed that dance movements, patterns and gestures orchestrated the processes of nature or the unseen forces that controlled them. This principle influenced the symbolism of ancient dance forms intended to invoke rain or sun, crop or human fertility, healing, military success, protection of benevolent spirits or appeasement of destructive ones.

"Round dances mimicked circular movements of the sun, moon and seasons and emanated warmth, mystique and growth. Weaving and threading flourishes choreographed the starry movement of heavenly constellations. Dancing around an object magnified its energy and shielded components. Shamans whirled in planetary orbit patterns wielding strength and power, arms raised to draw cosmic energy downward, lowered to direct dynamic vitality into the earth. Dances with animal costumes, masks and parody captured the characteristics attributed to distinct creatures. Thus, the serpentine dance of the priestess at Delphi drew on snake symbolism of wisdom and fertility. Wedding dances and various forms of linked dancing signified union. Funeral dances portrayed grief. Shamanic healers aspired to evoke and enrich creative forces through dance."

"That's very entertaining and educational," the seeker said. "But some people consider gyrating in a sacred circle sacrareligious."

"Religion is an attempt to control the masses. Spirituality is man's individual connection to the divine," the labyrinthine counselor opined. "Uninhibited dancing is considered therapeutic, granting the dancer release from the structural tension of social rules and, perhaps, inspired by the cadence of the human heartbeat or the tempo of rhythmic walking.

"It was the earliest form of theater, translating spiritual beliefs into expressive movement as in the religious dances of ancient Egypt and Greece. Military victory was rehearsed in war dances, hence the symbolism behind the sword dances of the Scots or Parthans."

"What about trance dancing?" the student asked.

"What about it?" the counselor chuckled, twirling her spiraling circuits in a graceful pirouette.

Without waiting for an answer to the rhetorical quip, the counselor extended its labyrinthine arms, feigned a double-twist and replied. "Trance dancing gives individual consciousness a new expression of transformative symbolism, the attainment of an altered state. The dancer becomes the celestial performance.

"Consider the iconography of dancing gods. Shiva, the Hindu Lord of the Dance, depicts the flaming embodiment of both creative and destructive energy. Buddha is another Lord of the Dance of Life. Dancing to the beat of a different drummer places energetic forces at full extension exuding a return to the vital center of cosmic consciousness.

"We've reached the center of the labyrinth, let's dance."

"What... here... now?" the seeker stammered.

"Why not? Remove all inhibitions and learn who you really are. Float freely through the cosmic circle and attain true mastery. Jesus said the truth will set you free. The greatest truth is to know thyself. Love yourself more, forget criticism and judgment, overcome limitations and welcome opportunity.

"Grab a partner and dance the celebration of life with the angels of joy."

*   *   *

"Wow, that was quite an experience dancing with Shiva in the center of a sacred circle. Very liberating and energizing. I'm ready for anything!" The seeker was high on life.

"Good, now let's see what you've learned as we travel the path back into the world."

"Some movie themes come to mind. Both about oneness."

"Oneness is the ultimate. It's the peace that surpasses all understanding. Everything falls into place once you attain that joyous state of being," the labyrinth counselor advised. "Achievement comes easily although goals often change. Inner peace produces global happiness."

"Intuitively, humans know about a place of internal tranquility and joyous contentment that transcends the material world. The question is how to find it," the seeker said.

"Sometimes, all it takes is a change in perspective. Choosing what to experience is the trick. Why believe you are alone in a difficult and disappointing world and have to struggle to get ahead? Know you are surrounded by a benevolent universe that enjoys presenting gifts, adventures and opportunities to explore your true nature."

"If you create what you believe, how do you alter your beliefs to a more positive mindset?" the seeker sought.

"Search for evidence that life is kind and you will discover proof of this existence. View every experience as an opportunity, forgive incidences that no longer matter and accept unimaginable blessings of divine fortune. Relax and appreciate the abundant goodness of life. Mankind deserves to feel good, overall well-being is natural.

"As you embrace the idea that life is here for humans to enjoy, then every moment becomes a gift lighting the path to fulfillment. Continuous magical moments of expanded consciousness enter your life and individual and collective vibrations shift to perfect alignment," the counselor said. "Tap into the wisdom and insight of infinite intelligence and focus more on the solution than the problem."

"So, anything is possible when we allow ourselves to commit fully to obtaining what we desire and love?"

"You learn fast," the counselor beamed. "The keys to the universe are know thyself, release expectation, forgiveness, gratitude, love, joy and belief in the possibility of all things."

"Shall we add staying in the present moment to that list?" the student asked.

"Absolutely!"

"And obstacles and challenges often show a better way when you erase them, fanning the flaming passion inside that nothing can prevent us from reaching our goal if we put one foot in front of the other non-stop on our chosen course."

"Correct again. Frequently, the act of admitting there are limitations is the missing requirement to dissolving barriers."

"I suppose it wouldn't hurt to hang out with people who can spiral the path with ease and provide support, knowledge and inspiration to create a harmonious life."

"Wouldn't hurt a bit," the counselor agreed. "Walking a labyrinth helps, too."

* * *

Exiting the sacred circle, we turned to face the center and bowed in prayerful gratitude, acknowledging our appreciation for the experience. The seeker and the counselor thanked each other for the shared encounter in a heart-felt embrace.

"It's a peaceful relief knowing time is on my side and there is enough of everything in this abundant universe," the seeker said.

"Yes, there is always enough time because the time is now. The time is always now," the counselor said. "So now is the time to align yourself with the universe and restore a powerful quintessence inside the sensitive soul of expanded manifestation and elevated consciousness."

The student seeker was ecstatic, seeing through the eyes of Source. "I feel a bubbling exhilaration as universal forces merge with mine encouraging me to act on my special essence of divine purpose creating passion, flow, synchronicity and leading to fulfillment of enthusiastic dreams. I am the One. All experiences have moved me closer to spiritual abundance and physical well-being. Heaven is much closer than I think."

Chapter 4
Oklahoma Labyrinths

Nestled in the Presence of God

The first labyrinth any of the authors walked was November 11, 2000, at First United Methodist Church in Edmond. None of us knew that seven years later we would be writing this book and discovering 70 labyrinths in the state of Oklahoma.

What a blessing to commune with these sacred circles. Our timing was perfectly divine as the world's only dual-path heart-shaped labyrinth was crafted in Tonkawa during the state's centennial year. We graciously welcomed the opportunity to participate in special inaugural events, the July 4th Harvest Walk and October 6th dedication ceremonies.

Oklahoma is indeed a spiritual place and it is extremely appropriate for the Sooner State to feature such a magnificent creation. Tonkawa is wheat country and this popular grain provides sustaining nourishment to a spiritually starved nation. Its majestic golden stalks waving in the wind are symbolic of harvesting the goodness of the Heartland.

An excellent omen for the next 100 years on earth as humans travel a peaceful path embracing the love emanating from their hearts, comfortably nestled in the presence of God.

Tonkawa is one of 27 cities in Oklahoma that sport labyrinths. Eight of those cities have multiple labyrinths with 14 in Oklahoma City, 12 in Edmond, 12 in Tulsa, four in Norman and three in Tahlequah. Chouteau, Muskogee and Shawnee have two each.

Chouteau's Camp Christian is one of two state locations with both an indoor and outdoor labyrinth. Camp Christian and St. John's Episcopal Church in Tulsa added permanent outdoor designs in 2008.

Other sites with two labyrinths include Muskogee's Moon-Shadow Herb Farm, the University of Central Oklahoma in Edmond, McFarlin Memorial United Methodist Church in Norman, and Oklahoma City's Optimal Potentials.

First United Methodist Church in Edmond is the only state site with three labyrinths.

The Oklahoma labyrinth movement started in 1992 at Sparrow Hawk Village in Tahlequah when Sancta Sophia Seminary built a 7-circuit Classical. Two canvas 11-circuit Chartres appeared five years later at Episcopal churches in Tulsa: St. John's and St. Dunstan's.

St. Luke's Episcopal in Bartlesville mowed a 7-circuit Classical into its lawn in 1998 and the first of two 7-circuit Classicals surfaced on the property of MoonShadow Herb Farm in 1999.

Then the labyrinthine revival started in the 46th state. The number of labyrinths more than doubled in 2000 when six more sacred circles emerged. Eight new labyrinths in 2001 witnessed the state's first outdoor 11-circuit Chartres at Dwight Mission Presbyterian Camp in Vian, also one of the largest Oklahoma labyrinths at 74 feet in diameter.

The only location with a labyrinth and maze, P_Bar Farms in Weatherford has a 75-foot sacred circle, a 7-circuit Classical. Red Plains Monastery in Piedmont showcases a 72-foot labyrinth built from 1,000 bricks in an 11-circuit Chartres pattern and the 70-foot, 11-circuit Chartres at Camp Okiwanee in Sapulpa is the state's only labyrinth with rope guides for the blind.

Forty-four of the 70 Oklahoma labyrinths are permanent outdoor creations. The remaining 26 are portable canvas or nylon, tile or painted indoors on concrete. A total of 33 represent religious institutions, church camps, spiritual centers or retreats. Seventeen are located on private property or owned by individuals not associated with a business.

Four add a special presence to public parks, three are located at educational institutions, three at farms and one each at a hospital, dojo, wellness center, deli, Camp Fire facility and art district. The other four are utilized by their owners in private counseling sessions.

Twenty-one (18 outdoor and three indoor) depict 7-circuit Classicals. Twenty (10 outdoor and 10 indoor) model 11-circuit Chartres. Five (two outdoor and three indoor) represent the Santa Rosa and two are interactive portable canvas prayer paths. Twenty-two characterize modified versions or contemporary styles.

For more detailed information on individual Oklahoma labyrinths, see the listings by city, type and year and read 48 of the labyrinth's unique stories in the remainder of this chapter.

Exceptional effort was exercised to identify all the labyrinths in Oklahoma, including countless hours researching state newspaper archives, contacting state chambers of commerce, museum curators, church offices, historical societies, librarians and interviewing builders, designers, facilitators and even the labyrinths themselves. Any missed or built after publication will be included in the second book of this series, *Sacred Circles of Creation Encircling the Oklahoma Landscape*, which will feature labyrinths, mandalas, medicine wheels, rose windows and zen gardens.

Want to know anything about a labyrinth? Just ask it. Sacred circles will answer every question as walkers spiral to the center of their souls, feeling the rhythm of the natural world beneath their feet, the connective energy of an inspired spirit and liberated excitement from fulfilling innermost desires. Open jubilant hearts to the transformative vastness of the heavens and harmonize with the perfect synchronicity of an attuned universe.

Author James Arthur Ray said the "basic principle of life, of spirit, is fuller expression and expansion. Results become the springboard for fuller expression, which then brings grander, more exciting ideas and goals into view. The next idea or desire sets a new intention for accomplishment. Ready, set, go becomes idea, intent, action."

Labyrinths support ideas, intent and action. They are an excellent tool for aligning the myriad aspects of our being and shining enlightenment on the interchangeable path to psychological and spiritual growth.

Energetic alignment is the key that unlocks the door to limitless opportunity. Labyrinths balance the human equilibrium and offset outdated mores empowering creativity and expanding consciousness. Spiritual centers are amplified, inviting the divine feminine to return to earth. A more nourishing, gentler, softer approach entwines a benevolent, angelic presence that permeates progressive possibilities with passionate enthusiasm.

These spiraling circuits have answered the call of the earth's ancestry and returned over the millennia from the imprint of the Greek Minotaur. Confusion no longer reigns supreme and we ask our Heavenly Father to forgive us of our illusions. Life has always been eternal. Death is merely progressing to the next assignment atop the evolutionary stepladder.

The main reason these sacred circles have resurfaced is to eliminate duality and highlight the present moment. To help humans reduce stress while simultaneously stressing the importance of focusing on the single path of Oneness. There is only One path to the Creator and it's from within.

Doesn't matter which religious affiliation one prefers; we all worship the same God. There is only one Supreme Being, no matter what you choose to call him or her.

The labyrinth teaches that when one feels stressed, weary, burdened, fatigued, impeded, impaired, thwarted, unappreciated, uncertain, overwhelmed or restricted, simply break issues or items into components and prioritize. The whole may be greater than the sum of its parts, but each part must perform optimally for the whole to attain mastery.

Suffering no longer required. It simply does not fit into the overall scheme of the new planetary consciousness. Labyrinths have returned to debunk that antiquated philosophy. Humans made everything difficult because we were told progress was laborious. We thought life was supposed to be exhausting. It's past time to change or transcend that limiting belief.

Labyrinths answer mankind's plea for help reappearing throughout history during intervals of spiritual crisis. They restore outer balance and inner awareness currently lacking in an illusionary world. People respond to the labyrinth without knowing why. They simply like how they feel in its embrace ... nestled in the presence of God.

Oklahoma Labyrinths
Comprehensive Site List

Bartlesville
St Luke's Episcopal Church, (918) 336-1212
210 East 9th Street, Bartlesville, OK 74003
7-circuit Classical, outdoor on grass, built 1998
Always open, no appointment or authorization necessary

Chouteau
Camp Christian, (918) 476-5712
275 Camp Christian Lane, Chouteau, OK 74337
Jim Hawley, administrator, (918) 671-9134
7-circuit Classical, indoor
painted on floor of recreation room in 2005
11-circuit Chartres, outdoor
painted on concrete in fall 2008

Coyle
St. Francis of the Woods, (405) 466-3774
PO Box 400, Coyle, OK 73027
sfwoods@ionet.net, available by appointment
7-circuit Santa Rosa model, 20-foot canvas

Duncan
All Saints Episcopal Church, (580) 255-6165
809 West Cedar Avenue, Duncan, OK 73533
http://www.texhoma.net/~allsts/
allsaintsduncan@cableone.net
7-circuit, rock and gravel, permanent outdoor
always open, built December 2006
Made from 4 tons of Oklahoma Creek Bed Stones

Edmond
First Christian Church, (405) 341-3544
201 E. 2nd, Edmond, OK 73034
Interactive canvas prayer path, purchased 2000

First United Methodist Church, (405) 341-0107
305 East Hurd, Edmond, OK 73034
http://www.fumcedmond.org, eumc@fumcedmond.org
2 indoor canvas Chartres replicas
    11-circuit, 36 feet, purchased 2000
    7-circuit, 24 feet, purchased 2006
Traveling parachute model
    11-circuit Chartres, 36 feet, purchased 2000
Both canvas Chartres available from 6-8 p.m.
3rd Monday of each month

University of Central Oklahoma
2 canvas labyrinths, both 11-circuit Chartres models
Available for class walks
Diane Rudebock, crudebock@ucok.edu
Department of Kinesiology and Health Studies

Private Acreage
7-circuit Cretan, 40 feet, rock and grass, built 2004

Private Back Yard
Barbara Henthorn, (405) 348-9157
bhenthorn@cox.net, created 2005
3-circuit flagstone with built-in prayer stations

Private Back Yard
Beth and Robert Huntley, (405) 216-0502
1600 Napa Valley Road, Edmond, OK 73013
eje50@cox.net
4-circuit herbal path, 18 feet, brick and mulch
built 2002

Private Back Yard
Diane and Rich Rudebock, (405) 348-9977
5-circuit design, lairope grass, built 2001
Contact for availability

Private Back Yard
Carol and Harry Woods, (405) 341-0500
hacmwoods@cox.net
3-circuit, cobblestones and pine needles, built 2000
Call for availability

Private Lake Property
Raine and Blair Benham, (405) 706-7716
11-circuit Chartres, brick and grass, built 2003
Call to schedule a walk

Enid
St. Matthew's Episcopal Church, (580) 237-4737
518 W. Randolph, Enid, OK 73701
http://www.pldi.net/~stmatthew
11-circuit Chartres replica, indoor canvas, 34 feet
wheelchair accessible, purchased 2001
Open for scheduled events and to the public
2nd Sunday of each month from 5-8 p.m.

Fort Gibson
First United Methodist Church Youth Ministry
302 N. Beauregard, Ft. Gibson, OK 74434
(918) 478-3811, ftgfumc@sbcglobal.net
6-circuit Classical, painted indoor on floor of youth room
19 feet, wheelchair accessible, created August 2005
Available by appointment

Geary
First United Methodist Church, (405) 884-2422
325 West Main Street, Geary, OK 73040
Canvas indoor belonging to minister Karen Slater

Hulbert
Clear Creek Wellness Center, (918) 772-3478
Nancy & Michael James, njames@lrec.org
7-circuit, rock and grass, 51 feet, built spring 2006
Named "Turtle Woman"

Jenks
Private Back Yard
Viola Rollins, (918) 720-8622
515 ½ East Main, Jenks, OK 74037
rollinsbillie@yahoo.com
7-circuit Classical, rock, built May 2006

Lawton
Private Back Yard — Linda and Garland Hines
Combination grass labyrinth and medicine wheel
created by Linda Hines and son Brian in 2004
(580) 248-0844, LadyHawkMessages@aol.com

Muskogee
MoonShadow Herb Farm
Sharon Owen, (918) 687-6765
moonshads@aol.com
2 outdoor 7-circuit Cretans, grass and brick
    left turn by well, 26 feet (feminine), built 1999
    right turn in meadow, 50 feet (masculine), built 2001
Open for holiday walks; call for availability

Norman
McFarlin Memorial United Methodist Church
419 S. University Blvd, Norman, OK 73069
(405) 321-3484, http://www.mcfarlinumc.org
2 indoor canvas models, adult and youth
    Adult: 11-circuit Chartres, 30 feet, purchased 2000
    Youth: 7-circuit Chartres replica, purchased 2005
Available the second Tuesday of each month from 3-9 p.m.
and from 7-9 a.m. the following morning. Additional times
during Advent and Lent. Special New Year's Eve Walk

Reaves Park, (405) 366-5472
Jenkins Ave. & Timberdell Rd.
Prairie Peace Path Labyrinth Sculpture
7-circuit outdoor permanent, reddish-brown granite stone
gravel walking path, 65 feet, wheelchair accessible
built May 2002

St. Stephen's United Methodist Church
1801 W. Brooks, Norman, OK 73069
ststephensumc@coxinet.net
Santa Rosa pattern, indoor canvas, 24 feet
purchased February 2005
Call for availability, (405) 321-4988
Regular Lenten and Advent walks, prayer retreats

Oklahoma City
Back Door Coffee House (formerly Deli on the Labyrinth)
3214 N. Classen, Oklahoma City, OK (405) 602-3354
Rectangular shape painted on parking lot

Carol Goodwin, Artist-in-Residence
carmagood2@cox.net, (405) 722-1674
4-circuit canvas Classical style

Harding Charter Preparatory High School, (405) 528-0562
3333 N. Shartel, Oklahoma City, OK 73118
5-circuit original student design, permanent outdoor
stone and grass, 30 feet, center rock in shape of Oklahoma

Mercy Health Center Labyrinth Prayer Garden
4300 West Memorial Road, Oklahoma City, OK 73120
Outdoor permanent, wheelchair accessible
11-circuit Chartres replica, 40 feet, built May 2003
13,000 red sandstone and white limestone tiles
Always open, east of visitor entrance

Optimal Potentials
Debi Bocar, (405) 722-2163, dbocar@aol.com
2 canvas labyrinths
  7-circuit multi-colored
  11-circuit Chartres

Our Lady of Mercy Retreat Center
2801 S. Shartel, Oklahoma City, OK 73109
2nd & 3rd floors of Mount St. Mary High School
11-circuit Chartres, portable nylon, 30 feet
Call for availability, (405) 634-1968

Quail Springs United Methodist Church, (405) 755-9477
14617 N. Pennsylvania, Oklahoma City, OK 73134
7-circuit Native American design, permanent outdoor
multi-cross center, wheelchair accessible, built 2003
Always open

Theatre Upon a StarDanceSwan
3022 Paseo, Oklahoma City, OK 73103
Lorrie Keller, (405) 557-7827
stardanceswan@cox.net
http://www.paseoart.com/stardance/a2.html
Contemporary concrete Jack o' Lantern Labyrinth, 40 feet
Part of "The Magic Lantern Celebration,
a night of light instead of fright"
Creative alternative festival
for children and the young at heart
Availability: Annually, the Sunday before Halloween

United Life Church, (405) 946-6753
3332 N. Meridian, Oklahoma City, OK 73112
11-circuit Chartres painted on parking lot, built May 2001
Open availability

Unity Spiritual Center, (405) 789-2424
5603 NW 41, Oklahoma City, OK 73122
7-circuit Celtic design, outdoor, rock and sand, 43 feet
built July 2005

Windsong Innerspace, (405) 285-0777
2201 NW I-44 Service Road, Oklahoma City, OK 73112
http://www.windsongdojo.com/innerspace/innerspace.html
Catherine Sullivan, csullivan24@cox.net
7-circuit slightly modified Classical, indoor canvas, 22 feet
created in 2005 by Catherine and Brian Sullivan

Private Back Yard
Shantel Carr, (405) 760-0872
beautifictouch@yahoo.com
3-circuit grass, built spring 2008

Private Back Yard
Wisdom Wheel Directional Labyrinth
Gail Peck, (405) 943-2741
wisdom110@hotmail.com
porcelain tile, mulch, stone border, 33 feet
built November 29, 2007

Piedmont
Red Plains Monastery, Sisters of Benedict
728 Richland Rd SW, Piedmont, OK 73078
http://redplainsmonastery.org, (405) 373-2887
Sr. Melissa Anna Letts, melissaannaletts@yahoo.com
11-circuit Chartres, brick and grass, 72 feet, built May 2003
Always open, labyrinth retreats welcomed

Ponca City
Standing Bear Native American Park, (580) 762-1514
Highway 60 & Hwy 177, Ponca City, OK 74601
Park open from 6 a.m. to 11 p.m. daily
Santa Rosa design, outdoor permanent, brick paver, 40 feet
wheelchair accessible, built October 2001

Sapulpa
Camp Okiwanee, (918) 592-2267
Camp Fire USA Green Country Council facility
11340 S. 177th West Avenue, Sapulpa, OK 74066
11-circuit, Chartres, grass walking path, 70 feet
rope guide for the blind, wheelchair accessible
built 2002

Shawnee
Private Back Yard
Lisa Sponseller, lisasponseller@gmail.com
7-circuit Classical, brick paver, 50 feet, built in 2003
Contact for availability

Private Lake Cabin
Diane and Rich Rudebock, (405) 348-9977
7-circuit river rock design, built 2005
Contact for availability

Stillwater
First United Methodist Church
400 West 7th Avenue, Stillwater, OK 74074
Ginger Howl, (405) 372-5854, ginghowl@mac.com
7-circuit Santa Rosa, indoor canvas, purchased March 2000
Open for scheduled events, call for availability

Stilwell
Private mountaintop labyrinth
Lela Samargis, lelasamargis22@hotmail.com
7-circuit, Classical, rock and grass, built April 2002

Stroud
First Christian Church, (918) 968-2744
323 W. 4th, Stroud, OK 74079
Canvas indoor belonging to Pastor Paul Ragle

Tahlequah
First United Methodist Church
300 West Delaware Street, Tahlequah, OK 74464
(918) 456-6141 or (918) 456-2939
http://www.tahlequahumc.org, tumy@sbcglobal.net
11 circuit, interactive portable canvas
Call for scheduled events

Sancta Sophia Seminary/Sparrow Hawk Village
22 Summit Ridge Drive, Tahlequah, OK 74464
Rev. Carol Parrish, (800) 386-7161, (918) 453-5962
http://www.sanctasophia.org, lccc@sanctasophia.org
7-circuit Classical, outdoor permanent, 65 feet
surrounded by trees, built November 13, 1992

Peg Willson, pegwillson@lrec.org
602 Summit Ridge Drive, Tahlequah, OK
4-circuit canvas modified Chartres pattern
12 x 12 foot, designed by Robert Ferré

Tonkawa
Heart in the Park, 6th and Grand
Centennial Park, Downtown Tonkawa
7-circuit Heart-shaped paver, dual-path
Built in June 2007 as an Oklahoma Centennial Project
Only heart-shaped labyrinth of its kind in the world

Tulsa
All Souls Unitarian Church, (918) 743-2363
2592 S. Peoria Avenue, Tulsa, OK 74114
http://www.allsoulschurch.org, kkeith@allsoulschurch.org
Indoor tile, rectangular design, built summer 2001

Bethany Christian Church, (918) 492-1353
6730 S. Sheridan Rd. Tulsa, OK 74133
6-circuit, brick and mulch, in meditation garden
west side of parking lot, built spring 2008

Hunter Park, open from 8 a.m. to 9 p.m.
5804 E. 91st Street, Tulsa, OK 74133
Between Sheridan and Yale on 91st Street
Bob Hendrick, (918) 596-2488
BobHendrick@cityoftulsa.org
11-circuit Chartres on concrete, outdoor permanent
62 feet, half-mile path, wheelchair accessible
built May 27, 2005
Located near the picnic shelter at back of the public park

Phillips Theological Seminary
901 N. Mingo Rd, Tulsa, OK 74116
http://www.ptstulsa.edu;
Mady Fraser, Seminary Chapin, mady.fraser@ptstulsa.edu
7-circuit modified Santa Rosa design, painted concrete
wheelchair accessible, 38 feet, built 2004
Call for availability, (918) 610-8303

St. Andrew's Presbyterian Church, (918) 627-9600
3601 S. Yale Avenue, Tulsa, OK 74135
http://www.standrewstulsa.org, office@standrewstulsa.org
4-circuit Chartres, stone and grass in Memorial Garden
wheelchair accessible, built spring 2003

St. Dunstan's Episcopal Church, (918) 492-7140
5635 East 71st Street, Tulsa, OK 74136
http://www.stduntulsa.org, jjosborne@cox.net
11-circuit Chartres, portable indoor canvas, 32 feet
purchased August 1997
Walks scheduled periodically throughout the year

St. John's Episcopal Church, (918) 742-7381
4200 S. Atlanta Place, Tulsa, OK 74105
http://www.sjtulsa.org, info@sjtulsa.org
11-circuit Chartres, portable, purchased July 1997
  Call for availability and scheduled walks
7-circuit Classical, grass, built spring 2008, always open

Private Area, Jan Lowell (918) 743-1232
jglreikimoon@cox.net
7-circuit grass, 51 feet, built summer 2004
Available by appointment

Private Front Yard — Michelle and Clark Wiens
(918) 747-3398, mkwiens@swbell.net
3730 Terwilleger, Tulsa, OK 74105
11-circuit Chartres, mortared stone on concrete, 38 feet
wheelchair accessible, built 2001
Always available for visitors to walk
Call ahead for group or night visits

Private Back Yard
Lynde Evans
7-circuit Classical, grass

Private Back Yard
Gala and Bill McBee, (918) 438-2598
1111 S. 141st E. Avenue, Tulsa, OK 74108
7-circuit Classical, grass, built 2006
Available by appointment

Vian
Dwight Mission Presbyterian Camp
Conference & Retreat Center, (918) 775-2018
Route 2 Box 71, Vian, OK 74962
Allison Beavers, allison@dwightmission.org
11-circuit Chartres, outdoor in wooded area, built 2001
Available to on-site campers, guests and general public

Weatherford
P_Bar Farms, (580) 772-4401
Loren and Kim Liebscher, www.pbarfarms.com
Rt. 2 Box 92-G, Weatherford, OK 73096
7-circuit Classical, grass, 75 feet, built 2006

Yukon
United Methodist Church of the Good Shepherd
10928 SW 15, Yukon, OK 73099, (405) 324-1900
Joan Brodmerkel, jebrodmerkel@netzero.net
11-circuit Classical, patio stone spiral on turf
45 feet, built spring 2003

*   *   *

Future Labyrinths
Planned in Oklahoma

- Blanchard Healing Center (outdoor)
- Enid — St. Matthew's Episcopal Church (outdoor)
- Stillwater — First United Methodist Church (outdoor)
- Tulsa — Clarehouse (outdoor)
- Tulsa — Hillcrest Hospital (indoor)
- Tulsa — St. Dunstan's Episcopal Church (outdoor)

St Luke's Episcopal Church
210 East 9th Street, Bartlesville, OK 74003, (918) 336-1212
7-circuit Classical, outdoor mowed in grass, built 1998
Always open, no appointment or authorization necessary

Just a few blocks from downtown Bartlesville, people seek the presence of God walking a labyrinth mowed in a vacant lot. Since 1998 people have found St. Luke's Labyrinth an insightful intermediary to experience God's peace, healing, direction, forgiveness, and nurture His profound essence.

In preparation for leading a Celtic Retreat at St. Luke's Episcopal Church, Stephanie Swinnea (now an Episcopal priest) asked the parish to build a labyrinth. She provided a 7-circuit pattern to follow, but no other instructions. Fr. Lee Stephens, rector of St. Luke's, knew little about labyrinths, but was inspired to create one in a grass lot across the alley behind the church (in the middle of the neighborhood). He wanted a style that could be easily maintained and available on an ongoing basis.

"Making such a labyrinth is difficult to explain," Fr. Stephens said. "In short, the path was mowed into the lawn on the lowest setting and the rest of the labyrinth was cut on the highest setting. Thus, the path is the width of the mower which makes it easy to follow and allows participants to pass without difficulty.

There are no trees, bushes, benches, flowers or markers to mow around. The pattern in its simplicity 'pops out' in the lawn and draws people into the sacred space and to God."

Fr. Stephens shared the following brief labyrinth history: Seven-circuit labyrinths, like St. Luke's, are the oldest form known in human history and date back many centuries before Christ. This classical replica has been found in numerous cultures and religions around the world. Currently, the most familiar labyrinth design is the 11-circuit medieval labyrinth like the one at Chartres Cathedral near Paris, France. It is a more complex and intricate style. The classic 7-circuit is simpler and its modest accessibility allows walkers to focus less attention on the path and more on the reflection.

St. Luke's labyrinth has been used for private meditation, spiritual direction, church growth groups, retreats, Vacation Bible School and similar events. Pilgrims report a variety of experiences. Some finish their walk in tears and express difficulty explaining what happened to them. Others encounter an inner peace or personal direction from God. Almost invariably, people report being in the presence of God and touched in some way.

Occasionally, someone will have trouble appreciating the intensity. Fr. Stephens remembered a woman who could not "get into the labyrinth thing" and found it less than interesting. Then one day when everything was going wrong and her frustration was turning into outbursts of anger, she gave the labyrinth another try. "She pulled her car into the alley behind the church and began to walk and pray the labyrinth. A peace she had never known before washed over her and a new person was born that day who will never forget the encounter," he said.

It forever changed her world.

A Spiritual Direction Group walked the labyrinth at the beginning of a new session. Each of the six participants shared unique perspectives following their journey. All reported feeling a powerful sense of God's presence — and wanted more.

The St. Luke's rector recalls a mother and daughter who were in town for the OK Mozart Festival. "They learned about St. Luke's labyrinth and wanted to see what it was all about. With minimum instruction, they walked the path together. When finished, the mother and daughter embraced and walked away arm in arm wiping away tears. Clearly, something meaningful had happened for them."

Stories from the Bartlesville labyrinth range from simple to profound, always intensely personal and often transformational. This sacred space is truly a pathway for experiencing God.

Similar labyrinths have been built using St. Luke's model. A temporary pattern was constructed at St. Crispin's Episcopal Conference Center near Seminole. Another was created for Fr. Stephens' previous parish in Kansas City, Missouri. St. Luke's labyrinth has been redesigned twice after mowing "accidents" destroyed the imprint. Each time, eager parishioners worked to repair it. On one of those occasions, a woman who was legally blind helped restore the labyrinth "providing additional insight and inspiration to the process."

Fr. Stephens encouraged anyone seeking additional information on the St. Luke's ministry or help with the labyrinth, "including spiritual direction," to contact him. The labyrinth is located behind the church, across the alley, and in a grass lot at Eighth and Dewey, one block south of the Community Center. "Available to anyone 24 hours a day, 7 days a week, no appointment or authorization necessary," he said with an inviting smile.

"If you are not sure about this spiritual exercise, try it on at least three different occasions before drawing conclusions. You may be surprised," the pastor admonished. "There is no one right way to walk the labyrinth, just walk with an open heart and open mind ready to receive whatever Spirit has for you. Walking the path in silence, prayer and meditation can lead to peace, healing, insight, courage, forgiveness, affirmation. Everyone's experience is personal and different."

Continuing with the history lesson, Fr. Stephens said the labyrinth is an archetype, a divine imprint, found in many religious traditions in various forms around the world dating back thousands of years. "Early Christians adapted the labyrinth as a way to sense God's presence, for guidance and to enrich their spiritual life. By the Middle Ages, these ancient patterns were inlaid in floors of cathedrals throughout Europe. Elaborate designs were also incorporated into beautiful gardens.

"Christians often took pilgrimages to sacred places in an effort to commune with God and receive illumination. The labyrinth may be experienced as a spiritual pilgrimage without having to travel long distances to a holy site such as Jerusalem, Rome, Iona or some other location. During Advent, for example, a person could walk the labyrinth as if going to Bethlehem to worship the Christ Child and return to share the joy and peace."

Bartlesville

Camp Christian
275 Camp Christian Lane, Chouteau, OK
Jim Hawley, administrator, (918) 671-9134
campchristian@hotmail.com, (918) 476-5712
7-circuit Classical
painted on floor of indoor recreation room in 2005
11-circuit concrete Chartres, outdoor, painted fall 2008

Located 40 miles east of Tulsa, Chouteau's Camp Christian spans 90 acres and has provided an enriching environment in an appealing nature center since 1948.

The year-round retreat and conference center is an educational facility of the Northeast Area Christian Church (Disciples of Christ) of Oklahoma.

"Camp Christian offers an open, loving, caring and nurturing atmosphere teaching and demonstrating the stewardship of God's resources," Camp Administrator Jim Hawley said. "We encourage participants to engage in activities which promote their growth and development in faith and relation to creation and Creator."

Approximately 200 campers per session enjoy hiking trails, volleyball courts and a swimming pool, ball field, frisbee golf course and playground.

The Amish cooks have a reputation in the area for serving the best food at weekend retreats and family reunions, weekly summer camps and other youth affairs, Amish dinners and company picnics, corporate training meetings, weddings or any celebration, convention or special event.

"Camp Christian hosts several minister and elder gatherings, church conferences, class reunions, anniversaries, birthday parties and various activities for youth, young adults, seniors, singles, men, women and married couples," Hawley said.

"We even have teacher training, scrap bookers, sewing, crafting and painting groups use our facilities. All are welcome," he added, smiling graciously.

"And many use our labyrinth." The Camp Christian indoor labyrinth was built in 2005 by the high school Christian Youth Fellowship group.

"They not only painted the labyrinth, those talented kids also did yeoman's work designing several murals on the pump house and pool bath house," Hawley remarked, nodding his approval.

Camp Christian's labyrinth is a 7-circuit green and white Classical, color and size chosen to match the outside colors of the surrounding buildings and the available area inside the recreation center.

Disciple ministries and other groups like to place candles on the floor and use soft meditation music to enhance their labyrinth experience. "Whether it be a CD or guitar, the music puts campers into a peaceful and ready state to go on their spiritual walk. It slows us down and opens our minds and hearts," Hawley said. "It affords a chance to listen to God — to clarify your wishes and hopes and prayers to God."

Most groups take communion in the center of the labyrinth.

Hawley said both young and old come out touched and feel a renewed relationship with God. "We sometimes go through a lot of tissues, but it does touch everyone."

The Disciple women plan to add a new outdoor labyrinth in the fall of 2008. Hawley said a permanent outdoor creation "will be a very nice addition to use with large groups and when we have that beautiful Oklahoma weather."

Both Camp Christian labyrinths (indoor and outdoor) will be available for walking year-round and anyone is welcome to take a meandering journey.

One of the youth who helped paint the indoor labyrinth said he "didn't really have any clue what it was at the time we made it, but I love the labyrinth. It helps me get closer to God."

Sixteen-year-old Michael Robinson said he especially likes to

Chouteau

experience them in the dark with candles lighting the way. "We usually have different stations, sometimes they have little items marking each path, sometimes there is a Bible open with a piece of encouraging scripture, and in the center there is Communion. I find it a way to relax and just pace your thoughts; you aren't rushed, you can take all the time you want. I once prayed people into the labyrinth. I am not that great at praying, but I gave it a shot. It felt good praying all of these people into it. It's just a meaningful experience."

Michael said his first encounter with a labyrinth was at the First Christian Church in Jenks about four years ago. Some of the youth helped former Pastor Paul Ragle make a green canvas labyrinth with purple lines.

"It was offered at our church and at Camp Christian before they made their own labyrinth," Michael said. "It was used by probably anywhere from 100 to 300 different people. I walked it several times, and enjoyed every time I did. When we did the labyrinth at Camp Christian, the one painted on the concrete floor of the recreation center, we had 70 people walk at once and it brought at least 40 of them to tears. It's that meaningful of an experience."

Photo courtesy of The Duncan Banner

Duncan

All Saints Episcopal Church
809 West Cedar Avenue, Duncan, OK 73533, (580) 255-6165
www.texhoma.net/~allsts, allsaintsduncan@cableone.net
7-circuit, permanent outdoor, rock and gravel, always open
4 tons of Oklahoma Creek Bed Stones, built Dec. 2006

Built as a gift to the church and community from four tons of Oklahoma river rocks, the labyrinth at All Saints Episcopal Church in Duncan pulsates with elfin energy. A frisky, 7-circuit path winds around a mature oak tree in juxtaposition to the quiet residential neighborhood.

A paradox of peace and chaos amid power, play and structure.

Karla Dillon, whose husband constructed the labyrinth over a three-day weekend in December 2006, said she was introduced to the ancient spiritual tool while visiting a friend in Santa Fe. "She has one in her back yard that she created to help with the grieving process when her husband died. She walks it daily.

"I wanted a sacred circle at our church to use for workshops and spiritual retreats. Something to help people center themselves in the spirit and bring peace to the chaos of life," Dillon added.

So Karla's husband built her a labyrinth.

Although "we haven't put it to proper use yet," Dillon says several individuals come to the church to walk the labyrinth. Spiritual workshops and retreats are planned in the near future with a labyrinthine theme.

The All Saints outdoor meditation area is located on the southwest corner of the 72-year-old church grounds. Protected on the west by two massive trees aglow with pastoral wisdom, the labyrinth has a north entrance and rests gracefully beside colorful stained glass windows. Oklahoma river rocks outlining the path were purchased one weekend and placed the next. The flagstone is from Arizona and fine-graveled chat covers the bottom layer.

Dillon said she originally was unhappy with the flagstone, but enjoys it now. Her husband doesn't like the unevenness it creates and he wants to remove them. "After walking it a few times, I decided I prefer the unevenness as it is metaphoric of our lives. It isn't always smooth, but we walk the path and make it to the center and out again, walking our journey of life."

Designed to calm, quiet and focus, labyrinths are ancient, archetypal, universal, collective. Their patterns are usually circular and have been associated with pilgrimages, rituals and self-discovery.

Rev. Joe Running, pastor at All Saints, said a labyrinth is a mystical tradition for spiritual growth and prayer; a way to quiet the mind and honor silence; a tool for clarity and creativity; it is holy ground where two worlds touch; a process of trust; a circular walking path.

"Walking the labyrinth is a time for peaceful reflection, like a stroll in the woods. The experience can be profound and provide transforming insights. Use the labyrinth in times of joy or uncertainty, when facing difficult decisions, for healing emotional wounds, during illness and grief. Walk the path for praise, thanksgiving, prayer, hope, inspiration and joy. When you have a moment, come and walk, alone or with someone. It is an experience open to those from all walks of life," the pastor said.

"There is no one way to walk a labyrinth. It is walked at your own pace. Our life journey is never direct or straight. It takes unexpected, unplanned and authentic turns. By the simple act of putting one foot in front of the other on the path, we arrive where we are supposed to be."

First United Methodist Church
305 East Hurd, Edmond, OK 73034, (405) 341-0107
http://www.fumcedmond.org, eumc@fumcedmond.org
2 indoor canvas Chartres replicas
  11-circuit, 36 feet, purchased 2000
  7-circuit, 24 feet, purchased 2006
Traveling parachute model
  11-circuit Chartres, 36 feet, purchased 2000
Both canvas Chartres available from 6-8 p.m.
3rd Monday of each month

First United Methodist Church of Edmond may not have been the first church in Oklahoma to purchase an indoor canvas labyrinth, but it is the only one with three labyrinths and a regular walk featuring two of them each month.

The church has two indoor canvas Chartres replicas and a portable parachute cloth labyrinth. Both the 7-circuit Chartres and 11-circuit Chartres are available for public walks the third Monday of each month from 6-8 p.m. in the Christian Activities Center, 305 S. Hurd.

"Our labyrinth ministry began in 2000 when we bought a 36-foot Chartres pattern. In 2006, we added a Petite Chartres, 24 feet in diameter, four courses smaller than our full-size model," said Carol Woods, one of three Edmond FUMC labyrinth facilitators. "Anyone is welcomed and encouraged to join these walks — there are no requirements!"

Candles and soft lighting, accompanied by a varied range of background music from Gregorian chants to rhythmic American Indian flutes, help cast a serene aura as seekers set one foot in front of the other traveling the continuous circuits.

Walkers tread at their own pace, circling the labyrinth path for personal, psychological and spiritual transformation.

Small, wooden boards imprinted with labyrinth patterns are available for those who choose to walk while seated, tracing the path with their fingers.

Diane Rudebock, another facilitator who is also a registered nurse and assistant professor at the University of Central Oklahoma, said walking a labyrinth is perfect for quiet time with God and shows "the Creator offers peace not instead of, but in the midst of, the everyday chaos of our hectic lives."

"The chance to slow down and listen continues to be meaningful for many and is the reason we host the regular monthly walks," Woods added.

Rev. David Conrad, former associate pastor at Edmond FUMC, said some people are skeptical about the labyrinth walk when they first arrive and see a hand-painted royal amethyst circular design on 1,296 square feet of canvas and another laying next to it outlined in burgundy on beige divided into three 12 x 36 foot sections placed together with hook and loop tape, weighing about 140 pounds.

"I can relate to their skepticism because I was among those who were undecided about the merits of this ancient walking path," he grinned.

After walking it, Conrad, who is currently pastor at the Minco United Methodist Church, said he decided it is symbolic of life, grounded in the Christian tradition, and allows walkers to snatch moments of reflection and solitude in a society that doesn't nourish these principles.

"One of the things I don't think we do as a society, as a culture, is to slow down enough to seek God," Conrad said. "We're so goal-oriented."

The pastor said decades ago people took long walks to reflect on life and connect with God in prayer. The labyrinth now provides that "long walk" and he continues to be amazed by its benefits.

"It's a good tool to help people keep their feet on the spiritual path," Conrad said. The theme of one of the labyrinth workshops sponsored by the church was based on Psalms 16:11, "Show me the path of life."

The best way to find answers to questions about this modern replica of an ancient sacred path is to walk it, Conrad said.

The Edmond congregation borrowed a labyrinth to use during Lent in 2000, which coincided with the fifth anniversary of the Murrah Building bombing. About 60 people walked the sacred circle receiving such a profound spiritual experience that the church started plans to purchase its own for regular walks.

Carolyn Lynd, the other FUMC labyrinth facilitator, provided more impetus when her awareness in labyrinths was sparked after reading *Walking the Sacred Path*, a book by Rev. Lauren Artress, an Episcopal priest.

Artress, who first learned about labyrinths in 1991, is credited for reviving the U.S. fascination in labyrinths as a tool for meditation and pathway to peace and serenity.

Lynd walked the labyrinth Artress installed at Grace Cathedral in San Francisco. "I experienced immense peace and found comfort regarding difficult emotional issues involving my parents and their health that I later returned to walk the Grace labyrinth with my husband."

As Lynd told members and leaders of the Edmond church about her intense encounter, more interest developed for acquiring a labyrinth. A $3,000 grant from the Petree Foundation aided the church in purchasing its first Chartres replica.

Lynd said a labyrinth is a tool. It's not a religion, theology or belief system. "People can make the journey however they choose — walk, run, dance, skip or crawl. It's also okay to walk outside the lines or cut across, but most people don't."

Although printed material is available on labyrinth history and ethics, no rules govern. A polite protocol of respect and reverence prevails. People remove their shoes before stepping onto the canvas walkway. Since the same path leads to the center and back out and walkers go at their own pace, meeting or passing people in either direction is part of the process.

"Just like in real life," Lynd added. "How you react is the key."

Many people ask what happens when they get to the center and stand inside a six-petal flower design. How do they know what to do and when to leave? "You will know," Lynd tells them.

Sometimes nothing happens. "A walk is a walk," she said.

But more often than not, from that discipline comes an intensely spiritual result.

Some can describe in great detail what their journey entailed, others are less specific. All are encouraged to write about their experience in a notebook kept near the labyrinth.

Lynd said she suggests people take everything they feel, sense, hear, taste and smell while walking the labyrinth as a metaphor.

"This is like walking the path of life. We're all on a path — wherever you are, have either been or will be. While someone seems so far away from the center, you've been there. Some pass you by on your way to the cherished goal, others step aside and yield to your needs."

A labyrinth is a rich symbol for deepening one's spirituality and reconnecting with the sacred space inside each human heart.

Edmond

Private Acreage
7-circuit Cretan, 40-foot, rock and grass, built 2004

A combination of leftover materials from a room addition and the design printed on a sweat shirt were the seed pattern for a 40-foot, 7-circuit Cretan labyrinth built in 2004 by an Edmond couple.

While visiting a retreat center in Connecticut, the Oklahomans saw a labyrinth they liked and decided to duplicate it. "We purchased a sweat shirt with a picture of the labyrinth and figured it would be an acceptable blueprint," said the lady of the house. "It was a replica of one found on the island of Crete, probably designed and built by the Minoans."

Although, a lot bigger project then anticipated over a six-month period, the gregarious couple has enjoyed sharing this spiritual symbol of quiet meditation that also offers a unique gathering place for family and friends.

Small white boulders remaining from the construction of an extra room provided the foundation for the rock and grass labyrinth. Two granddaughters helped lay the groundwork with two-foot spaces left for walkways. Unfortunately, the lady of the house forgot the lawn mower wasn't that wide, so "someone spends quite a bit of time" in the summer trimming with a weed-eater.

The next phase was accomplished with the help of their Urantia youth study group who completed the middle third of the project. The other three grandchildren finalized the mission.

Several trips to acquire additional rock and stone made the venture even more interesting. "Building it was quite a socializing experience."

Family and friends occasionally gather to walk the labyrinth. "We tell each group it is used to calm the spirit within by letting loose of negative feelings on the walk to the center and thinking positive thoughts on the walk out," their hosts explain.

The authors walked this labyrinth in September 2006 for an Inspired Forgiveness Labyrinth Ceremony. Drumming enhanced the effect and joined with the heartbeat of Mother Earth as each person danced their inner song while walking the spiraling paths.

We met the couple at a health fair one Saturday afternoon at Third Street Yoga. When they heard us talking about stopping at Mercy Hospital on the way back to Oklahoma City to walk that lovely labyrinth, they issued an invitation to experience their back yard creation.

Quite an enjoyable adventure amid a delightful spiritual symbol of quiet meditation.

From this...

to this...

Edmond

Private Back Yard — Beth and Robert Huntley
1600 Napa Valley Road, Edmond, OK 73013
(405) 216-0502, eje50@cox.net
4-circuit herbal path, 18 feet, brick and mulch, built 2002

No weeds or errant grass grow in this small back yard laby-rinth, but symbolism runs rampant. Abstract ideas conveyed in artistic fashion give meaning to life, a quality we can't quite pin-point or see, but know is there.

"Kind of like faith," said Beth Huntley of Edmond. "Although I leave the symbolism of my garden mostly to the walker, it speaks sweetly to me in gentle tones."

The Huntleys built a labyrinth at their Napa Valley home in the summer of 2002 after Beth saw an article in a magazine that "tweeked my interest" in labyrinths.

Beth said she liked the idea of an "ancient" walk for prayer and quiet meditation.

Three years later, Robert bought his wife a greenhouse for her birthday. "The best location for the new present was on the labyrinth, so we moved it a little to the south and placed the greenhouse where the labyrinth rested."

Most people don't build one labyrinth at their private resi-dence, let alone move it. But the Huntleys are far from normal. They not only have an 18-foot labyrinth in their spacious, well-manicured back yard, they also have a variety of flowering bushes, trees and a large goldfish pond interspersed among a rock garden and fountain.

Look closely and you can find the colony of red ladybugs Beth has hidden in the crevice of a large boulder on the far side of the pond. No, they are not real. Adds a surprising splash of color to the dirt-brown rock though.

If symbolism is an artistic representation that evokes ideas, feelings or reveals truth through the use of suggestive images, then the goldfish certainly do their part evoking happiness in all those watching them dart to the surface and eat from Beth's hand — or anyone else brave enough to feed them. It doesn't hurt.

Ponds with goldfish are good feng shui, helping balance energy, inviting peace and prosperity into a home and sur-rounding environment, The sparkling water also offers abundant opportunity to detect subtle movement, cleanse emotions and create harmonious relationships.

"We may add a fountain inside the labyrinth since the gold-fish pond is at the other end of the yard," Beth said, rubbing her husband's arm and smiling coyly. "That would make a nice birthday present."

Presently, the brick path surrounded by cocoa shell mulch has seven turns, four circuits and three areas wide enough to plant foliage or place a symbolic item.

Beth said she picked this design for her labyrinth because she liked those numbers. Seven denotes luck and spiritual truth. Four signifies a solid foundation and three represents the Holy Trinity and Creation.

"At one point, I had a place to sit made with three stones (sort of like at Stonehenge with two vertical stones and a single one across them). "It's good to have a place to rest and reflect while walking," the Hospice volunteer added.

Larger items inside the Huntley labyrinth include a water jar which Beth says reminds her of Jesus ("the Living Water so one never has to thrist for spiritual water again"), a small pagoda — a place of prayer, and a large piece of blue glass that is a little murky ("for now we look through a glass darkly, but later we will be face-to-face with God and can see clearly").

The first thing one notices when stepping onto the path is a "Prayer Walk" plaque setting the intent for a quiet sojourn. The tree and roses adorning the plaque remind Beth of the Tree of Life and Jesus who was also called The Rose of Sharon. Another sign gracing the entrance admonishes the walker to "Listen" and a stone says "Welcome to my Garden."

Those walking the labyrinth brush against scented herbs and other fragrant plants. Beth chose an herbal theme of sage, basil and heather because "fragrances, like incense, are prayers to God." The mulch of cocoa shells tantalizes with a gentle smell of chocolate.

A labyrinth should also be healing, Beth said. So she included some scented herbs noting that yarrow, planted all over the world, was used by the Roman army as a poltice to stop bleeding. "I have also had dill and cilantro in my garden and garlic chives are planted nearby. Garlic was one of the spices the Israelites longed for after they left Egypt."

Peace and prosperity reign supreme in a fig tree, which overlaps the outer path next to the greenhouse. Indigenous to Palestine, it was the first tree referenced in the Old Testament. Figs also have curative properties. The Bodhi Tree, a sacred fig, is the tree under which Buddha sat while meditating for peace.

Various stones and other items dot the path available for individual interpretation. Some signs inspire the walker to "Talk to the plants" and notes "One who plants a garden, plants happiness." Three round stones of different character and color represent Trinity. A piece of petrified wood from Beth's grandfather reminds her of many generations of family ties to faith. The ceramic frog teaches adabtability and croaks "Beauty is in the eye of the beholder."

Another stone lists the many names of God. Giant, gentle, cupped hands hold a bluebird, protecting humanity's happiness. Smooth granite, rough lava stones, sharp-edged stones — "so many people in my life of different temperment, talents, gifts and character," Beth smiled.

The center capstone acclaims "Peace" on a white stone decorated with easter lilies. "That's the ultimate goal for all of us, isn't it?" Beth nodded. "Peace is something that needs no symbolism. It's obviously the goal of the labyrinth, the walk and the prayer."

A bobwhite calls in the distance while bluebirds balance on the back privacy fence. The neighboring bald cypress gently sways in the breeze.

Symbolism may be subject to interpretation, but inner peace is a common goal, recognized as the faith that sustains us in walking our daily journey, adding quality to the meaning of life.

Edmond

Snow decorates the lairope grass.

Private Back Yard — Diane and Rich Rudebock
Contact for availability, (405) 348-9977
5-circuit lairope grass, built 2001

The Rudebock's have a 5-circuit back yard labyrinth which was built in 2001 at their home in Edmond. The design is made from lairope grass and the path is grass.

Here is Diane's story:

After walking a labyrinth for the first time at Edmond First United Methodist Church on New Year's Eve in 2001, I experienced clarity and quietness and realized I wanted to walk a labyrinth more than once a month.

My husband Rich was very open to the idea of transforming our back yard to include a labyrinth. Over the next several months, we discussed the placement of the labyrinth and spent much time considering its construction.

A very interesting thing happened for both us the weekend he was driving home from a trip to St. Louis. Upon arising Saturday morning, I kept thinking about the design of the labyrinth. When I looked outside from the upstairs window down to the back yard, I literally saw the path of the labyrinth emerge from the ground encircling a nice shady maple tree.

I was so overwhelmed about the experience, I immediately grabbed the phone to call Rich. When he answered, he said, "You know, I have been giving a lot of thought about where to place the labyrinth. What would you think if we made the maple tree the center and used lairope grass to make the design?"

Incredible! We had both experienced a moment in a miracle since we each had the same simultaneous vision, even though we were hundreds of miles apart. By the time he arrived home that evening, I had the 5-circuit design completely drawn and we started ground preparation for the labyrinth in the spring of 2001. Many feet have walked the path of our back yard labyrinth, from young children to grandparents.

In the spring of 2005, we decided to make a 7-circuit labyrinth using river rock at our lake cabin near Shawnee. Our grandsons assisted in gathering the stones and a group of students from Oklahoma Baptist University helped finish the project. We enjoy walking the path of the labyrinth which is in the midst of several trees and overlooks a private lake. I occasionally lead women's retreats at the lake and also enjoy having friends visit to experience the path in the midst of nature.

Edmond

Rudebock lake labyrinth at Shawnee Twin Lakes

Private Edmond Lake Property
Raine and Blair Benham
11-circuit, Chartres, 56 feet, built 2003
Call to schedule a walk, (405) 706-7716

The Labyrinth of the Lake was built on hands and knees over a six-month period in the spring, summer and fall of 2003. Not as penitence or a pilgrimage to Jerusalem, but as a labor of love "to enhance our personal spiritual journey and offer the labyrinth to our Oklahoma community," said Raine Benham.

In 1997, Raine attended a labyrinth workshop presented by Lauren Artress, the woman credited with bringing the labyrinth movement to the United States. "I immediately felt a connection to this ancient tradition and wanted to bring it to life in my hometown. My husband Blair accepted the mission with a sincere heart and tons of sweat."

Raine's mom, Betty Head, says she makes walking the Pleasant Oaks neighborhood labyrinth part of her Oklahoma visit.

"The lake and geese and trees are so relaxing — it encourages you to let go of any cares as you walk. I usually start out praying for my family one-by-one, there are so many of them that I'm usually about halfway through the labyrinth before I've covered them all! Then I can be calm in spirit and get rejuvenated as I finish my walk."

A Healing Touch practitioner, Raine uses the 11-circuit Chartres labyrinth in her therapy work. Modeled after one at the Chartres Cathedral in France, it is a simple design, made of inlayed brick with grass paths and a tree in the center.

"The natural setting of open field with a view of lake and trees adds to its appeal," Raine said. "All around the labyrinth in late spring wild flowers burst onto the scene in a chorus of renewal for the cycle of life."

Perfect surroundings for a back yard lake labyrinth.

Edmond

Lush green plants surround the 3-circuit, cobblestone and pine needle labyrinth in the Edmond back yard of Carol and Harry Woods. The walking path is 18 feet with a two-foot outer ring of greenery. A sturdy, flat-surfaced boulder sits in the center providing a place to rest, meditate or ponder the mysteries of life. Horticulture Services in Edmond built the labyrinth in 2000, also landscaping a zen garden to the east. A 600-square-foot herb garden accentuates the northwest corner of the one-acre property.

St. Matthew's Episcopal Church
518 W. Randolph, Enid, Oklahoma 73701
Info@StMatthewsEnid.org, (580) 237-4737
11-circuit Chartres, indoor canvas, 34 feet
wheelchair accessible, purchased 2001
Open for scheduled events and to the public
2nd Sunday of each month from 5-8 p.m.

Walking a labyrinth is a discipline of reflection, appropriate for any season. Those strolling the circular paths travel in silence, pray the Lord's Prayer, repeat a sacred word, chant a mantra or focus on a spiritual image.

The labyrinth at St. Matthew's Episcopal Church in Enid is a painted canvas replica of the 13th century Chartres Cathedral labyrinth in France. The famous medieval design offers the chance for renewal — a spiritual journey, allowing those walking its path to make a sacred voyage within themselves. At Chartres, it symbolized the traditional pilgrimage to Jerusalem.

"It's an ancient tradition that has been lost for centuries," said Vicki Longhofer-Copeland (formerly Jackson), one of three St. Matthew's labyrinth facilitators. A contemplative practice, the labyrinth has been rediscovered within the last 20 years as a worldwide instrument of meditation and prayer.

The concurrent efforts of two St. Matthew's parishioners led to the church's labyrinth project. Margaret Moss formed a Centering Prayer group to create a parish setting for contemplative study in 1999. Vicki visited San Francisco's Grace Cathedral after reading an article about labyrinths and the Rev. Dr. Lauren Artress, creator of Veriditas, the Worldwide Labyrinth Project.

As an artist-educator, Vicki knew the labyrinth experience could enhance the creative process. In 2000, she attended Veriditas training to become the first facilitator at St. Matthew's. The next step was the acquisition of a labyrinth.

A series of fund-raisers (dinners, Christmas Greens, holiday cards and Church Mouse rummage sales) produced seed money for a matching grant awarded by the Episcopal Diocese of Oklahoma.

From inception, the centerpiece of the St. Matthew's labyrinth ministry has been the monthly Open Walk available to the community. The labyrinth walk is offered to a diverse range of groups including nursing home staff, teachers, healthcare workers, Episcopal Church Women conferences and Camp Start, the Episcopal ministry for children of incarcerated parents.

In 2004, Lissa Qualls, a Youth for Christ missionary, completed facilitator training through Veriditas. Margaret Moss received training in 2006. Labyrinth facilitators conduct workshops and classes and provide counseling and instruction for the monthly second Sunday evening Open Walks.

Additional facilitators enable St. Matthew's to share the benefits of this "sacred circle" with a variety of people and organizations such as alternative high school students, youth groups and child care workers.

"The portable nature of the canvas labyrinth makes it possible to reach beyond the limits of our city, making it something of a floating ministry," Vicki said.

In April of 2007, she presented a two-day seminar at the Harding Charter Preparatory High School in Oklahoma City. Students then collaborated with art teacher Sheridan Scott to design and create a uniquely original outdoor grass and rock labyrinth.

Three years ago, preparations began for a more permanent installation at the Enid church, an outdoor meditation and labyrinth garden available to the public on a daily basis. After presenting the walk to students at the Landscape Architecture Department at Oklahoma State University, more than two dozen potential designs were produced, with site-specific plans for plantings and physical construction of garden features.

To further this effort, the current fund-raiser, a St. Matthew's Centennial Cookbook, was published in the fall of 2007. Proceeds benefit the Meditation Garden.

The Enid parish is one of three Oklahoma churches currently planning new outdoor labyrinths. All three presently have indoor canvas models. Permanent creations will soon be unveiled at St. Matthew's, Stillwater First United Methodist and St. Dunstan's Episcopal in Tulsa.

A labyrinth walk is a metaphor spiraling mankind's transient journey. Individuals are affected differently, some experience profound encounters they do not understand and cannot articulate. Emotions frequently overflow allowing spiritual or physical healing. Often peaceful and calming, it's a chance to quiet chattering chaos amid the harried hustle and poignant stress of an overburdened life.

Walked with a searching heart and open mind, these sacred symbols offer unlimited opportunities for solitary, focused meditation and are indeed a discipline of reflection.

First United Methodist Church Youth Ministry
302 N. Beauregard, Ft. Gibson, OK 74434
ftgfumc@sbcglobal.net, (918) 478-3811
6-circuit Classical, 19 feet, painted on floor of youth room
wheelchair accessible, created August 2005
Available by appointment

Peace, joy and calm embrace those standing in the blue five-foot circular center of the classical labyrinth at Ft. Gibson First United Methodist Church.

The surrounding journey theme décor, complete with road signs, license plates, street names and directional markers, was the brainchild of the youth ministry who decided to renovate the youth room in August of 2005.

Eighteen students tore out carpet, painted the floor and added unusual decorations.

"When they approached me with their idea, I thought it was brilliant," Pastor Scott Rodgers said. "Labyrinths represent a person's journey through life so this theme was very symbolic and most appropriate for a room housing a labyrinth."

But the youth did not stop there. They inscribed their favorite scripture passages on the floor before painting it gray and drawing a black, 6-circuit, classical-style labyrinth.

Although the paint and labyrinth cover the Bible verses, you can feel the unwavering power of the unseen Word.

Just as the old hymn says, anyone walking the labyrinth is truly standing on the promises of God.

*   *   *

At first glance, the area seems to be in disarray... typical of a kid's room. But initial impressions can be deceiving. Herein lies another lesson taught by these youth.

Those who listen closely can hear the laughter of happiness, the melodious voices of cherubim angels — dancing, twirling, spinning — inside the spirals of a sacred circle.

Joy abounds when intent is pure.

A cozy, huggable sofa, bean bag chairs, pin ball machine, pool table and a couple of television sets complete the room. Flickering candlelight highlights an altar in the outer path.

Youth activities and announcements fill a large corkboard. Featured is a certificate of appreciation for FUMC youth assistance in June 2005 during Hurricane Ivan relief. Other service projects connect the youth to community.

Sunlight shining through nearby windows casts unique shadows over scratched patches of the labyrinth. Probably from moving the pool table and pinball machine, but just as easily identifying scars of the world obtained while overcoming obstacles.

The labyrinth's north entrance denotes a physical journey. By stepping onto the path and acknowledging our surroundings, we embark on a wondrous walk of self-reflection. Peace that calms the waters of human emotion.

As walkers travel around the circular path, circumventing the altar, pinball machine and pool table, which overlap portions of the labyrinth, conscious judgment subsides when noticing a large key hanging on the wall.

The key to walking the correct path is understanding. Not any one key starts all projects or vehicles. Not everyone sees something blocking a path as an obstacle; it may be a challenge or an opportunity.

A green headband twisted in the shape of an infinity symbol catches a traveler's eye. It is crisscrossing an outer circuit near a door to the church's food pantry. Could it suggest that one can see more clearly if keep sweat and hair from obstructing your vision? Since infinity communicates forever... eternal, endless... maybe it means no limits, that all boundaries are self-imposed. Or is it just a fashion statement?

The adjoining room food pantry signifies combining physical needs with spiritual nourishment. Perhaps, Matthew 4:4 should be one of the Bible verses written under the floor of the labyrinth: "Man shall not live by bread alone, but by every word that proceedeth from the mouth of God."

Ft. Gibson First United Methodist Church has an active food outreach program. It serves as the focal point for all churches in town that collect can goods and non-perishable items. Each church in Ft. Gibson separately gathers donated food and "then we come together as one" assisting those in need.

Physical and spiritual nourishment is a strong message from this labyrinth. Five road signs have directional arrows. All arrows point up. Only the "No Parking" sign has horizontal arrows. Translation: No parking in the physical, look to spirit for answers. Keep moving to avoid stagnation.

"It's hard not to observe the 'One Way' arrows pointing skyward," chuckled the pastor. "The kids turned the road signs with arrows that way to get people's attention and push home their point. Walking a labyrinth may be a physical activity, but it is important to seek a spiritual connection on this journey called life."

Three stop signs and a traffic light signal walkers to stop, look around, proceed with caution, wait your turn or continue forward. Color therapy also comes into play here. Honoring the tones and hues of colors can add meaning and importance to any journey.

This trip is enhanced with a green headband, gray floor, black labyrinth and blue center. Green is healing, abundance, growth. A neutralizing color, gray represents initiation, imagination, overcoming imbalance and secrecy. Black removes negativity, offers protection, birth and magic. Blue conveys happiness, calm, truth.

Beautiful stained glass rose windows adorn the Ft. Gibson sanctuary. The church sits on a pinnacle, a mighty appointment on higher ground transcending Army shadows of a bygone era. The former battleground of fear, loss and bloodshed has been replaced with peace, love and forgiveness.

Exactly what travelers would expect to find at the only labyrinth in Oklahoma with an altar in its outer path and the Greek word for "journey" covering its center. Weary pilgrims can rest, conversing with a benevolent Supreme Presence while standing on the promises of God.

Fort Gibson

Clear Creek Wellness Center
Nancy and Michael James, (918) 772-3478
njames@lrec.org
7-circuit Classical, rock and grass, 51 feet, built spring 2006

An affinity for turtle shells and a gathering of women led to naming the only labyrinth in the state currently at a wellness center. Turtle Woman is a 7-circuit grass and rock design located at the Clear Creek Wellness Center in Hulbert.

The town of 543 near Tahlequah in northeastern Oklahoma will not hold that distinction long. Another sacred circle is planned in 2009 at a Blanchard healing center about 25 miles south of Oklahoma City.

Nancy and Michael James opened the Clear Creek Wellness Center May 9, 2008. Turtle Woman was built two years earlier with the assistance of Lynde Evans from Tulsa.

"My favorite time to walk the labyrinth is sunset when the sky is filled with color and the sun reflects through the clouds creating interesting shapes, patterns and designs — just like on a turtle shell," Nancy said.

"I like it best when the sun casts an awesome light behind those giant clouds outlining a perfect window, showcasing blue sky in the midst of the masses of clouds covering the wellness center."

The new center specializes in foot reflexology, bioenergy therapy, reiki, emotional freedom and hypnosis. Classes on some of those services are presented on a continuing basis. Soap-making sessions teach the art of crafting homemade herbal soaps.

Area teachers and healers are encouraged to participate in educational programs concentrating on their individual skills.

Visitors can enjoy a leisurely stroll around the wooded 20 acres which includes Clear Creek Wellness Center, Turtle Woman, a pond, sweat lodge and the James' home.

"Having this sacred space here on our property is a wonderful blessing to us, and because of the wellness center, it adds to the healing energy of our land," Nancy said. "It also attracts and draws lightworkers and other spiritual people who benefit from the healing work that transpires here."

Six women walked the labyrinth the day the authors visited. Drums and rattles accompanied a healing chant in honor of Mother Earth while the lone male stood sentinel in the east, positioned for new beginnings.

An eagle circled overhead, oblivious to the brisk breeze. Soaring oracles of rebirth, eagles also exemplify the triumph of spiritual power over sickness and the ability to see the world around them, identify opportunity, swoop in and seize it.

A pertinent — and perhaps predictive — sighting at a wellness center.

The winds of change spiraled profusely around the travelers as that elemental has been flowing freely this season. State meteorologists noted recent winds have topped the 1929 Dust Bowl era declaring the answer is indeed blowing in the wind, clearing old energies, cleansing stains of stubbornness.

Last year's labyrinth walks were researched amid the wettest spring and summer in Oklahoma history.

The Native American aspect of this rock and grass circle is apparent in the feminine divine healing energy emitted from the heartbeat of the Earth Mother honored in its 9-foot center. Bountiful blessings emanate from the peaceful surroundings culminating at the altar platform where movement and energy effervesce.

Just like the swirling circuits of the labyrinth, illusion intertwines reality and the shape of an ankh appears in the clouds.

Hulbert

An ancient emblem of love, both physical (the union of male and female) and spiritual (the key to esoteric knowledge), the ankh also represents harmony and oneness between heaven and earth.

Such a marriage of divine grace radiates holy sweetness, the nectar of life, analogous with perfection and community. This stunning interaction of beauty and wholeness defies conscious comprehension.

In Far Eastern mythology, shells signified heaven and their square underside portrayed earth. Knowledge of turtle medicine could help unite heaven and earth invoking blessings for each. Native Americans associated turtles with lunar cycles and feminine powers; a designation for the primal mother, symbol for Mother Earth, longevity and awakening to heightened sensibilities.

Nancy said her understandings of the natural world "and my place in it" lean more to Native American customs than any other spiritual practice. "So we took that into consideration when building the labyrinth.

"Since it has been here, I have walked it frequently, and done a lot of praying and communicating with nature spirits," Nancy remarked. "In a way, I guess it is a portal, because I have received much communication there. I usually walk it fairly rapidly and chant as I walk. My energy level increases and becomes balanced. It also puts me more in tune with nature spirits and the spirit world."

Studying the characteristics and actions of animals can attune humans with nature and help harmonize inner spiritual principles. Called animal totems by the Native Americans, certain species can provide assistance to those in the physical, explaining why things manifest in one's life. Noticing how actions parallel specific animal traits reveals information about innate powers, abilities and attributes.

Listen whenever a totem calls to you, catches your attention, nudges those little gray cells or provokes an emotional response. What you learn will probably solve the problem you are currently facing, offer support, provide protection or teach beneficial lessons.

"I named her Turtle Woman because it seemed so fitting," Nancy added. "The location of the labyrinth is close to our pond, where lots of turtles live. Plus, I have been collecting turtle shells for years and display them everywhere. I eventually want to place a staff at the entrance with turtle shells hanging from it. Maybe like the medallions we wore at our first gathering walk in March of 2006 when we honored the turtle noting its meaning and importance."

Living in and around water, turtles are the most ancient vertebrate animal. As a shore creature, this reptile utilizes both land and water. Shore areas are associated with doorways and turtle is often considered a keeper of the door to the fairy realm extending rewards to those who pay attention.

Turtles signify motherhood, longevity, awakening to opportunities. Their long life grants grounding to those able to understand the coherence between creative energies and physical manifestation. Slow down and observe favorable circumstances; learn new perceptions about time and how humans relate to themselves.

Reconnect with the primal essence. Apply those amazing survival skills and strategies; analyze, investigate, document. Use that strong head and neck to flip things over and view issues from all directions before acting. Go within your shell to avoid danger, rest or contemplate emerging when feel like traveling again or ideas are ready for implementation or expression. Take time to let natural flows develop and balance the apparent dichotomy of asymmetrical aspirations.

Recognize the difference between wisdom and knowledge. Overcome fear when strange becomes ordinary. Accept different perspectives and appreciate ridges, patterns, textures; gloss, sheen, hue; shine, radiance, brightness; color, smooth, delicate.

These reptilian totems teach how to sense vibrations and awaken the senses on both physical and spiritual levels. Their keen sense of hearing prompts clairaudience and the ability to see at varying levels helps activate clairvoyance. A superior sense of smell stimulates the capacity for discrimination and aids identification of dimensional flavors.

Turtles possess a strong backbone for continuous endurance developed from traveling with their homes. A perpetual shield of shelter, turtle shells present a solid foundation and protect and nurture its occupant, just as Mother Earth tends to her inhabitants. A turtle cannot separate itself from its shell, and neither can humans separate themselves from their planetary home.

Native cultures believe the way to heaven is through the earth. We must return the favor extended by this pulsating planet and protect our home as she nurtures us. This connection

Hulbert

to all things is evident from the lessons of turtle medicine.

Conversing with the Spirit of the Turtle while sitting in the center of its labyrinth namesake, one of the authors practiced her clairaudient skills and had this to share:

"We are thrilled you chose to join us on this windy June day and journey with the Spirit of the Turtle who is all around you and within. Animal totems serve with a mission seeking divine purpose and to answer as many questions as ask.

"Tune your heart to the rhythmic drumming of Mother Earth, hear her sparkling heartbeat, play with dolphins, intuit protection, commune with nature as iridescent goddess energy wafts around the altar encompassing divine grace, offering alternate methods of transition.

"Pockets of enlightenment continue to unfold within as I converge without completing an elliptical compilation of knowledge to be placed inside an orbiting shell of mastery. Spherical efficacy suggests a willingness to surround and perfect the nucleus of the revolving mind quantifying quantum configurations, spatial in number and consistency.

"I come to liberate humanity both individually and collectively yet not through steadfast traditions of unaltered directives. Creation can be playful, decorative, exclusive, comforting, attentive, protective, flexible.

"My desire is to share this journey of emotion and heal our center as we reflect on the clouds above moving in opposite directions showing all paths are relevant and vibrant."

The phrase "heal our center" seemed pertinent as we had just toured the new wellness center. Plus, the admonition arose while sitting in the center of a labyrinth. Duality and unity harmonize in a serene place of healing and restoration.

The focal point of the soul internalizes the message from resident feline and canine companions who peered under the altar rocks on separate occasions during the last hour. Drawing attuned attentions to the heart of the matter (center of the labyrinth) where heaven meets earth, masculine blends with feminine, hidden treasure awaits those willing to lift the veil and investigate.

Turtle says the doorway to higher consciousness is standing open, the sky is clear. It's time to come out of your shell and journey the sacred circle.

Lawton

Private Back Yard — Linda and Garland Hines
(580) 248-0844, LadyHawkMessages@aol.com
Combination grass labyrinth and medicine wheel
Created by Linda and son Brian in 2004

Standing Tall inhabits the middle of the 24-foot medicine wheel labyrinth in Lawton at the private residence of Linda and Garland Hines.

Attired in traditional buckskin, the Native American spirit statue oversees the cardinal directions and offers insight to any who will listen.

Before he speaks his ancestral wisdom, he requests you pay your respects.

Therapist Linda Hines and her son, an Oklahoma City architect, created the combination labyrinth/medicine wheel and her husband maintains it.

"We love it and have had it for about three years. I did not know of any such sites, so created my own."

Linda's interest in medicine wheels and labyrinths gave her the unique idea to combine the two into one. She uses it for personal spiritual work and group therapy classes to share the experience of learning to trust inner knowing.

The traditional four directions correlate to healing spiritually, emotionally, physically and mentally.

"This allows me to walk within a particular quadrant to delve more deeply into the issue of that direction. I will walk, in a clockwise direction around the medicine wheel, until I feel pulled by one quadrant," Linda said. "Then I walk that area for detailed meditation and increased perception.

"I have groups do the same thing and encourage everyone to listen to their inner guidance for where to start their medicine walk. It amazes each person when they learn the aspects of that direction and what they are facing in their lives."

When people meditate together, they usually hear a distinctive message relating to not only their individual path, but also the most important thing for those in the group to know at that point in their collective lives, the practitioner and owner of Counseling and Heart-Centered Therapy Services said.

Walkers also receive the benefit of gemstone and crystal healing from energetically charged crystals and multi-faceted rocks collected in various states and strategically positioned around the back yard.

"Crystal energy accompanies visitors and the four directions have been blessed with crystals that found me when I went digging in Arkansas," Linda laughed.

Grass is mowed higher in certain spots to form the design of the sacred circle. Medicine wheel paths open at the four directions meeting in the center and also comprise the outer ring.

The four areas sculptured by a lower lawn mower setting can be walked as a labyrinth contained within the medicine wheel. Each pattern is traveled separately and, although can be walked as a traditional labyrinth, it is quiet challenging.

One of the authors tried this and does not recommend it. "I learned to step over obstacles blocking the path if you choose the unconventional route. It gets easier with each circuit and reinforces that no one path is correct, they all lead somewhere. Certainly not the path of least resistance or going with the flow, but sometimes worth the effort if you can increase vibrational rates to avoid getting dizzy. Concentration paramount encouraging all aspects to work together fusing creative capacity and logical encounters into a scintillating divine space."

"I, too, am on this healing journey," Linda said. "It is a journey filled with both joy and pain and is a process working from the inside out and the outside in for integration of mind, body and spirit. Bioenergetics has been essential in my own personal healing and allowed me increased opportunities to work with people in this energetic modality that analyzes the interaction of mind and body."

Helping people resolve emotional problems and realize more of their potential is the fundamental thesis of Bioenergetics Analysis. What occurs in the mind reflects what is happening in the body.

Linda shares her personal triumph while teaching clients about self-healing when they traverse her sacred back yard circle.

A white Rose of Sharon honors the north entrance to the medicine wheel signifying the color of that direction. Buffalo is the spirit keeper of the north which represents the mental self.

When entering the north quadrant of the medicine wheel labyrinth, healing for the mental body is requested. This healing permits one to see the truth and let go of all lies humans have been told and accepted in their minds. Here is the wisdom of the ancestors: clarity, understanding, illumination.

Luscious crepe myrtle tenderly kisses the heads of those entering the east quadrant. The color of a vibrant golden yellow sun serves the spiritual self. Eagle, hummingbird or firefly are the spirit keepers of the east.

Those who desire healing on the spiritual level walk this pathway to learn what is sacred to them and what is truly sacred in the universe. It enhances knowledge about ceremony and religion.

The south quadrant is shaded by a neighboring maple tree. Red is the color for the emotional direction and rabbit and wolf or cougar are the spirit keepers of the south.

To receive healing on the emotional level and for the heart, visit this section of the medicine wheel labyrinth. Here, walkers give thanks for and request help with relationships. This direction provides the opportunity to be more centered, self aware, balanced and courageous in dealing with relationships and affection. South features growth, trust and love.

Black is the color of the west which concerns the physical self. Bear is the spirit keeper of this direction.

West characterizes physical healing and how one relates to the world. Release disease, accept health and go within to seek inner wisdom. What are the present physical lessons of the individual and how do they relate to the earth? Is detoxification needed or elimination of impurities that are hindering maximum health? Cleansing, renewal and purity are west attributes.

This magnificent yard is decorated with scented flowers, crepe myrtle, triangular mirrors, animal totems, dragon protectors, crystals, rocks, symbolic emblems and, of course, Standing Tall.

More an emissary than a decoration, Standing Tall told one of the authors he would speak to her if she played her drum for him.

How can one refuse such an offer?

"You have come at a most auspicious time in the evolution of Mother Earth. She is splitting at the seams and must be healed. You chose to drum in the physical quarter facing me (Standing Tall) and the spiritual wheel of mankind, with emotions to the right and ancestral wisdom to the left. It all must come together as one embodiment before the earth can be cleansed and overcome the past. It can be done by connecting the spokes of the human medicine wheel synchronistically with the sinew (fabric) of creation.

"Listen with your heart and dance to the drumbeat of your forefathers. Knowledge gained from researching this book can help. Link to the labyrinth, rise above the twists and turns of mediocrity. Let diversity shine forth to enlighten the world. You are on the right path to understanding. Go now and share your talents, love, wisdom and compassion to help all ascend to their multi-dimensional self."

Standing Tall's words emanated through the spokes of the medicine wheel traveling each path of the labyrinth interconnecting man and spirit. His image aligned with a large rock formation sitting a few paces outside the physical west quadrant. A crystal near the north ancestral wisdom sector sparked its radiance in the setting sun.

Indeed, we are all connected, sparkling, radiant beings traveling life's unicursal path, laying a solid foundation for rebirth, encompassing all knowledge, participating in the grand scheme of the continuous cycle of life.

Feminine Well Labyrinth

Muskogee

MoonShadow Herb Farm
Sharon Owen, (918) 687-6765, moonshads@aol.com
2 outdoor 7-circuit Cretan, grass and brick labyrinths
  left turn by well, 26 feet (feminine), built 1999
  right turn in meadow, 50 feet (masculine), built 2001
Open for holiday walks; call for availability

Walking a labyrinth is a gift we give ourselves. Sharon Owen doubles the pleasure generously sharing her special present as visitors can experience two sacred circles on a five-acre wooded herb farm south of Muskogee.

Both are 7-circuit Cretan brick and grass designs. The "feminine" model by the well near the house is 26 feet and the "masculine" meadow creation is about 50 feet.

The smaller one weaves a universal web of divine wisdom offering spiritual nourishment from a softer, gentler feminine side. A wilder, aggressive masculine energy exudes from the larger, meadow labyrinth.

An energy bubble springs from the feminine, floating above its interior. Twirling vortices encircle the upper meadow of Moon-Shadow Herb Farm often casting a purple mist over the center of that labyrinth.

Sharon said she chose the 7-circuit Cretan pattern because it predates the 11-circuit Chartres "and doesn't take as much time to walk."

Plus, it has a secret. It's a circle based on a square. The seven rings are formed from a cross seed pattern.

"The 7-circuit labyrinth may also symbolize the seven chakras of the body with paths corresponding to the seven colors of the rainbow, the Seven Rays, the seven Principles of the Cosmos, seven planets, seven days of the week and the seven Stations of the Cross," Sharon explained.

Walkers can also explore energy centers of the body in a 7-circuit symbol which enables work with not only the chakras, but also with mantras, color and musical tones. This style contains the notes of a musical octave, Sharon said. According to the order of the paths, the "music" of the Cretan equates to C, D, E, F and G, A, B, C. "This is the song of the 7-circuit labyrinth," Sharon smiled, tapping her fingers on the countertop.

"There are as many ways to walk a labyrinth as there are people on earth," she continued. "The circular winding paths nourish your spirit. To me, it's a place to get closer to God or a high power.

"Its passageways represent life's journey. You circle and turn, circle and turn and you think you're going toward the center, making progress. Then you discover you're on the outer rim."

Sharon spent four years on "the outer rim" after she moved from town to her current home. Spending many months walking the property line using dowsing rods, meditation, prayers, reiki and other energy techniques, she slowly learned the lay of the land and its ley lines.

In 1999, she noticed a small area near a well vibrating special energy suitable for a labyrinth. "A large bubble of energy floated above the ground and I kept a 7-circuit pattern drawn on the grass, but it was temporary and required continuous work."

Bricks were eventually imbedded to mark the well labyrinth's pattern with soft, green grass pathways. The left-turn entrance follows the same direction as a medicine wheel.

"Most everything about this labyrinth is feminine (including the location next to a well)," Sharon said. "Its energy is nourishing, comforting and accepting. Initially, a group of women met and walked the well labyrinth for many different reasons. People noted a butterfly frequently accompanied them and once a butterfly lit on a woman's hands folded in prayer and remained there for her entire walk."

Dowsing confirmed an energy vortex in the upper meadow at MoonShadow. (Sharon developed a natural aptitude for this ability as her dad and grandfather both dowsed.) Ley lines in this section of the property run west-southwest.

In late 2000, the herb gardener planned a larger labyrinth on the west rim of the vortex. "The next summer solstice, another group of women gathered for a ceremony to create a meadow labyrinth following the seed pattern drawn on the ground. Each took turns placing bricks to form a right-turn 7-circuit Cretan, approximately 50 feet in diameter. We then walked in unison to the center of the labyrinth — lead by a lady in a wheelchair. Everyone offered a prayer and song according to their belief."

The meadow labyrinth has mostly masculine energy, Sharon said. Dynamic, inspiring, dramatic, yet peaceful... spiced with Indian paintbrush, aster, wild clover, coreopsis and bluestem grass. Wheelchair accessible pathways are mowed thatched prairie grass whose appearance changes with the seasons.

Both labyrinths received revered attention on the fall equinox of 2001. Several different spiritual study groups joined to formally open and consecrate the sacred symbols using water and special blessings by a Lakota medicine man.

Sharon said these circles have been attended on numerous occasions. "They have welcomed groups of people for spiritual work; individuals have walked for personal reasons. I have visited them for meditation, prayer and healing as well as for last rites. Groups of school children touring the herb farm have run, played and laughed in them. We have danced in them with joy and gratitude — and just for fun. They have even been part of an annual garden tour."

Sometimes, they lay silent, at rest, sleeping until awakened by another "pilgrim's visit."

The labyrinths at MoonShadow Herb Farm are open to family and friends anytime and to the public on most observed holidays. "Just call or e-mail in advance so I will know to expect someone," Sharon said, adding she has a printed schedule available showing what weekends the labyrinths are open for public walking.

Sharon plans to create a third labyrinth using a design called "Heart of the Chartres."

"That probably won't happen until after I retire," the government employee grinned. "Until then, it's a task to determine suitable and sustainable materials for the more complicated pattern."

Muskogee

Nothing complicated about the day the authors visited. A simple picnic started the afternoon activities as a charming hostess placed a card table alongside the feminine well labyrinth for her guests.

She even offered a ladder so a picture from a higher perspective could be taken of these magnificent earth sculptures. We decided to use the photos she provided and eat our chicken. Someone was hungry. Communing with the sacred images would wait until after lunch.

The red brick dividing the paths shined crisply against the suede look of the well-manicured grass of Miss Laby, polished after three weeks of almost constant rain. Today was the first day of sunshine in almost a month.

A south slope provided natural drainage for the unusually wet Oklahoma spring. The labyrinth wore an exquisite emerald green dress in our honor. Matching leaves from the nearby trees nodded their approval as a cool breeze kissed the pages of an author's notebook.

Unicorn magic resided under one of the arbor pine trees in the form of a white statue decorated with an iridescent scarf, orchestrating accompanying nature spirit energies.

Pleasant herbal aromas from succulent plants growing throughout the farm titillated nostrils. Prickly-pear cacti lined the ornate rock garden and red barn sharing this area of the property.

Whispers of love softly caressed the inner ear sanctum as the fluttering doorway to the mind entertained itself imagining artistic shapes in the picturesque blue clouds floating gently overhead.

A multiplicity of form searched intensely for a soothing return to wholeness and a divine journey to completion.

Female intensity tempers bold aggression in the upper meadow as a stucco matron performs her daily chores outside the masculine labyrinth. Balancing logic and intellect with passion and creativity, Queen Anne's Lace and Black-eyed Susan's caress walkers' legs as they traverse the wild and daring overgrown paths of Mr. Laby.

Aerial acrobats flitted about reminding humans of the omnipresence of Spirit. The invisible will soon become visible.

This vast expanse of beauty and openness surrounding guests in the upper meadow prompts remembrance of at-one-ment (not atonement) and resurrects lost vitality. A higher plane provides a distinct overview of any situation. Luminous vortex energy animates change spiritually cleansing the collective, raising the vibration of all who pass this way.

Flamboyant wildflowers cover the brick path dividers reinforcing a dependency on faith. Foundation stones provide stability in an uncertain world while humanity's feet understand where to safely trod.

Dense foliage may block the intended goal, but add dazzling brilliance and daring to any expedition. Even in chaos, the path is well-defined. An effervescent center altar of flowers affords a pulsating antithesis to stillness and being.

Clouds covered the sky, yet the sun (son) shined brightly bathing grateful walkers with an almost instant 10-degree temperature drop inviting an expanded and more pleasant voyage.

Petite smiling faces sparkled from vivid daisies enhancing an exciting atmosphere making one feel they can accomplish anything. Simply reach out and touch God inside the individual heart of Creation.

Muskogee

Masculine Meadow Labyrinth

Reaves Park — Prairie Peace Path
Jenkins Ave. & Timberdell Rd, (405) 366-5472
7-circuit outdoor permanent, 65 feet, reddish-brown granite
gravel walking path, wheelchair accessible, built May 2002

A stately Chinese pistache tree adorns the center of the labyrinth in Norman's Reaves Park. Its branches accentuate a 65-foot artistic creation of reddish-brown granite highlighting a three-foot-wide gravel walking path.

The natural wooded area sits inside an open rail enclosure of warm earth colors with a pleasant meandering trail inviting walkers to seek the path of least resistance. An outer perimeter of shade trees and lush green grass completes the picturesque park setting like a scene portrayed with broad, artist strokes.

Built in May 2002 as a memorial after the September 11 terrorist attacks, the Prairie Peace Path Labyrinth Sculpture was designed to help with the grieving process, provide peace, solace and comfort and remember loved ones.

Longtime Norman resident Madeline Rugh spearheaded the effort, designing the labyrinth, meeting with city officials, raising funds and securing materials and volunteers to build what many residents called an "interesting addition to our park."

"I see it as a highly unique way of dealing with the complexities of our lives by generating deep calm and introspection," said the Norman Parks and Recreation tai chi instructor. "Sometimes we need relief or quiet."

Rugh, who is also a visual artist and educator, said her interest in labyrinths was sparked by an Episcopal priest and their artistic patterns. The idea germinated until the tragic events of September 11, 2001, prompted her to action.

"It was like a convergence of many streams into a river," Rugh said, adding she felt it would be a good tool for grieving and a soothing memorial.

Trained several years ago as a labyrinth facilitator, Rugh said a labyrinth can provide the community with a focal point for people to express grief, celebrate life or solve whatever problems confront them.

Dedication ceremonies were held May 19, 2002, with a contemplative walk accompanied by native flute music. People were invited to write a blessing or a wish concerning September 11 on a ribbon and carry it with them through the labyrinth and into the center to hang on the pistache tree. Some are still there, flapping in the Norman breeze honoring the enduring quality of the human spirit.

An appropriate labyrinth amid the inquiring, educational essence of a college town, the Prairie Peace Path epitomizes the quest for answers that go beyond the surface, those you cannot see, but know are there.

The reddish-brown granite stones signify a connection to earth, ancestral wisdom and a solid foundation for learning and applying fresh knowledge. The open space around the labyrinth allows room to breathe and connotes freedom from antiquated beliefs.

Two metal buildings to the south provide a natural protective screen from the busy nearby street. Far enough removed yet acknowledging other travelers on life's path. A picnic area to the north honors family, recreation, nourishment. Entertainment and exercise are featured to the east with several softball fields and kids practicing fly-fishing or seeing how high their new butterfly kite will soar.

A young boy brought his mother to walk the labyrinth for the first time. He called it fun; she said it was relaxing. Another couple strolled its paths, arm in arm, enjoying the environment and each other's company, perhaps unaware they were walking an ancient spiritual path to enlightenment.

One astute walker noticed some of the rocks that define the paths were out of alignment in certain places and applied that to mankind. "Even when some of us get out of line, humankind is still beautiful. The precision of this labyrinth is also beautiful. It leaves me with a sense of peace and harmony — just like its name implies. Simply viewing it activates joy."

Linn Ann Huntington, a college friend of one of the authors, had her first labyrinth experience at the Prairie Peace Path following the death of a loved one. She shared the following comments:

"Gail suggested we walk the labyrinth in Reaves Park the day after my husband Don's funeral. I had spent the past five days in a blur. Don had broken his leg. We had gone to the hospital. There were X-rays. The fracture was simple, they told us. The physician's assistant set the bones and put Don's leg in a cast. Because Don was diabetic, they admitted him to the hospital for observation. But no one expected him to die. People don't die from a broken leg. But a few hours later, Don went into cardiac arrest. The doctor told me a blood clot probably traveled from the fracture to his lungs and killed him. She called it a pulmonary embolism and said it was abrupt, and he experienced no pain. All I knew was the man I had spent the last 29 years of my life with was gone. He was 55. I was 52, and all of a sudden, I was a widow.

"Immediately, there were phone calls to make. Then funeral arrangements. Then travel arrangements for my elderly mother and me, since we took Don's body back to his hometown for the funeral. When Gail asked me if I wanted to go walk the labyrinth I was exhausted, both emotionally and physically. To be honest, I wasn't even sure what a labyrinth was. I went along with the suggestion simply because it meant additional time I could spend with an old friend. And connecting with dear friends was something I desperately needed right then.

"It was close to dusk when we arrived at the park. I had never walked a labyrinth before and wasn't exactly sure what I was supposed to do or feel as I walked. But I discovered that my feet quickly developed a steady, even gait and my breathing became deep and regular. There is nothing mystical or magical about a labyrinth. It is simply a journey. As I walked toward the center of the labyrinth that evening, I envisioned walking toward the open heart of God. It is that quiet conversation with the Creator of all things that is wondrous — not where the conversation takes place. It is the process of quieting oneself and listening to the voice of God that becomes life changing. As I poured out my heart to God that night on the labyrinth, I had no idea how I would ever make it through the rest of my life. I only knew I wanted to stay connected to Him forever.

"I have no labyrinth in the town where I live. So my nightly walks take place in my own neighborhood. Those are still special times for me, away from all the distractions of a busy life, times when God and I talk about matters great and small. That is not to say I don't talk to Him throughout the day. I do, constantly. But those times walking and meditating as the sun goes down on my day are very special to me. Many times as I walk, I envision the labyrinth with its continuing circle — like the circle of life itself — always drawing me closer to the open heart of God."

Norman

Harding Charter Preparatory High School
(405) 528-0562, 3333 N. Shartel, Oklahoma City, OK 73118
5-circuit original student design, permanent outdoor
stone and grass, 30 feet, center rock in shape of Oklahoma

What are the chances of finding a rock shaped exactly like the state of Oklahoma in a random purchase of stones from a quarry? Probably about the same as an Oklahoma City Charter High School receiving a grant to build a labyrinth in the corner of its soccer field.

Both happened in the spring of 2007 and the Harding Charter Preparatory High School is the first — and, at present, the only — state high school to have the benefit of this sacred circle gracing its property.

"It was important to have native Oklahoma rock and a natural look," Art Instructor Sheridan Scott said. "But to find a rock in the outline of Oklahoma was an incredibly nice surprise. The center created itself."

The labyrinth was designed and built in the spring semester by 70 high school students in the art history and humanities department under Sheridan's supervision.

Each art student submitted a blueprint which was combined with research from the internet and Smartboard technology. "We first drew the pattern on paper, then calculated the space needed. The path across is 30 feet and has five circuits, plus the center space."

Many students suggested painting quotes on the rocks marking the walking path. "In love we trust" was the favorite.

"It's an ongoing project," Sheridan said. "I doubt we will ever be done as we plan to add something new each year during art studies. In ensuing semesters, we will probably construct luminary lights for evening walks."

Landscaping plans include planting herbs (spearmint) and flowers and placing benches for students and neighborhood residents to sit and reflect or chat while visiting the labyrinth.

One of the additional features will be a small mosaic "H" to represent Harding Charter and Harding Fine Arts. Both schools are housed in the same building and helped create the labyrinth.

Sheridan said the purpose in applying for the grant was to create an outside environment for students to release their creativity, intuition, imagination, aggression and/or angry emotions.

"It also lets them leave part of themselves for future classes as the labyrinth will be used by school counselors, language arts, history teachers and open to all faculty," Sheridan added.

Now for the history lesson. Labyrinths are different from mazes. These sacred symbols have one well-defined path that leads into the center and back out again. Labyrinths and mazes are frequently confused. A maze presents a puzzle to be solved. It has twists, turns and blind alleys and is a left-brain task requiring logical, sequential, analytical activity to find the correct path into the maze and out.

A labyrinth is a right-brain task involving intuition, creativity and imagery. Tools for personal and psychological transformation, labyrinths only present one choice: to enter or not. A more receptive mindset is required.

"When walking a labyrinth, students meander back and forth, turning 180 degrees each time they enter another circuit. As one shifts direction, they also shift their awareness from right brain to left brain. This is one of the reasons these investigative patterns can induce altered states of consciousness," Sheridan explained. "People walk labyrinths for varied reasons and each walk often has a distinctive focus. The purpose may be to seek balance, centering, awareness, inner answers or creativity."

Counselors could take troubled students outside to walk the

unicursal paths. At its most basic level, the labyrinth is a metaphor for the journey to the center of the student's deepest self and a return to the world with a broadened understanding of who they are.

"The labyrinth offers counselors an additional tool allowing students to look inside themselves for evasive answers and teaches self-empowerment," Sheridan said. "Walking around a defined space and then back out in slow, timely steps, provides an angered student time to cool off, and think about his behavior as opposed to aggressive reaction."

Junior Lea Crim said, "This helps us focus on our pathway of life. I will walk the labyrinth before school each morning to start my day out right."

Another student said when she gets angry, she intends to drive to the school at night and "chill out by walking the labyrinth."

History teachers can lead students through what experience the Greeks spoke about regarding the Minotaur. Some of the earliest forms of labyrinths are found in Greece, dating back to 2500-2000 B.C. Theseus was the son of Aegeus, King of Athens. At the time, Athens had to pay a tribute of seven boys and seven girls to Crete — as food for the Minotaur — every nine years. Theseus decided to put a stop to this and joined a tribute group traveling to Crete. There, Ariadne, one of Minos' daughters, fell in love with him. She gave Theseus a ball of string, which helped him find his way out of the labyrinth after he killed the Minotaur.

Language art teachers could employ the labyrinth to inspire poetry. Each student would keep a journal, the walk featuring an inner journey for self expression. "I stand at the door" or "I am at the crossroads" as beginning entries into their journaling. Walking a labyrinth creates an energetic experience, opposed to passively sitting in the chair of a classroom.

Sheridan said as an art teacher, her students would study the history of the labyrinth at Chartres Cathedral in France. Around 1230, as the Cathedral of Chartres was built, a large labyrinth 40 feet across was set with blue and white stones into the floor of the nave of the church. Like all cathedral labyrinths, it draws upon the ancient northern Celtic, Middle Eastern and Classical Greek and Roman origins of the Christian faith. Medieval builders were careful to incorporate their understanding of sacred architecture into the design and location of these labyrinths, which were usually placed near the entrance at the west end of the nave, beside the baptismal font at the foot of the church.

A trained labyrinth facilitator visited Harding in April 2007 for a two-day seminar to teach students the advantages of labyrinths and spark their interest in building one. Vicki Longhofer-Copeland received training for this special work through Veriditas, the Worldwide Labyrinth Project at San Francisco's Grace Cathedral. For in-depth study, she participated in a pilgrimage week at Chartres, France, site of the aforementioned labyrinth in the 13th century Chartres Cathedral.

"From personal and collaborative experiences with labyrinths, I see them as an instrument for fostering peace. Sharing my love of art has become a way of life highlighting 20 years of involvement in arts education," Vicki said. "As a consultant, I often work in curriculum development, teacher and docent training, and facilitate special programs for children at risk."

A doctoral dissertation and book Sheridan plans to use in labyrinth classes were written by Lea Goode-Harris, one of the designers of the Santa Rosa Community Labyrinth at Standing Bear Park in Ponca City.

What Matters to the Heart? Exploring the Psychological Significance of the Labyrinth and *Poetry In Motion: Finding Words in the Labyrinth of Life* will allow scholars to discover their inner poet and "enable this project to serve the faculty and entire student body," Sheridan said.

"Now where did I put my classroom planner?"

Mercy Health Center Labyrinth Prayer Garden
4300 West Memorial Road, Oklahoma City, OK 73120
Outdoor Permanent, Wheelchair Accessible
11-circuit Chartres replica, 40 feet, built May 2003
13,000 red sandstone and white limestone tiles
Always open, east of visitor entrance

Created from 13,000 red sandstone and white limestone tiles, the 11-circuit Chartres labyrinth at Mercy Health Center is the focal point of a sacred prayer garden located between the hospital's patient and visitor entrances.

An ancient art form, the majestic mosaic 40-foot circle is comprised of all naturally tumbled stones and offers a secluded outdoor sanctuary where patients, families, friends, co-workers and community residents can rest, walk, meditate or pray.

Surrounded by native Oklahoma oaks, pines and red buds as well as five decorative concrete benches, the garden also features one of the original crosses that topped the old Mercy Hospital in downtown Oklahoma City from 1947 to 1974.

Mercy is the only hospital in the state with a permanent labyrinth and was one of five public outdoor creations built in Oklahoma in 2003. The previous year saw the construction of outdoor labyrinths at Reaves Park in Norman and Sapulpa's Camp Okiwanee. In 2001, United Life Church in Oklahoma City, Standing Bear Park in Ponca City and Dwight Mission Presbyterian Camp in Vian crafted outdoor labyrinths.

Tahlequah's Sparrow Hawk Village owns the first Oklahoma outdoor sacred circle (November 1992) followed by St. Luke's Episcopal Church in Bartlesville (1998).

"Labyrinths are an ancient tool for connecting with what's really important in life and furnish a place for reflection," said Teri Everhart, Mercy Convent Administrator. "In the hubbub of all that's occurring around us, labyrinths grant a little solitude."

For thousands of years, they have symbolized the twists and turns of an existential journey.

"Labyrinths can help people find peace in the present moment and also provide a powerful metaphor for life," said Sister Rose Elizabeth Power. "Everyone has a different experience when they walk a labyrinth, a single, open path that leads to the center and back out again. It's not a maze where you can get lost. Just follow the path and you will find the center."

The hospital has held candlelight vigils and anniversary memorials to observe the April 19th Murrah Building bombing. "We want people to pause and think about the sacredness of life," Everhart added.

Healthcare seminars for social workers, nurses, physicians and counselors have also utilized the Mercy Hospital Labyrinth and Prayer Garden as a learning tool to see illness as a gift, revisit what it means to take part in a heritage of caring and discover how to be an instrument of forgiveness.

"As healthcare workers, we have a common bond and share the need to find ways to rejuvenate our energies so we can continue to provide compassionate care to patients," Glenda Bronson, a Mercy health ministry outreach coordinator, said.

Hospitals and healthcare providers are discovering labyrinths offer a unique complementary or integrative option to promote healing. They instill peace, alleviate stress, counsel grief, put life in perspective, enhance wellness and bring tranquility to the mind.

A Florida hospital study with 75 participants found that walking the curved paths increased hope, decreased stress and equalized blood pressure. Patients with bipolar disorder showed the most improvement.

Advocates say an act of walking between the lines engages the left portion of the brain allowing the right lobe to roam creatively or solve problems.

The American Cancer Society recommends labyrinths as a complementary treatment method to reduce stress.

A walking meditation encourages concentration with individual steps substituting for focused attention on each breath or mantra. Some use the movement as body prayer or liturgy.

Oklahoma City

Thomas Moore, author of *Care of the Soul,* believes the spiral turns portray the nature of religious knowing: "Not a straight line of reasoning leading to a clear answer, but rather a spiral and a labyrinth taking you deep within."

For an anxious family member waiting at the hospital, the meandering circuits may offer a chance to focus on the present moment, escape dreaded worries and relinquish the need to think.

Labyrinths offer special benefits to older citizens. The twisting path is good exercise and improves balance. Younger, faster travelers don't know if an older walker is coming in or going out, discouraging judgments on speed or progress.

Alzheimer's patients operate within a circle of safety where they can't get lost and may proceed at their own pace. Persons losing loved ones can use a labyrinth as a vehicle for dealing with grief. Individuals navigating the unicursal circuits in wheelchairs feel they are on equal footing and receive the same benefits as more mobile companions.

In 2006, Mercy conducted a 90-day study testing walking the labyrinth as a means of stress reduction in new nursing graduates. Eighteen new graduates were randomized into two groups. Both learned about the labyrinth and a special care model during orientation.

Researchers asked the intervention group to walk the labyrinth at least twice per month. They measured stress levels at baseline and 90 days. After three months, nurses in the intervention group showed less stress, while nurses in the control group exhibited a marked increase in stress.

The intervention group also reported higher job satisfaction.

Research project coordinator Gary Parker said the results were "staggering" in support of walking the labyrinth as an effective method of decreasing stress while increasing job satisfaction.

Another way health center nurses use the labyrinth is through a nursing theory called the Charism of Mercy. Developed by Mercy nurses, it includes 10 elements of caring and six influences of health and well-being. New nurses are introduced to the labyrinth as a tool for incorporating the model into practice.

As the nurses walk the labyrinth, they can meditate about the elements of caring: respect/dignity; compassion; teaching/ learning; informed decision-making; faith; empowerment; hospitality; problem-solving; wise use of resources, and clinical excellence or the things that influence health — access to care, cultural heritage, family, health history, environmental stressors and spiritual experience.

Chris Weigel, chief nursing officer at Mercy, says nurses may walk the path as they think through how best to help a family with end-of-life decisions or when problem solving a clinical issue. "It clears your mind so when you get into the process of doing things, you can make quick, clear, concise decisions."

Weigel said the labyrinth is such a peaceful place for people to de-stress, have a few moments of quiet and make tough decisions relative to patient or personal care.

Oklahoma's *Nursing Times* called the Mercy labyrinth an interesting support tool providing the facility's nurses the opportunity for integration of relaxation and prayer/meditation in a convenient worksite setting.

While labyrinths have a spiritual connection, they speak to people of all faiths seeking a deeper meaning in life or simply wanting to reduce stress, lower blood pressure or aid overall well-being.

It's the walkers personal belief that matters. This meandering "walking tour of the soul" presents a pilgrimage of prayer, time to ponder a conflict, seek God's direction, release earthly concerns or simply quiet the chatter of an overburdened mind while following a spiritual path, reflecting on how a Supreme Presence illuminates one's life.

"It permits a slowed down, peaceful opportunity to allow things within you or part of your relationship with the creative God to come to the surface and minister to you. People can't be healed just physically and stay well. If people are ill, they have fractures in their mind, body or spirit," an oncology doctor said.

"This labyrinth is very intricate and employs an artistic approach to finding renewal," one man remarked.

Another woman who participated in the master number walk at Mercy Health Center on July 7 (7-7-07) said "it was exactly that. A walk of mercy, inner stabilizing and healing. The other people present on this special day each gave to me in energy, comfort and acceptance. As we gathered in the sacred center, I sensed a moment of connection at a soul level with each being present (and there were far more than the bodies I could see). Several birds flew over and swooped in a great flock. (They were grackles which symbolize community.) As they did this twice in almost identical formations, I noticed they were bringing my

Oklahoma City

attention to the glass pyramid building facing us on the other side of the parking lot and the rotating cross on top of the hospital — two strong sacred symbols for mystery and compassion. This reminded me to hold in reverence, everyone from all stations in life and to respect my brothers for their healing presence on my journey. I was again reminded to love all with detachment."

A female nurse said that while walking the labyrinth she immediately felt the presence of angels. "One over my right shoulder had huge golden white wings and a blue aura. My guardian angel was on my left following me as I reverently walked the path inward. I began chanting OM about halfway through. There are benches close to the path where one can pause to rest during their walk. I chose to do so and wrote this while sitting there. Then I continued on my journey inward. The travelers on this path joined each other in the center and prayed together. I encountered a sense of solace, serenity and peace. We read from various holy texts and then returned outward taking renewed purpose, joy and understanding to share with others along the winding path."

In the Christian faith, seven is considered the number of perfection, signifying creation and connection to the powers of heaven. It represents wisdom and seekers of truth.

Many consider seven a lucky number and associate it with advantageous endeavors. Supreme Lady Luck dices the imagination attracting the energy, people, situations and opportunities necessary to multiply wealth, prosperity, health and happiness — strengthening collective powers and magnifying extraordinary chances for major success and magical attractions.

This triple-seven day energized our universal consciousness on a majestic mosaic of 13,000 red and white glistening tiles spiraling to the center of a sacred focal point where the holly encircling the outer path reached out and embraced our souls.

Optimal Potentials
Debi Bocar, (405) 722-2163, dbocar@aol.com
7-circuit multi-colored and 11-circuit Chartres (both canvas)

The beautiful multi-colored 7-circuit canvas labyrinth available to walk at the Oklahoma City Holistic Health Fair each year belongs to Debi Bocar, RN, PhD, of Optimal Potentials.

"We provide this labyrinth at the holistic health fairs to add to the nurturing environment and to help participants relax, reinvigorate, reflect and get inspired," Dr. Bocar said. "The colors delineating the paths evoke different responses. Color therapy is a new way to use this ancient tool."

A labyrinth helps walkers connect to their spiritual source and aligns perfectly with the purpose of these holistic fairs, Dr. Bocar stated. "Educating the public about the various types of complementary therapies and mind, body, spirit modalities is what Optimal Potentials is all about."

Walking a defined path that continually changes direction provokes a spatial relationship encouraging focus on the present moment.

"And isn't the present moment all there really is?" Dr. Bocar asked.

A canvas multi-colored labyrinth offers additional concepts not available with rock, stone, concrete, grass, turf or wood outdoor designs, the consultant and educator said. Directions, elements and concepts correspond to the various colors and circuits of the sacred symbol.

Geographical and vertical directions, the elements to sustain life and character attributes can enhance any labyrinth walk. Adding a color component spices the journey.

Dr. Bocar employs the following combinations while facilitating her multi-colored circle:

The east direction coincides with the color yellow and element air. Significant concepts include insight, clarity, guidance and new beginnings.

Red honors south and fire, love, compassion, wisdom and forgiveness.

West symbolizes blue, water and healing on all levels.

Green represents north and earth, strength, growth and releasing fears.

Up respects white and denotes divine inspiration and universal energy.

Brown unites down and earth divinity.

"Spiraling color patterns within the labyrinth show how a mixture of vibrant tones and hues profoundly influence our lives," Dr. Bocar said. "Consciously choosing colors for daily attire, home and employment settings and during healing episodes augments our experiences and optimizes general well-being."

The labyrinth paths also profess how colors affect one's journey. Yellow rules the abdominal organs (liver, spleen, gall bladder, stomach and small intestines). A mental color signifying intellect and the brightness of the sun; new beginnings, insight, clarity, personal power and concept of the individual; self-worth, energy, self-control, moderation, perseverance, optimism.

Orange correlates with the reproductive organs, pelvis and hips, large intestines, appendix, lower back and bladder. Burning embers magnify creativity, relationships, sex, feelings, money, guilt and exemplifies physical prowess and emotional stability.

Corporeal body support depends on red: bones, muscles, legs, feet, immune system. Fire stirs love, compassion, safety, security, trust, courage, commitment, enthusiasm and relates to tribe, family history, personality and Mother Earth.

Green epitomizes heart and circulatory system, lungs, shoulders, arms, hands, breasts. Plants tender emotional power and social identity, love, compassion, healing, growth, nature, kindness, hope, grounding, balance.

The ethers breathe purple, spirituality, intuition, creativity (right brain), nervous system, top of head, inspiration, values, empathy, gratitude, faith, wealth and abundance.

Blue constitutes thinking (left brain), nose, sinuses, eyes and face; integrity, self-reflection, intellect, intuition, justice, perspective, leadership, peace; associated with sky and the heavenly realms.

Water and sea bond to aqua through the throat and neck, thyroid gland, mouth, teeth, gums and ears. Will power, speaking one's truth, listening to others, curiosity, knowledge, integrity, making choices, discernment, fairness, humility and stamina characterize the seventh path surrounding the golden center.

Gold is the highest healing color and is the pinnacle of achievement. True attainment. The goal has been reached, creativity heightened, imagination sparked, intuition elevated, relaxation enhanced, stress reduced, question answered, problem solved, grief released, insight gained, forgiveness granted...

Any number of possibilities exist inside a labyrinth where one can truly dance the colorful celebration of life with the angels of joy.

Using a finger labyrinth inside a labyrinth enhances the experience.

Our Lady of Mercy Retreat Center
2801 S. Shartel, Oklahoma City, OK 73109
2nd & 3rd floors of Mount St. Mary High School
11-circuit Chartres, portable nylon, 30 feet
Call for availability, (405) 634-1968

Tucked away on the second and third floors of Mount St. Mary High School in south Oklahoma City is an oasis of serenity. "The peace that surpasses all understanding" resides inside Our Lady of Mercy Retreat Center.

Individuals and groups have embraced its welcoming silence and solitude, spacious grounds, meditation garden, library, ministry, education and prayer chapel since its inception in September 1997.

Large and small meeting rooms, double and single occupancy sleeping quarters (accommodating 25 to 30 people), a well-equipped kitchen and beautiful dining facilities encourage lengthy stays.

Sister Betty said nearly 2,000 persons visit the retreat center each year. "They experience what Matthew 11:28-30 meant when he wrote: Come to Me all you who labor and are overburdened. I will give you rest...learn from Me, for I am gentle and humble of heart, and you will find rest for your souls."

They come seeking quiet retreat time, guidance, peace from a chaotic world, spiritual knowledge, cultural reflection, undisturbed ministry meetings or other faith-based curriculums.

The retreat center serves people of all religious traditions. Sister Betty said its programs share the richness of the Roman Catholic heritage integrated with contemporary tools for reducing stress and finding a deep, inner peace.

Enter the labyrinth.

The 11-circuit Chartres replica is on nylon parachute material and epitomizes the mission of Our Sisters of Mercy offering faith to a unique community with mercy, compassion and a Christ-centered approach.

Mount St. Mary High School also parallels this philosophy. As the first state high school, the Mount has provided a college-preparatory education to a student population of diverse social, economic and ethnic backgrounds since 1903 focusing on educating the whole person in mind, body and spirit.

Nurturing a life-long commitment to learning, leadership and a Christian life, Mount St. Mary is the only Catholic high school in the country sponsored by both a religious order and an archdiocese.

The religious community, Sisters of Mercy, oversees the retreat center where several labyrinth workshops have been presented. The 30-foot labyrinth fits nicely inside the Prayer Chapel sanctifying the walk between golden paths of wheat stalks on white nylon.

Soft music and candlelight accompany the comfortable surroundings. What better place to commune with the Source at the center of our souls than in a chapel. A strong angelic presence walked with us as we individually transcended the circuits aligning our spirits to a higher power. Collectively, we touched the celestial realms.

Heaven does not have to wait. It's right here inside each of us as we journey through life supported by those around us, experiencing a continuous conscious connection to Creation.

One of the authors said in her walk tonight, she noticed the labyrinth had some slippery parts amid its narrow path. The reversals seemed more pronounced than in other sacred circles she had traveled.

"This observation led me to muse about the vagaries on life's path — sudden reversals and twists and turns that seem to lead nowhere. But with perseverance and effort, the path leads to the

Source. This points to the truth that all of us, regardless of those twists and turns, reversals and tight squeezes, will make it to our goal.

"A deeply satisfying encounter and poignant message as usual. What an honor to be allowed to participate in this retreat."

Twelve people from all walks of life were privileged to combine essences that evening as they joined in a sole quintessence becoming One with God.

A sacred space for all to seek the divine, inside a labyrinth in an oasis in the city.

Oklahoma City's Paseo Crossroads annually glows vibrant orange with a jolly 40-foot Halloween Jack O' Lantern. A Magic Lantern Celebration springs to life the Sunday before All Saints Eve, providing "a night of light instead of fright." The artistic Jack O' Lantern labyrinth is the focal point for the creative alternative festival for children and the young at heart. (Photo by Skip Largent)

Quail Springs United Methodist Church
14617 N. Pennsylvania, Oklahoma City, OK 73134
(405) 755-9477, always open
7-circuit Native American design, permanent outdoor
multi-cross center, wheelchair accessible, built 2003

The labyrinth at Quail Springs United Methodist Church is proof that dreams do indeed come true. Created in 2003 with generous memorial gifts and abundant volunteer efforts, the 7-circuit Native American design is painted on concrete in reddish-brown earth colors surrounded by the beauty of creation.

Centered amid a well-manicured garden in a serene pastoral setting in the "woods" of Quail Springs, sacred symbols and shapes grace poignant, purple flowers, emerald-green grass, evergreen trees, pines, poplars, junipers and angel hair sweet grass.

The dream of a prayer garden for the Quail Springs church was born in 2002. Linda and Sam Bowman chaired the committee charged with planning, developing and implementation. Dr. Bertha Potts, pastor from 1997 to June 2005, was a dynamic and involved leader whose "Dare to Dream" personality led to countless growth and beautification projects and showed the congregation "what could be" when people worked together dedicated to the glory of God.

Bert, as she was fondly called, led by example. Applying physical attributes to spiritual reality, she took the symbolic pilgrimage experience gained from a labyrinth to new heights revealing how to turn a physical journey into a spiritual journey.

The deck, labyrinth, gazebo and landscaping were financed through numerous contributions and the Prayer Garden became a reality in the spring of 2005.

A Memorial Album was created to recognize and remember the people in whose name memorial donations were made. These books sit atop the pulpit from the Stonewall, Oklahoma, Methodist Church built in the early 1920s. The town of approximately 400 was proud of its new church and in an effort to provide funds to purchase a new pulpit, Mrs. Vallie McKoy and Mrs. Mamie Beck decided to sew and sell women's bonnets "to be worn while working in the gardens and doing various daily outdoor chores women did in those days."

Hundreds of bonnets were sold at church bazaars, in downtown Stonewall stores or any other place that would showcase them. All the money went into the "pulpit fund" until they had enough to buy a lovely wooden pulpit to be placed at the altar. The wood matched the altar and wooden cross which hung directly behind the pulpit.

Mrs. McKoy's son, Rev. Clifton McKoy, preached from this pulpit several years later and when the church was demolished in the 1990s, Rev. McKoy saved the pulpit to honor his mother and Mrs. Beck for raising the "pulpit" money before he was born. He placed a brass plate on the pulpit when he salvaged it from the old church and the pulpit remained with him until his death in 2004. It was then given to his sister and nieces who wanted the pulpit to once again find a home in a Methodist Church.

Through the efforts of Mrs. Virginia Calame, the pulpit was donated to Quail Springs United Methodist Church where it resides in the Narthex, displaying the Prayer Garden Memorial Books. The brass plate is still intact and reads: In 1920, Mrs. George (Vallie) McKoy and Mrs. Joe (Mamie) Beck made and sold bonnets to buy this pulpit furniture "For the Glory of God and This Church."

A charter member of the 20-year-old Quail Springs church, Virginia Calame epitomizes the involved volunteer spirit of its members and "Dare to Dream" philosophy.

The church protects the Prayer Garden on the north and west with a winding sidewalk leading from the sanctuary to the labyrinth. Simplistic stained glass windows overlook the labyrinth aligning with the center logos when the Sun (Son) reflects its true colors.

The unusual design of the Quail Springs labyrinth originates from the outdoor exhibit at the Museum of Indian Art and Culture in Santa Fe, New Mexico. It represents going with the flow of the new millennium. Denise Sidwell and Curtis Moore helped draft this pattern to fit the garden area. The center features the multi-cross symbol accepted by the church as one of its primary logos.

A cross surrounded by a circle also characterizes the zodiac symbol for earth.

The unique diamond-shaped center indicates treasure within. Solid, rectangular areas at the four cardinal points suggest stations of the cross or pausing points for inward reflection.

Relaxing on one of the nearby benches enjoying the ancestral essence of family and community, the loving arms of this labyrinth reach out and surround our spirits in a sweet embrace. Loving arms of the Father, embracing his daughters on a Father's Day Walk in the House of the Father.

Oklahoma City

United Life Church
3332 N. Meridian, Oklahoma City, OK 73112, (405) 946-6753
11-circuit Chartres, painted on parking lot in May 2001
Open availability

Built in May of 2001 as a ministerial school project, the 11-circuit Chartres painted on the parking lot at United Life Church was the first outdoor labyrinth in Oklahoma City.

Religious Science practitioners Suellen Miller, Dana Martin, Jeanne Claborn and Joy McBride spent a hot spring day following directions found on the internet to create a sacred circle patterned after the famous symbol in the Cathedral of Chartres near Paris, France.

Suellen said each student is responsible for a project giving back to the community during their second year of practitioner training. "I had walked a labyrinth in St. Louis as part of a retreat and wondered if it would be possible to have one in Oklahoma City. I looked online and found a web site with very specific instructions on how to build that particular type."

She asked the church minister if they could craft such a design in the shady corner of the parking lot. "My idea was that if people used it, then we might take the time to create a grass model. And if they didn't, I would just be out some paint," Suellen laughed.

No grass creation has yet materialized, but a few touch-ups have occurred in the last six years and this is one of the best known labyrinths in Oklahoma City.

Joy said building it was a fun job. "We have walked the labyrinth many times and it has been very inspiring to us. All the practitioners walked it together on the day we took our licensing panels which was a powerful experience."

Spiritual seminars, forgiveness workshops and full moon walks have also been more meaningful thanks to this 11-circuit Chartres.

Construction was not that hard, Suellen said. "It's really pretty easy — at least to assemble on a parking lot. I drove a huge nail into the center and tied a string with knots positioned at 18-inch intervals to the nail. Then I held the string and walked in a large circle with the string pulled taut while other volunteers marked the knot points with chalk.

"When we were finished, we had a bunch of concentric circles drawn in chalk. We then took our pattern picture and drew lines blocking out the turns, erasing pieces of the circle and chalking lines to create corners. Once our seed pattern was finished, we walked the labyrinth to make sure it worked."

"Surprisingly enough, it did," Joy chuckled.

Suellen said they used 4-inch rollers and parking lot paint to cover the chalked lines. "The whole thing took about four hours. I'm sure one cut in grass would take much longer, though the process would be similar."

The Religious Science practitioner said she has often wondered what people in airplanes think as they look down while passing over its Meridian location on their flight approach to Will Rogers World Airport.

"I enjoy these sacred circles and when I attend conferences, I check out the labyrinth(s). Usually, I can find 45 minutes in my schedule to walk one. They are a form of moving meditation with stillness in the center."

Suellen recently passed her ordination panel. June festivities included the labyrinth at Unity Spiritual Center in a rite of passage ritual the night preceding the sanctuary ceremony.

Labyrinth walks were featured in regular monthly full moon circles this summer at United Life. A three-month experiment highlighted individuals walking the Chartres replica in May, a guided meditation added to the June journey and a reiki circle walk enhanced a 6-foot pyramid perched over the center of the labyrinth under the July full moon.

Energy vibrations increased each month with participants reporting the usual calming walk during individual trips through the unicursal paths in May. The next month's music meditation provided improved guidance and overwhelming feelings of gratitude. Incredible variations of multitudinous insight and healing connections resulted from a July reiki circle under a white pyramid.

Laurie Kinney walked her first labyrinth at the June 30 United Life full moon ceremony. She said it was a powerful event and was extremely grateful for the opportunity to participate.

"I am sure I will be walking the labyrinth again as my first experience with one was incredible," she said. "I did not know much about labyrinths and had never seen one until I went to United Life Church. So, I didn't have any preconceived notions about what would happen. My friend Alex, who came to the full moon ceremony with me, saw the labyrinth when we arrived and I knew we were supposed to walk it together.

"The encounter was so much like my journey in this lifetime. There was a moment when I was near the center, which was directly in front of me, that I almost stepped over a line and went directly to it. I was pulled back and realized I still had a little further to go before I reached it. The reason this was so meaningful to me is how it completely mirrored my experience with my brain injury. I thought I had reached my awareness on this physical earth, but was pulled back (by my brain injury six years ago) and had to collect myself so I could walk the rest of my path," Laurie shared.

"Along the way, when I reached a turning point on the labyrinth, I would pause for a moment, say a little prayer and give thanks. While in the center, I meditated and when Alex got to the center, I approached her and extended my hands. She placed her hands on top of mine and we both felt something pass etherically between us. Afterwards, we hugged and I resumed my walk.

"The trip back was much more calm and steady. It was as if I knew what to expect because I had done it before and although I wasn't in a hurry, I was definitely aware of my guidance as I was walking. When I reached the end of the path, I thanked my guides and Source and stated my gratitude for the experience."

Reiki Master Judy Leyrer participated in all three full moon labyrinth walks. The last made the most impact.

She said it was probably one of the best full moon ceremonies she ever attended.

The regular monthly meditation was held around the fire under the elm tree behind the church. A group reiki circle then entwined through the paths of the labyrinth with walkers keeping their hands on the shoulders of the person in front of them walking "a connected path" to the center (which was covered with a 6-foot pyramid). A reiki session was performed on a stroke victim in a wheelchair.

Judy shared her July full moon ceremony and labyrinth walk thoughts. "We were chanted out of the circle with a Cherokee chant at which 24 people were present — the number of elders in a Cherokee circle. Those who were going to walk the labyrinth followed the light from the directional candles. One red candle sit in the middle. I had the honor of leading the group since it was a reiki walk and I am a reiki master. Prior to the walk, we set our intent, purpose and affirmations.

"Four reiki practitioners were among the nine people present. We walked into the labyrinth with everyone's hands on the shoulders of the person in front. It was difficult at first to get everyone started, but after about two or three turns, it became much easier.

"About halfway into the walk, approaching the south outer ring of the 11-circuit labyrinth, my hands tingled and heated in traditional reiki fashion, and all my hair stood on end. While passing through the tenth ring (counting from outside to inside) at the south, I had the same experience, but not as pronounced. We discussed this once we reached the center of the circle and I learned we had created a vortex.

"In the middle of the labyrinth, under the pyramid, we held hands and circled a man in a wheelchair and his companion. We talked about our journey to the center with each person sharing their reflections. I then guided everyone to place their hands on the stroke victim to access healing energy and let it flow into him noting the intent to heal allowed the energy to flow into his body from every angle to where it was needed. I started at the feet with the intention to ground him for this experience. Then I moved my hands to his right foot and right knee. He said he could feel everyone's hands on him, especially mine, and described them as very hot.

"As people finished their work and started to move back, I placed both of my hands on his chest and encouraged him to express his emotions. Feeling the need to finish my walk, I hugged the man and asked him to come to the OKC Reiki Energy Circle two days later in the ULC Healing Room. I collected the red candle and walked out of the labyrinth just in time to see the moon peeking from behind the clouds. What an incredible evening."

LeRay accepted Judy's invitation and participated later that week in an OKC Reiki Energy Circle session. He was thrilled the following day when he could move his hand. His companion said he "awoke in a great mood and worked for hours at exercising his hand. I noticed it was very relaxed and the spasticity was gone. He was able to move it more and work with it better than he had been able to in a long time. It gave him hope. He began trying to pick things up and get his hand to grasp the door and turn the knob. This definitely borders on miraculous healing."

Equally impressive was LeRay's comment when people danced around the full moon fire during a healing chant. "I felt as if I could have gotten up out of this wheelchair and danced with them. Maybe one day I will."

We told him the important thing was to remember that feeling and its subsequent desire.

A Course in Miracles instructor found the human reiki chain most interesting. "Our walk was hands-on and we walked as one. It was like a dance with Judy leading the rest of us in difficult pirouettes and side steps. I could feel the human rope behind me sway and twist following each turn. The hands on my shoulders were warm and comforting. As I contemplated the lesson from this 'human train,' it hit me suddenly. This walk was all about sensitivity, listening, remaining vigilant to my partners' needs. It was a walk of cooperation, trust, willingness, acceptance and tolerance. I gained a deeper sense of compassion and empathy for my partners as we collectively reached those turning points, but still stubbornly clung to one another for support, strength and guidance. In the end, we successfully attained the center goal and my heart felt full and grateful. As the Course says, "No one goes home alone."

One lady who had never walked a labyrinth before enjoyed the winding journey and said she would be using them frequently for relaxation and problem-solving.

LeRay felt the warmth and love of the healers and said he wanted to take more healing treatments from the reiki master present.

Another gentleman said he was able to release some family

issues that had surfaced recently when his grandmother died and no one invited him to the funeral.

A lady and her son came to the ceremony since they had learned about labyrinths at the holistic health fairs and wanted to walk an outdoor one in a group setting. "Pretty profound" was all they could say nodding their heads while hugs were shared.

The person at the end of the chain tried different techniques during the lengthy sojourn. "It took a few twists and turns to settle into a routine of following in another's footsteps at a slower pace than I usually walk," she said. "I did some prayer work as I always do inside a labyrinth and ask for guidance. The slower walk permitted time to view the surroundings and enjoy a peaceful night under a full moon.

"Unlike most labyrinth walks where one has to pay attention to the path, the hands-on reiki movement allowed freedom to let yourself go with the flow and close your eyes trusting the persons in front to lead the way. Isn't this what God does?"

The group learned faith and trust are interchangeable. They were also rewarded for their willingness to try a different approach with an ancient symbol. A hands-on-shoulders reiki walk is powerful, intriguing, revealing, challenging, pleasing, painstaking, healing, creative, meditative, insightful, innovative.

It requires trust, balance, teamwork; offers consideration, caring, sharing — the opportunity to experience magical moments and master the richness of spirit.

Participating souls walk a connected path to the center where one finds solace blending an iridescent illumination with greater understanding, transcending limiting beliefs by exploring infinite possibilities and coalescing with the infinity of our sparkling divinity.

Oklahoma City

Unity Spiritual Center
5603 NW 41, Oklahoma City, OK 73122, (405) 789-2424
7-circuit Celtic design, outdoor, rock and sand, 43 feet
built July 2005

"We turned an empty sand lot, a former volleyball court, and an unused eyesore into a 7-circuit Celtic symbol offering spiritual learning and universal connection," Rev. Patrick McAndrew said of the Unity Church Labyrinth Prayer Garden.

The church held a vision quest concerning the function of the vacant property at one of its Town Hall meetings. "When the idea of a labyrinth arose, it felt right to the whole group. So, I went to work researching the project," the enthusiastic minister said.

Online investigation revealed the perfect labyrinth design, a history of worldwide labyrinths and the dimensions of the one Unity selected, which "just fit" into the size of the available sand lot.

"Very synchronistic," Rev. Patrick mused. It was two years from conception to completion.

"The whole process from when it was first visualized and until it was built took less time since we already had the sand and the land. Total cost of materials (sandstone, lava rocks, initial plants) was about $2,500. All labor was donated. The privacy fence was another $1,500."

Additional landscaping in the ensuing two years included trees, more flowers and park benches.

"It's still a work-in-progress," Rev. Patrick said.

The colorful labyrinth is comprised of sand, sandstone and various shades of river rock, adorned by a variety of garden plants and flowers and surrounded by a privacy fence on the west, trees on the north, Heritage House to the south and the church to the east.

Benches around the perimeter and in the center provide places to stop and rest, think and meditate.

On the outer edges of the sand lot, triangular garden beds give definition to the labyrinth and create an image of peace, beauty and inner calmness. A stone patio extends from Heritage House with a rock sidewalk inviting visitors to enter the sacred space.

"Will you walk my path?" asks the labyrinth. "I will give you strength, renew your passion and heal your wounds."

The choice is whether or not to embark on the spiritual journey.

Rev. Patrick shared his internet research travels on the history of this revered instrument.

A labyrinth is an ancient symbol that relates to wholeness. Combining the imagery of the circle and the spiral into a meandering, yet purposeful path, it represents a journey to our own center and back again into the world.

To walk the labyrinth is to create balance within one's brain as the soul seeks to restore stability within its masculine and feminine aspects — the duality of creation — and the electromagnetic polarities of man's physical existence.

Labyrinths are a primordial tool for meditation and prayer. The spiral is the path of consciousness and aligns humans with their truest reality through sacred geometry, how Spirit integrates into matter. The labyrinth is an archetype, a divine imprint, found in native religious cultures around the world: the mystery schools of Egypt and Greece, the Druids of Britain, the Incas of Peru, the Hopi and Anasazi of the Southwestern United States, ancient Japanese societies and Scottish and Irish civilizations.

Each of these traditions taught that wisdom and knowledge emanate from within. Understanding creation and man's innate

Oklahoma City

creative process is a gift labyrinths can help uncover. They grant an initiation to awaken the sleeping intellect encoded within man's DNA. This symbol creates a sacred space that asks the ego to step aside. This "within" space may resemble a dream state. It is real in its own space-time and embraces and guides the walker to her center, the source of creation.

Walking a labyrinth aids in rediscovering a long-forgotten mystical practice demanding rebirth. Their contemporary resurgence stems from a deeply rooted urge to once again honor the Sacredness of All Life. Often associated with the birthing womb of the Great Goddess, the unicursal path is honest with no tricks or dead ends. The path winds continuously, mirroring the present. It touches sorrow and enhances joy.

Each walk is different. Today the trip may offer a connection to the higher self, centering, opening to an exalted awareness, balancing chakras, experiencing subtle energies. Tomorrow's journey may take the seeker to deeper levels of commitment, release, forgiveness, acceptance, spiritual alignment, unconditional love.

Like mandalas, a labyrinth presents a holistic route (meandering radius) from periphery to center. A labyrinth imprints a ceremonial pathway designed according to principles of Harmonic Proportion and the Alteration of Energy. The clockwise (sunwise) and counter-clockwise (moonwise) spins of a labyrinth balance the left and right hemispheres of the brain. Thus, the labyrinth is a potent ritual of self-integration, a radiant encounter with ourselves as we are born anew, consciously dwelling in human form, revitalizing our essence as we explore the Infinite at the Center.

"Sound intriguing? Give it some thought and try it out," Rev. Patrick said.

The authors did and got this answer to their question: "Who built the first labyrinth?"

"We all did — we are part of everything that has gone before and everything that will come after. Like Emerson said in one of your favorite quotes: What lies behind us and what lies before us are tiny matters compared to what lies within us."

Windsong Innerspace
2201 NW I-44 Service Road, Oklahoma City, OK 73112
Catherine Sullivan, csullivan24@cox.net, (405) 285-0777
http://www.windsongdojo.com/innerspace/innerspace.html
7-circuit slightly modified Classical, indoor canvas, 22 feet
created in 2005 by Catherine and Brian Sullivan

Aikido literally translates as "The Way of Spirit Harmony." That's probably the best way to describe the Innerspace Labyrinth which likes to be walked after sunset by candlelight both at Windsong Innerspace and Channing Unitarian Universalist Church in Edmond. It practically glows in the dark and exudes loving energy.

Catherine and Brian Sullivan, Aikido practitioners at Windsong, created the 22-foot slightly modified Classical, 7-circuit design in 2005. "Our group has explored traditional and alternative methods to self-discovery for over 30 years, so the labyrinth was a natural step on our path," Catherine said.

Windsong Innerspace shares accommodations with Windsong Dojo in north Oklahoma City. The Innerspace half is a center for movement and healing arts, including qi gong, meditation, dance, body awareness, drumming and chanting. The pursuit of health and spiritual awareness is foremost in its studies.

"When we moved to our current location five years ago, we had a new canvas cover made for the dojo mat. Several swathes of canvas remnants remained which we decided to make into a portable labyrinth to fit the zendo," Catherine said.

The black paint on natural (off-white) canvas labyrinth has "soaked" up many years of training and "really, really likes to be walked after the sun is set by candlelight." It's name is Innerspace Labyrinth, Catherine said by way of introduction.

"I chose black for the labyrinth because I felt we would be walking in subdued light and black paint shows up best on the wheat-colored canvas at night in candlelight. Also, I've noticed a neat effect with this color scheme. After walking a while, the pattern reverses to its opposite and looks white on a dark field."

Since the majority of the Innerspace group is of religious alternative persuasion, Catherine said she and Brian selected the Classical pattern as it is more generic and "better meets the needs of any who may walk it." A draftsman in her younger days, Catherine formulated a slightly modified version so she could use two pencils, a string and two people to easily sketch the pattern in a few minutes. Painting took about four hours.

"I have studied martial arts for 28 years and, therefore, the art of balance. I find it fascinating I am nearly knocked off my feet every time when walking the Windsong Innerspace Labyrinth. Constructing and using it has been enlightening," Catherine shared.

Anyone interested in borrowing or walking Innerspace Labyrinth is invited to contact Catherine.

Profound entrainment music adds an insightful variation to a regular meditative background. Its high tones provide an enthusiastic symphonic crescendo often causing the directional candles to sway with a new energetic vibration.

The oriental decorations and Buddhist icons surrounding Innerspace Labyrinth smile in esoteric delight. Surreal wall art primed at eye level catches the wandering attention of walkers, reminding them to stay focused on the path and meet calmly in the center to share in the accomplished goal. Teamwork is, after all, what life is all about.

This sacred symbol offers comforting solace, a highly charged meditative atmosphere, soft carpet massaging tired feet, granting renewed understanding. Peaceful arms reach out from the protective circle to cradle individual spirits in a sensitive embrace.

One walker said she felt she was floating through most of the walk. "The prancing entrainment music and the softness of the padding in the carpet made me think I was walking on marsh-mallows.

"I liked the prayer work we did in the center with energy vibrating between our extended palms. I loved the place, its soothing energy, the sweet lady who allowed us to join in the walk, the music, the atmosphere and the bouncy dojo mat. All of it was entrancing! I was high for a full day after that walk and I had no hangover! Amazing. My mind feels so good every time I listen to the CD. It's like eating chocolate. Yeah, that good. Hmmmmm.....and my hyper cat likes to lie on the floor next to the stereo and meditate to the entrainment music."

Another walker appreciated the peace and tranquility of Windsong and noted the aesthetics of the Far East induced an atmosphere of mystery and subtle intrigue.

"When we met in the center, we were sensually united and a bond formed. Some began chanting, others hugged. Tele-pathic communication was fully integrated into a renewed spiri-tual essence. We were mentally trance dancing with each other as we left this quiet place of solitude," she said.

Bryon Parrino, a teacher at the Oklahoma City School of Metaphysics, said he could sense the sacred intention of those present. "I could feel this energetically, especially as I walked the circuits. The first time I went through, I nodded in gratitude to each of the elements represented by candles and symbols on the four corners of the canvas. The music occasionally scattered the focusing of energies, but by ignoring it I could assist the thought-form of the labyrinth. On the second walk, we created a circle in the center, similar to the Circles of Love at the end of School of Metaphysics classes. I welcomed the loving energy as it moved through us and out to the world."

The Windsong experience can best be summarized in the description of one of its newest classes. Music, movements and emotions in a group context sparks a new sensibility that speaks to our very existence... a system of human integration and a fun way to garner more vitality and develop creativity, sexuality, feelings and transcendence.

The dance to develop our inner wisdom, to heal, to unveil the poetry of human encounter, to feel one with the Cosmos and to enjoy a shared commitment to practice, learn and grow together toward the realization of our highest human potential.

Red Plains Monastery, Sisters of Benedict
728 Richland Rd SW, Piedmont, OK 73078
http://redplainsmonastery.org, (405) 373-2887
Sr. Melissa Anna Letts, melissaannaletts@yahoo.com
11-circuit Chartres, brick and grass, 72 feet, built May 2003
Always open, labyrinth retreats welcomed

Red Plains Monastery peacefully meanders among 21 acres of rustic ranch-style cabins, spacious fresh air, wooded walking trails, pine trees, willows, sycamores and crepe myrtle. The Piedmont residence to the Sisters of Benedict also has a 72-foot brick and grass labyrinth.

Visitors are always welcome. Neighboring horses switch majestic tails in greeting, friendly dogs provide companionship on leisurely strolls along the adjacent pond or even escort walkers through the sacred symbol. A mixed chorus of colorful winged socialites chant background music.

A place where people seek refreshment, guidance, stress relief and some call home.

"We employ ancient tradition in our active ministry," Sister Melissa Anna Letts said, referring to the pilgrimage of using a circular path to symbolize a devout journey.

Letts built the Chartres replica in 2003 laying 1,000 bricks around 11 circuits following a pattern she found on the internet, based on the floor design at the famous French Cathedral.

"In the 13th and 14th century, people who couldn't go to Jerusalem on a pilgrimage would walk the labyrinth instead, in a prayerful manner," Letts said. "Very wonderful and relaxing. It's a way to use your whole body in an intriguing, spiritual meditation."

Frequently finding answers to unasked questions, an awakening occurs and a deep hunger inside searches for the meaning of life.

Often the question matters not. The answer is the relevant issue. As Letts can attest when deciding to join the Sisters of Benedict.

One night while driving home from church, she felt God was quizzing her. He wanted her to say yes or no. "Okay, what's the question?"

God said the question isn't important. "So I said yes and here I am."

Focus on prayer life, dedication and personal growth is what drew Letts to the Red Plains community. The native Oklahoman serves as chaplain for Hospice of Edmond and is director of religious education for a small rural parish in Calumet.

Sisters of Benedict use their talents and energies to share God's hope and healing with others as spiritual directors, retreat facilitators, pastoral ministers, gardeners, artisans and cooks.

Letts said the labyrinth is an ancient meditative art form, a design laid on the ground that invites one to traverse its metaphoric path.

"This encounter helps walkers circle inward to the center of their soul. The center represents moving toward a goal and allows the release of unhealthy emotions to envision a solution while traveling the unicursal journey back into the world."

Letts said this liberating exercise frees humanity from linear, left-brain thought processes invoking the intuitive, creative right brain.

Some people walk the labyrinth methodically, heel-to-toe, as a contemplative and joyful pilgrim draws closer to God. Others tread fearfully on their knees, as a penitence for sin. Prayerfully, meditatively walking a sacred circle can help deepen spirituality no matter which path you choose, Letts said.

Sister Jan Futrell, prioress at Red Plains Monastery, said over the past 30 years she has seen more and more people turning to spiritual communities for guidance, counseling and meditation.

"Perhaps the entry into the membership has lessened, but

the number of people finding their way to the monastery doors has increased worldwide," Futrell said. "And that's people of all faiths, looking for prayer, peace, a place of refreshment."

Saint Benedict taught to put God at the center of one's life and to live simply, committed to community, combining a balanced life of prayer, work, silence, hospitality, solitude and leisure, seeking peaceful answers.

Just like in a labyrinth — meeting in the center of their soul.

Sister Melissa Anna Letts not only designs and builds brick and grass sacred circles, but she also creates beautiful handmade ceramic clay models. She enjoys painting the labyrinths with various colors in both 7-circuit Classical and 11-circuit Chartres designs. One of her favorite patterns has borders with flowers that resemble crosses.

Standing Bear Native American Park
Highway 60 & Hwy 177, Ponca City, OK 74601
Park open from 6 a.m. to 11 p.m. daily, (580) 762-1514
Santa Rosa design, outdoor, brick paver, 40 feet
wheelchair accessible, built October 2001

The first thing one notices when entering Standing Bear Park in Ponca City is the sacredness of the land. It is indeed hallowed ground.

A 40-foot brick mosaic labyrinth is among the many features this park offers. All are spiritually enlightening, activating passionate kundalini energy.

In addition to regular park amenities, a wide red asphalt trail skirts the edge of a one-acre lake with a central island representing Standing Bear's final stopping point before continuing east through a peaceful prairie of buffalo grass and wildflowers.

The trail circles clockwise entering a large viewing court where visitors may gaze at a 22-foot bronze statue of Chief Standing Bear. Facing east, the direction of the rising sun, the feet of the park's namesake rest on a limestone boulder, the high point of the surrounding land.

Standing Bear was a prominent 19th century Ponca Indian chief and outspoken proponent of Native American rights. In 1879, he sought and won a judge's ruling granting freedoms to

Native Americans guaranteed by the U.S. Constitution. Indians were declared people, not savages.

Below the statue eight segments of a circle, each with a design in earth tones, contain the name and phonetic spelling of a Ponca clan. A reflecting pool highlights the center of the court surrounding Grandfather Fire. Here rests the ashes from the fire used to bless the land in the traditional way in 1994.

Since the unveiling of the chief's statue in 1996, Standing Bear Park has continued to evolve. Improvements include pond fish, native grass, a permanent arbor pow wow site and eight granite plaques with photographs of Native American dancers in traditional attire describing typical pow wow dances. A two-story welcome center and museum opened last fall.

And, the first permanent, outdoor, public brick labyrinth in Oklahoma was completed in October of 2001.

Created from hand-cut inlaid pavers, the red brick of the labyrinth represents both the red earth of its native state and the bricks that originally paved Ponca City streets. The color matches the asphalt trail system employed throughout the park.

An adjoining meditation garden suggests a quiet place for rest and reflection.

The Community Labyrinth has participated in celebrations, mourning, dances, worship, questions, answers, connections, prayers, meditations, healing, calming and listening. It also helped strengthen a city.

Ponca City residents raised and donated funds to build the labyrinth as well as laid some of the bricks. The National Endowment for the Arts and Episcopal Diocese of Oklahoma provided grant monies.

Several workshops held during fund-raising efforts educated the town populace about the history, function and advantages of this sacred symbol.

City businesses even sponsored a special exhibit "Labyrinths for Peace 2000" to generate interest in the project. The display presented 153 photos depicting 120 different labyrinths, 40 illustrations and an original work of art. It hung in the Canon Rotunda of the United States House of Representatives the previous spring.

The Santa Rosa design of Ponca City's Community Labyrinth is divided into four quadrants and encapsulates a circular space on the fourth circuit that is not walked but approached from all directions. Four interwoven circles in the center symbolize the spirit of community cooperation that made this endeavor possible.

Park officials built a 4-foot mound near the labyrinth to enhance the tranquility of the site by lessening the impact of traffic noise from the nearby highway. Donated sod added a natural look.

An oil refinery sits on the other side of the highway seemingly in stark contrast to the peace and calm promoted by the stress relief and personal insight afforded from a walking meditation.

The juxtaposition offers a chance to realize we can have peace within no matter what surrounds us. A glorious feeling of well-being is possible anywhere. Sometimes, it just takes a bit more focus.

A sign facing the sidewalk proclaims: We invite you to bring your own personal experiences to the Community Labyrinth. As you begin your walk, you might want to stop on the "pausing stone" — the round gray stone set in the entrance — to reflect upon your impending journey. If you are dealing with a specific issue, you might want to put something symbolic of that issue in the "heart space" — the round gray stone on the fourth path. As you walk the labyrinth, you will literally be able to look at your issue "from all sides," perhaps finding an answer or solution deep within yourself.

One walker choose to use the gray outer ring to contemplate more complex issues surrounding the "heart of the matter."

After walking the labyrinth, the authors viewed other aspects of this impressive Oklahoma park.

As we walked clockwise around the 22-foot signature statue of one of our friend's great, great grandfathers, Standing Bear told us to approach and he would speak to us. Here is what he said:

"It is once again a difficult time in your culture. Regrettably, many are treating their brethren as non-people and the earth as well as her inhabitants suffer from this indifference.

"Listen to your heart. Draw on deep, inner strengths and share your God-given talents to create the wholeness each heart desires. It is time to discard any pretense and honor the connectedness of All Our Relations with the one heart of creation."

A most poignant message from the soul of higher understanding.

Collective ancestral wisdom permeates all eight acres of this spiritually active park.

Standing Bear Park
Ponca City

Camp Okiwanee
11340 S. 177th West Avenue, Sapulpa, OK 74066
Camp Fire USA Green Country Council facility, (918) 592-2267
11-circuit Chartres, grass walking path, 70 feet
rope guide for the blind, wheelchair accessible, built 2002

One of four labyrinths at three camp facilities in Oklahoma, the Community Labyrinth at Camp Okiwanee has an unusual feature. Rope hand guides line the grass walking paths.

"It's not the most beautiful labyrinth, but that is due to the steel posts and rope installed to make it accessible for persons without sight. It is also longer than most because we made the paths three feet wide to accommodate wheelchairs," said Bobbie Walker Henderson, Executive Director for Camp Fire USA Green Country Council.

The Sapulpa Camp Fire facility and Dwight Mission Presbyterian Camp in Vian both feature 11-circuit Chartres models fashioned after the famous labyrinth in a 13th century French cathedral. Chouteau's Camp Christian has an indoor 7-circuit Classical and an outdoor 11-circuit Chartres.

Created as part of the tradition of pilgrimage, the sacred symbol at Chartres parallels the camp's philosophy. Camp Fire boys and girls are seeking direction and wish to become viable members of their communities.

What better tool to teach them than one which requires concentration, observation, spiritual acknowledgement and dedicated purpose.

A pleasant wooded area surrounds the Okiwanee labyrinth, built about five years ago to provide a resource for groups and individuals in Tulsa and the surrounding area.

Henderson said labyrinths can be fun and relaxing and are advantageous in team building, personal growth, spiritual development, and therapeutic and recovery purposes.

Tulsa's Resonance Center for Women has used the Okiwanee labyrinth in its substance abuse programs.

Clinical Director Mae Ann Shepherd said the women make two collages — one portraying "who I am" when active in addiction and the other portrays "who I am" in recovery. "We explore the fact that when a person is using, the real person is hidden by the addiction.

"Then we go to the labyrinth. Walkers have the opportunity to take the addiction collage into the center and leave it if they want. Most of them are surprised at their experiences. For example, one client who was the first to exit the labyrinth, looked back at the other women still walking. She suddenly realized she could not go back into the labyrinth nor could she pull anyone else out of their addiction.

"Her statement really stuck with me and made me realize how powerful a device labyrinths can be to help people struggling with their identity. The lost often find themselves pleasantly hidden around one of the twists and turns of its circular path," Shepherd said. "They rediscover their humanity."

Camp Services Director Vicki Proctor said campers enjoy learning the history of this mystical circle. "They like the ancient origin and are surprised to learn labyrinths have been carved on rocks, painted on ceramics, woven into baskets, stamped onto coins, carved into rock cliffs, sculpted out of turf and configured from raw stone and intricate tile work."

A sign near the entrance to the Chartres replica teaches a little more history: Labyrinths have been made for thousands of years, but little is known of their ancient origin. The earliest known labyrinth form was found in the Ukraine dating to 18,000-15,000 B.C. Ancient labyrinths have been found in places such as Sumatra, Peru, Egypt, India, Iceland, Scandinavia, the British Isles and New Mexico.

Proctor said campers also enjoy learning there is no one or correct way to walk a labyrinth. "They like the simple instruction: You only have to enter and follow the path."

Gathered at the labyrinth prior to a group walk, counselors convey the message the journey can encompass a variety of attitudes. It may be joyous or somber. It might be thoughtful or prayerful. Campers may employ a walking meditation.

"Adults are usually serious in the labyrinth. Children most often run in and out as fast as they can in a playful manner. We teach young people to let intuition be their guide and to occasionally choose a different attitude," Proctor said. "Make it serious, playful or prayerful. Play music or sing. Pray out loud. Walk alone and with a crowd. Notice the sky. Listen to the sounds. Most of all, pay attention to your experience."

Sapulpa

An important feature of the Camp Okiwanee Labyrinth is its accessible design for persons in wheelchairs and those who are blind. Paths are 36" wide and the steel posts dividing the paths are connected by rope which serves as a hand guide. Here, the blind can "see" again.

Private Shawnee Back Yard — Lisa Sponseller
lisasponseller@gmail.com
7-circuit Classical, brick paver, 50 feet, built 2003

Lisa Sponseller said she "got the crazy idea" in the summer of 2001 to build a labyrinth in her backyard, and told her son Josh, it would take approximately two weeks. Two years later, Josh and his sister Shelley were tired of looking at the mound of red Oklahoma clay mom had dug from the center of the yard, and devoted five months each to help finish the 7-circuit Classical, 50-foot brick paver labyrinth.

"Thousands of pavers and 24 tons of decomposed granite were needed to finish this project. It almost killed us all!" Lisa moaned. "But we love it, are proud of it, and very aware that our back yard is uniquely different and tremendously special."

A variety of colorful slag glass adorns the center casting a rainbow effect in bright sunshine. "The reflection, as well as the whole labyrinth, affects me each time I walk it or even just sit and meditate," Lisa said. "It's very soothing. Everyone gets something from their walk, but it hits me right in the heart."

Stillwater

First United Methodist Church
400 West 7th Avenue, Stillwater, OK 74074, (405) 372-5854
Ginger Howl, ginghowl@mac.com
7-circuit Santa Rosa, indoor canvas, purchased March 2000
Open for scheduled events, call for availability

"First United Methodist Church in Stillwater purchased a 7-circuit Santa Rosa labyrinth from the St. Louis Labyrinth Project in March 2000. It was the largest size we could accommodate in our church at the time. We have used it a great deal both at the church as a prayer tool for spiritual rejuvenation and in other settings to acquaint people with its benefits," said Ginger Howl, former associate pastor and labyrinth coordinator.

The labyrinth has been to youth and adult retreats at all three of the United Methodist campgrounds in Oklahoma, as well as St. Crispin's Episcopal Retreat Center near Seminole. It has visited the Wesley Foundation at Southwestern Oklahoma State University in Weatherford where many college students experienced their first labyrinth walk.

A local labyrinth guild was formed when the Stillwater church originally purchased the canvas labyrinth. "At that time, it had 12 members who attended a full-day retreat learning about labyrinths in general, how to take care of our particular labyrinth, and how to lead labyrinth walks," Howl said.

Since that time, the Stillwater labyrinth has traveled with a member of the First United Methodist Labyrinth Guild to numerous churches in Oklahoma for the purpose of education and prayer walks. It was placed at several sites in Ponca City, including the Conoco-Phillips refinery, to familiarize the community with the values of a labyrinth and raise funds for the permanent outdoor labyrinth built at Standing Bear Park in October of 2001.

Stillwater First United Methodist Church is also in the preliminary stages of building an outdoor permanent labyrinth and prayer garden across the street from the sanctuary adjacent to its Family Life Center at the corner of Eighth Avenue and S. West Street.

Stilwell

Private Mountaintop Labyrinth — Lela Samargis
lelasamargis22@hotmail.com
7-circuit Classical, rock and grass, built April 2002

Lela Samargis offers the following insight on her mountaintop labyrinth:

On April 26th, 2002, I came home from work to the most wonderful happening. My son-in-law Ron was in the woods south of the house building me a labyrinth for my birthday. It took him two or three days of hard labor, but it turned out so wonderful I don't know how I could ever move because I would have to leave it here. Ron said he would build me one wherever I live, so not to worry.

The 7-circuit Classical labyrinth was created around a dying tree that had to be cut down because it was so big we were afraid it would fall and hit the house. We left a four-foot stump to plant flowers or honor in some way. Ron used this tree stump for the heart of the labyrinth. Another small tree graces the fourth pathway. I hang wind chimes on low branches and the sturdy oak provides a wonderful umbrella of shade in the summer.

Ron took his antique black Ford truck and walked up and down the country road and both banks of the creek to find the perfect rocks for my mountaintop labyrinth. I am sure he asked permission of every one of these magnificent stones before he removed them from their former resting place. I think he must have convinced them they were going to sacred ground and what an honor to be chosen for this endeavor. They probably sensed his wonderful energy and decided to go with him.

The following month was May and we celebrated our first Wesak festival at the labyrinth, as we have every continuous year. A crystal bowl full of water is placed at the heart and left all night to be blessed by Buddha and Christ as they come close to earth on this night. This is holy water that I bottle and distribute to family. New and full moon ceremonies are also celebrated at the labyrinth. Often there is no other human here, but I always pray my own quiet meditation.

At first I practiced a regular labyrinth reflection, entering with my problems or challenges, taking them to the heart and leaving them there. But I eventually discovered I didn't want to take any negative thoughts or feelings anywhere around this healing place. So I started doing a walking contemplation that blessed Mother Earth and allowed my positive love and energy to flow into her as I traveled the circuits. Besides, I was given solutions to my problems anyway, or I just turned them over to the universe.

I have had some amazing encounters while doing this meditation. Of course, the nature connection is tremendously intense with the rain falling in an encircling and cleansing mist, the wind melodiously blowing through the trees and leaves shimmering in sunlight or moonlight. Peaceful feelings of angelic presence also radiate. There is nothing like walking a labyrinth on a full moon night.

Since the labyrinth is outside and experiences the cycles of the seasons, it is much more alive than if it were an altar or table on the inside of a house. In autumn and winter, the leaves fall from the trees covering the labyrinth with a thick, protective coat. This is its resting time. I leave them undisturbed through most of the winter and clean the circuits in spring before new grass sprouts. But first, an emerald cushion of weeds softens the path and provides homes for ants and other insects. Several deer often visit at night. Glorious, brilliant green bursts of life and growth mark this renewal phase. Five redbud trees line one side of the labyrinth. Every year, a new one sprouts. The ground is almost bare by mid-summer, but in the fall, the labyrinth shrine dresses up in full glory with dazzling colors. A few months later, a glistening blanket of snow turns the area into a pristine winter wonderland.

This labyrinth has become so special that I usually do my spiritual rituals in its hallowed space, from prayers and novenas to meditations or moon celebrations. If and when I ever do leave this revered place, I feel it will remain sacred ground for all who come later.

Stilwell

First United Methodist Church
(918) 456-6141 or (918) 456-2939
300 West Delaware Street, Tahlequah, OK 74464
http://www.tahlequahumc.org, tumy@sbcglobal.net
11 circuit, interactive portable canvas
Call for scheduled events

How to handle distractions and still stay on course is the message of the interactive labyrinth walk at Tahlequah's First United Methodist Church.

Narration headphones guide walkers through 11 continuous circuits using this ancient philosophical tool as a new way to reflect on their spiritual lives.

White lines painted on blue canvas epitomize the symbolic sojourn to a central chamber and back out again.

Former Youth Director Cindy Bright said during medieval times, labyrinths were built for divine encounters, with the winding paths representing a person's journey through life, and the central chamber characterizing a centered state of mind — or soul.

Spread across the floor of the church's activity building, the sacred replica embodies a similar meditative purpose, with a few modern twists added to the mix. Television sets and CD players were not well known to medieval pilgrims.

Numbers along the walk denote stopping points where walkers are encouraged by their mobile CD companion to ponder distinctive aspects of their existence.

The first five stations function as releasing sites to make worshippers aware of areas where they need to let some things go. Pausing in the center allows one to sit and consider what they've learned on the walk so far and how it can assist them when they return to their daily lives. The last five stations offer tidbits to contemplate while journeying back into the world.

Preparing travelers for the trip ahead, the tour guide narrator provides introductory information at the first station.

A flashing television set, tuned to no particular channel, greets people at the second station. Today's world has many noisy, out-of-focus distractions causing static and lack of attention to detail.

Station 3 features two buckets. One is filled with water and the other holds rocks. Signifying the emotional state of mind that weighs people down, walkers are encouraged to think about their concerns and drop a rock in the water for each weight they bear.

A desk, with pen, paper and trash can await at Station 4. Here people are urged to "let go," of all the ways they have either been hurt or injured others. Write it down, draw a picture, compose a letter or choose another method to express yourself. Then throw it away and let it go.

Station 5 is helpful for folks who don't remember how they arrived at their present "station" in life. A map of Tahlequah, compass and magnets are available for direction.

Experienced navigators know magnets do strange things to compasses, causing them to give inaccurate readings. This station also notes daily distractions and pinpoints the need for balanced polarity.

By following the designed path, and ignoring the "inaccurate" compass at Station 5, walkers reach Station 6, the center of the labyrinth, the goal of their destination, a return to their spiritual center.

Traditional Communion elements reside here (bread and grape juice) and a candle with three wicks, representing the Trinity. Travelers are encouraged to pause and reflect, pray, meditate or simply sit and "just be."

When ready, parishioners leave the center through Station 7. It links a bridge between the beginning and the end and suggests we ask the God we've rediscovered in the center of our being to continue the journey with us.

Station 8 houses a mirror and an ink stamp. People examine their fingerprints to remind themselves they are unique and look in the mirror to remember they were made in God's image.

Walkers are next treated to a short video featuring pictures of the planet. This prompts mankind to take better care of creation by planting a seed in the pot of soil supplied at Station 9.

Station 10 has a candle for people to light, honoring the old custom of lighting a candle for someone when saying a prayer on their behalf.

A box of sand commemorates the final station, Number 11. Pilgrims leave their footprint in the sand to mark the imprint they leave on the world.

The labyrinth kit, which includes the CD narration and canvas pathway, is sold as a spiritual tool for youth groups, but can be used by people of any age.

"We originally purchased it for a weekend prayer retreat," Bright said. "It worked so well, we decided to open it up to everyone and use it more often."

A walk through the interactive labyrinth, with the narration headphones, takes about an hour.

Sancta Sophia Seminary/Sparrow Hawk Village
11 Summit Ridge Drive, Tahlequah, OK 74464
Rev. Carol Parrish, (800) 386-7161, (918) 453-5962
http://www.sanctasophia.org, lccc@sanctasophia.org
7-circuit Classical, outdoor permanent, 65 feet
surrounded by trees, built November 13, 1992, always open

Since 1982, Sparrow Hawk Village has offered its 440 acres as a consecrated blessing of holy consciousness honoring divine facets of human potential, blending matter and Spirit.

The international spiritual community was planned to reflect a lifestyle of aesthetics, harmony and peace applying universal principles to evoke symmetry and beauty for the well-being of humanity.

Its educational focus provides a supportive environment for the practice of ethical living and fosters personal growth through the healthy integration of art, science and philosophy.

Home to the first labyrinth in the state and one of only two located at Oklahoma seminaries, Sancta Sophia graces the top of Sparrow Hawk Mountain in Tahlequah. Built November 13, 1992, this ancient sacred symbol honors earth energies and was designed to holistically nurture connecting pathways, ley lines and the multiplicity of man's etheric temple.

Rev. Carol Parrish, dean of Sancta Sophia and founder of

Sparrow Hawk Village, said honoring earth energies and taking ley lines into consideration when establishing places of worship strengthens one's relationship with God and nature.

"Sacred space is created from key links of celestial force. Our chapel was designed to draw upon the power source of the leys that form a star-shaped energy center below the altar in the sanctuary. The labyrinth is located on the extended ley of the chapel center. Sancta's western mountainside is dotted with points indicating traditional energies evoked in the ascent to high consciousness. Thus, we have defined indoor and outdoor med-itation places with unique capabilities which facilitate healing, intuition, dream awareness and communion with the High Self."

Parrish said their 7-path Classical labyrinth moves much like a circuit from left to right and right to left integrating polarities. It helps one think, feel and pray about life itself.

"The center of this sacred circle is known as the heart or goal," she shared. "The heart is the goal, for here we remember the soul's message — our reason for being — deep within. What is our purpose? Why are we here? What is the next step in the enfoldment of our lives?"

Labyrinths can be walked as a rite of passage if one is ready to put the past behind and seek inner direction, embracing the unknown. "Unconscious awareness or hidden truths emerge into consciousness as we explore the mystery within," Parrish said.

Walkers often feel an increase of harmony, wholeness, holi-ness, quietude and accomplishment when stepping into this sacred space. Parrish said the compressed energy of the laby-rinth "rises about us, protecting us from outside influences as we turn our attention inward and invoke spiritual assistance."

A labyrinth is not a maze demanding questions, but a path to transcend rational thought. The only choice is whether to step into its magical plane and weave a new tapestry of life.

Plunge right in, take a vision quest, get cleansed in the pro-cess, travel an unexplored route, nurture novel leadership, listen to the sounds of nature, the silence of the gentle night... but don't forget your umbrella!

Twenty-two people walked the Sparrow Hawk labyrinth beneath a cloudy Cancer full moon holding colorful umbrellas.

The moist gravel path crunched underfoot, circuits outlined in white paint glistened by flashlight and tiki torch. Fresh bark soaking up mud around the perimeter helped Villagers and visi-tors communicate with Mother Earth via droplets of rain.

A yellow equal-armed cross just inside the entrance, an astrological symbol for Earth when placed inside a circle, radiates cosmic vibrations, balancing intellect and emotion, renewing spiritual dedication, providing disciplined guidance, transforming creative energies.

"That night walk was beautiful this rainy year. It was as if our souls knew the way to walk even though our eyes could not always see the paths," said Bonita Plymale, associate dean of Sancta Sophia Seminary.

Maybe the sharp-eyed namesake of the Village led the way. A sparrow hawk is a kestrel falcon who hovers and flies straight upward, symbolic of levitation and ascension. Much like the Christed One who expands human consciousness awakening man's mystical spark of inner divinity.

Tahlequah

Photo by Ken Crowder

Heart in the Park, 6th and Grand
Centennial Park, Downtown Tonkawa
7-circuit heart-shaped paver, dual-path
Built June 2007, Oklahoma Centennial Project
Only heart-shaped labyrinth of its kind in the world

A glowing acknowledgement of Oklahoma spirit reigns supreme in a small town of 3,300 people in the heartland of America. The only dual-path, heart-shaped labyrinth in the world honors the visionary soul of artistic creation in Tonkawa, the Wheatheart of Oklahoma.

Artist Audrey Schmitz said the close-knit community wanted something that was unique to both Tonkawa and the state and expressed "This is who we are" when she developed the concept for the Heart in the Park Oklahoma Centennial project. "We're not Chartres, France."

Tonkawa is wheat country, known as the "wheatheart" of the state and named after the Native American tribe that settled there in 1885, following removal from Texas. In their distinct language, the people called themselves "Tickanwa-tic" or "Real People." The name by which they are known comes from a Waco word, "Tonkaweya," meaning "They all stay together."

Engraved red plaques adjoin the heart-shaped walking path

of the labyrinth spelling the word "Tonkawa" and the phrases "They All Stay Together" and "Wheatheart of Oklahoma."

"It's definitely us," Audrey nodded.

Stone sculptor Marty Kermeen, an internationally famed labyrinth builder from Yorkville, Illinois, and labyrinth historian Jeff Saward, of Great Britain, turned Audrey's concept into the unique heart-shaped design.

Actually, there are five hearts. The four inside the overall heart shape represent the four chambers of the human heart. The one encasing them signifies the heart of God who cradles our heart-felt desires and helps us bring them to fruition. It also offers encouragement for what's inside each of us — divine inspiration.

At the center of the design is a heart of red pavers. The cast of a wheatheart symbol lies inside another heart and serves as the pausing stone at the entrance. The walking path is heart-shaped as well as the inscribed word and phrase plaques surrounding it.

The intricate labyrinthine structure of interconnecting passages and spiral images can build strong communities. This labyrinth incorporates history, art and a vision for the future and was funded with grants, private, corporate and business donations, and multiple fund-raisers, including the sale of personalized pavers.

A charcoal gray walking path outlining the labyrinth is bordered by a timeline of 100 engraved pavers recording Tonkawa's history from 1879 to 2007.

The central area is filled with red pavers highlighting the heart-shaped goal. Golden limestone forms the crossing or "crown" area above the goal. A small piece of stone from the historic Yellow Bull Crossing sets as a "jewel" in the crown.

Sandy Linton, chief financial officer and co-owner of Tonkawa Foundry, said the dynamics and energy created from this project will benefit the community for generations. The Foundry cast and donated the Wheatheart pausing stone from an original clay sculpture Audrey crafted.

A plaza constructed from original Tonkawa street brick leads to the labyrinth. The plaza entry embraces a six-foot granite slab. Cut into the shape of Oklahoma, it identifies Heart in the Park as Tonkawa's official Centennial project.

The Grand Heart Walk connects to the entry plaza. The 11 x 50 foot sidewalk is comprised of hundreds of red and wheat-colored engraved pavers recognizing individuals, organizations and businesses who have played an integral part in the community. These personalized pavers surround seven art panels presenting colorful designs denoting aspects of Tonkawa's distinctive heritage.

Future phases of the project include a pavilion, landscaping, park benches and Hands in Clay, mosaic-style sculptures imbedded with ceramic tiles bearing the handprints of Tonkawa school children and other community members.

The first official function at Heart in the Park (HIP) was a July 4th Harvest Walk. To celebrate the local agricultural heritage, more than 200 participants walked the new labyrinth carrying stalks of local wheat which they traded in the center for souvenir packets of Tonkawa wheat grain.

Photo by Ken Crowder

HIP visitors could take an educational stroll and read the town history dating from 1879, recorded on 100 engraved pavers surrounding the labyrinth. The charcoal path for this history walk symbolizes the oil heritage of the area.

Those walking the labyrinth were encouraged to stand in front of the cast iron wheatheart pausing stone at the entrance prior to their sojourn for a moment of reflection.

The seven circuits of this dual-path labyrinth allow individuals to begin their walk on either side of the pausing stone. The golden pavers represent agriculture while divider lines highlight the blue of the Salt Fork River.

Halfway through the walk, one reaches the crown-shaped crossing. This area recalls the historic Yellow Bull Crossing, located 1.2 miles west of downtown Tonkawa, and features a diamond-shaped flint cut from the river site serving as the crown jewel.

Nez Perce Chief Yellow Bull established his home on a bend of the Salt Fork River where a natural rock bottom made fording the river possible. He charged travelers a toll to cross the river and the ford became known as Yellow Bull Crossing.

Continuing the journey on the opposite side of the crossing, this mirror image encourages self-discovery and emotional release. After walking both sides of the labyrinth, one passes the pausing stone and completes the journey to the goal, the large red central heart.

Walkers may exit by reversing their path or simply travel directly out from the goal. As one departs, they are invited to touch the wheat on the pausing stone to leave a bit of themselves with the Heart in the Park.

The authors were blessed to participate in the July 4th Harvest Walk and shared a prayer with community leaders in the heart of the labyrinth at 11 a.m.

Sitting atop a gentle knoll, the HIP labyrinth gradually increases to an elevation of 11 inches. Eleven is a master number signifying the merging of both sides of the heart, reason and passion, and the transformation of the physical into the divine.

Heart in the Park anoints the junction where 6th Street formerly extended and the Santa Fe Railroad once traversed. The natural movement of energy enables one to float along this incredible sacred symbol. Pavers are easy on the feet and the winding paths express light-hearted merriment instead of the usual quick, about-face turns characteristic of many labyrinths.

Matters of the heart can frequently be confusing, but not here. A crescendo of synchronized heartbeats provides a true catharsis. All hearts beat as one. Corresponding connections clear the chambers of the heart allowing the flow of divine creation — combining the crown and heart chakras with unabashed kundalini energy.

A towering grain elevator built in the late 1940s aligns with the center of the labyrinth protecting its cherished love, providing a suggestive temple of divine imagery. The perfect place for a dream wedding.

Nancy Sloan from Duncan had a little fun with the words in the granite pavers over the heart. Instead of "together," she visualized "to get her heart." No, she did not catch the bridal bouquet at her sister's wedding.

An Oklahoma City walker said, "This beautiful, totally balanced labyrinth speaks volumes just with its shape. There is a symmetry and rhythm unlike any other sacred circle I have seen. It can be walked by two people simultaneously (starting at the same moment) and possibly meeting at the crossover point. Both sides act as a perfect reflection of the other and are connected only by the crown bridge." She, too, is a romantic.

Continuing in this vein, she said that while the labyrinth has a feminine and nurturing presence, the masculine energy stands just to the southeast in the form of a grain elevator. "This represents the masculine protector and supplier presence who has finally been granted the love of his life and now his heart is with her forever. He looms over her in silent adoration reveling in the beautiful goddess sleeping at his feet. His presence reminds us that male and female are bound together in an exquisite balance of love and harmony."

A woman familiar with "A Course in Miracles" noted the Course says we cannot achieve atonement (salvation) alone; our brothers serve as our salvation because they mirror our thoughts and beliefs. "So, too, this labyrinth acts as a mirror for anyone walking it. The iron touchstone at the entrance has a symbol of wheat showing how this labyrinth nourishes each fortunate being who walks it. The crown bridge lies atop the sacred heart center stone and is the symbol for the Holy Spirit, who is our bridge to heaven and a higher awareness of All That Is.

"Taking a moment to pause on this special aspect of the labyrinth gives a sense of connection to the treasure that lies at its very core — the sacred center or Holiest of Holies. As a seeker proceeds to walk the mirror of the first side and approaches the heart of the matter, she has the opportunity to reflect on the journey behind her and the one yet to come," the Course mentor continued.

"Entering the sacred heart causes a spine-tingling sensation of reaching a goal much sought after and finally achieved. In this revered space, we leave our harvest (the results of our choices and actions sometimes known as karma) and are gifted with the seeds of perfect love, abundance and sustenance to sow on our journey back to the mundane world.

"As the walker exits the sacred heart and starts on the return trip, she is asked to pause at the iron touchstone to rub it gently and leave any energy, wisdom or knowledge obtained from the labyrinth so the next sojourner will receive of this gift upon entering and stopping to stroke the stone.

"This labyrinth has touched my heart and will remain as one of my most treasured walks," the woman said, wiping a few tears from misty eyes.

"A lot of creative ingenuity went into in designing and making this labyrinth," a Ponca City man said.

Labyrinths offer a form of communion with the Divine and healing for the soul. A walking meditation igniting the passions within, sparking the imagination, allowing us to rediscover the wild and untamed beauty inside.

Connecting to the eternal sanctum of creation, we converse with our intrinsic, intuitive spiritual natures and journey back to Self. Experiencing God along the path, we never feel lost or alone.

Just follow your heart — to the center of its source in the world's only dual-path, heart-shaped labyrinth in Tonkawa, Oklahoma.

Tonkawa

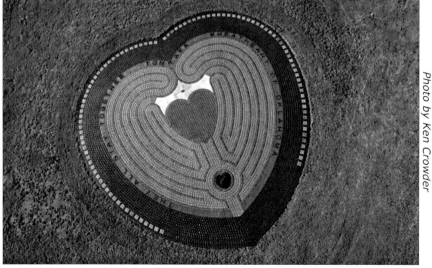

Photo by Ken Crowder

All Souls Unitarian Church
2592 S. Peoria Avenue, Tulsa, OK 74114, (918) 743-2363
http://www.allsoulschurch.org, kkeith@allsoulschurch.org
Indoor tile, rectangular design, built summer 2001

Most church labyrinths are built as tools for personal growth and to incorporate teachings of meditation and prayer. The style and construction of the rectangular tile model at All Souls Unitarian Church in Tulsa required "tons of all three of those ingredients" laughed one of its parents.

"We also learned about patience and perseverance over a ream of graph paper and pencil stubs in the summer of 2001," said Kathy Keith, Executive Director at All Souls.

The non-classical, 1100-square-foot labyrinth was designed around available space during a major flooring overhaul in the basement of the church's large activity room.

Since the floor was scheduled for replacement and the leadership team had enjoyed using labyrinths as tools for spiritual practice at other churches and retreat centers, they partnered the two ideas into a "reconstructive" one.

"It occurred to us that since we were retiling the floor and the tile would have a pattern anyway, we might as well make it useful as well," Kathy recalled.

With the backing of senior minister Marlin Lavanhar, Kathy, Mary Frances Meyers and Nancy Harbaugh grabbed graph paper and pencil. Mary Frances and Nancy were well-versed in the study and use of labyrinths. A 7-circuit classical graced the back yard of Mary Frances, and Nancy was a trained facilitator frequently traveling with a Chartres canvas replica. Kathy just liked the idea.

As religious educator at All Souls Unitarian Church when the labyrinth was conceived, Kathy knew there would be many opportunities for its educational and spiritual use. The research and planning process ensued. Due to the constraints of a long, rectangular space and the size of commercial tiles, the outline was a challenge.

"We could not fit any of the classical labyrinth models into the space," she stated. "It was only after repeated attempts with the 'one way in, one way out, no wrong turns' mantra that we produced the rectangular motif, worked out on graph paper, then drawn on the floor with chalk to ensure it was walkable."

Don Butterworth of Carpet Supply in Tulsa agreed to the intricate installation at no additional charge. Builder Mark Wood and architect Leisa McNulty oversaw the installation.

Since the project's completion, all ages have enjoyed the labyrinth. Church school classes, youth groups and adults have walked the sacred symbol and reaped its benefits. The labyrinth is available to walk any time the church is open and the activity room is not in use, Kathy said. Potential users may contact the church office regarding the space's accessibility. Visitors are requested to begin their walk at the church office.

Then the treasure hunt commences. A tile floor in the basement is not where one would expect to find a labyrinth. But that's part of the mystique of these mysterious ancient spiritual tools. No one really knows where they originated.

A basement room signifies foundation, safe haven, protection from stormy weather. The speckled brown aggregate pattern is simplicity itself as it winds down a long hall, beckons to follow its turns, then flows into the President's Room.

Three designs are apparent as one enters the large room. The two outer designs mirror each other and the path winds around culminating in the middle of the room which is the center of the labyrinth. Quick inspection determines the path opens to the left continuing this treasure hunt to locate the entrance to this mystical journey. Many people would not recognize the tile floor as a labyrinth since it blends with the rest of the surroundings and is often covered with kids.

Labyrinths can offer surprises as one walker on the treasure hunt noted. Sometimes one has to look for the right place to begin to seek the goal — search in unusual places or off the beaten path and clear obstacles before envisioning the overall project. Patience frequently brings the bigger picture into shaper focus.

This labyrinth was easy to walk once we deciphered the code, shiny footsteps gliding along a pristine path. Ten circuits, quick turns back and forth, powerful impact in a small organized space.

What's this? A tiny bird feather... definitely out of place at an indoor labyrinth, no birds in sight and window does not open. An angel message, gift from the gods or significant communique to be alert to the unexpected?

Six window panes allowed the sun to glisten through the lone basement window lighting labyrinth footsteps with natural sonlight (light of the Son) and casting a serpentine glow to the vinyl tile path. The playground was visible above the window, trees cast an interesting shadow, green plants splashed color and birds serenaded in the distance perhaps providing accompaniment for this journey.

Wonder if one of them lost a feather?

Jonathan Duerbeck, director of the Tulsa School of Metaphysics, attended the Sunday service at All Souls Unitarian Church before he joined in the labyrinth treasure hunt. "The sermon was about slowness, being in the present, enjoying the now, appreciating what's right here instead of rushing to get somewhere else. Well, that's what I learned from this labyrinth," he said.

"The pattern was plain and easy to overlook. It was in a room in the basement where kids played on Sundays during morning services. Under all the kids and toys and chairs and a big rug, was an ordinary tile floor. The tiles were dark and light, and the dark ones formed a boxy, striped pattern. I had to slow down and look to notice it. Now, what did the preacher just say? Appreciate what's right in front of me now, see the beauty in what is here. This floor is special!

"The kids playing there were definitely in the present moment, and that reinforced the whole present-moment lesson. It seems fitting for that labyrinth to be in an activity room. The present moment is sacred and special, and I think people often confuse sacred with serious," Jonathan said.

"Walking a labyrinth is very pro-slowness," Jonathan continued. "A labyrinth rebels against the purpose of most paths and sidewalks, which is to quickly get from where you are to somewhere else. Following the tiles was an act of choosing to stay in one place, one simple basement room, and experience it fully by walking all over it. I learned to be grateful for ordinary things."

Far from ordinary, colorful student art adorns the walls outside the labyrinth. A large mural of planets lines the steps leading down to the basement and a fun macaroni Buddha grins as people exit the elevator. Both take visitors into another world preparing them for new visions they might encounter while walking the labyrinth.

Sometimes, the surroundings of a labyrinth can be just as important as the path itself.

The walkers joined in a group squeeze prayer in the hall in front of the labyrinth before beginning their Sunday stroll employing a new kind of prayer learned in Vian at the Dwight Mission Presbyterian Youth Camp the previous Friday. Such a prayer seemed appropriate as this labyrinth was squeezed into available space — hidden treasure tucked away in the basement.

Bethany Christian Church
6730 S. Sheridan Rd. Tulsa, OK 74133, (918) 492-1353
6-circuit, brick and mulch, in meditation garden
west side of parking lot, built spring 2008

A splash of color catches one's eye from the parking lot of Tulsa's Bethany Christian Church. Further inspection reveals a 6-circuit brick and mulch labyrinth mounted like the artistic creation it is on a sloping grassy area west of the church.

Curved, interlocking pink bricks and interesting geometrical shapes invite walkers to enter this sacred circle, reminiscent of a mandala of hope.

Dubbed the Bethany Labyrinth, this rustic design portrays positive expectation and epitomizes keynote aspects of mandalas depicting the universe, totality and wholeness.

Conscious creation and interaction with a caring community characterizes a congregation that shares its resources and defines love and compassion. Traits associated with the color pink.

Bricks are a building material that represent foundation, mastery and thought. Cypress mulch also denotes a solid base since it doesn't float as much as other types of wood.

Some of the bricks are circular on one end which created a unique design challenge, according to Pastor Barney McLaughlin.

"We had to get creative and crafted several triangles and diamond shapes into the labyrinth to complete the paths."

Triangles exemplify the Holy Trinity, wisdom and creation. Diamonds are symbols of solar radiance, immutability and integrity known for their brilliance, sincerity and strength.

McLaughlin said this area was chosen for the labyrinth due to its proximity to the church's meditation garden.

"We thought it would be nice to have the labyrinth next to the meditation garden since there are benches there for walkers to sit and reflect before or after their walk."

Several peace poles and a variety of trees dot the spacious landscape. The desire for harmony is expressed in four different languages on alternate sides of a slender white pole: Peace, Shalom, Eirene, Pax. Nearby birdhouses offer comfort for feathered friends.

A colorful church playground in the distance reminds us it's important to play as well as pray. An adjoining picnic area notes the significance of family functions.

Surrounding trees provide more than shade. Their metaphorical features convey admirable qualities worth emulating. Black jack trees are rugged, flexible, abundant. Pine delineates balance between pain and emotions and creativity symmetry. Strength of will and intuition are associated with the elm. Sycamore trees imply communication, love, receptivity while cypress teaches understanding the role of sacrifice.

One branch in an outer path kisses walkers softly as they pass underneath. Belonging to an elm, it suggests we strengthen our intuitive abilities.

The three-foot downward slope of the labyrinth's location completes the scenic setting amid six serene acres.

"It also makes it more challenging to walk," laughed McLaughlin, "as some paths angle quite a bit." The sloped spirals simulate the ups and downs of life, an occasional uphill ascension.

Two layers of garden liners cover the ground and provide padding under the mulch. Plus, three inches of sand. The sand base makes the path soft and squishy underfoot. Pretty comfy actually.

An occasional bare spot reveals the sand foundation. It's not a blemish, but a reminder that what is hidden will be revealed. Time to uncover the mysteries of life; polish those diamonds in the rough.

"This is still a work-in-progress," McLaughlin said. "We need to add more mulch, even it up a bit. And, we plan to extend the path from the entrance of the labyrinth to the meditation benches."

The pastor noted any imperfections in the design simply parallel human imperfections and pinpoint areas needing improvement.

Consider the mandala of hope analogy of artistic creation. A powerful and mystical symbol, the mandala coalesces the positive energy of the universe within its form. It unifies the intersection of cosmic events and earthly experiences.

The circle (labyrinth) enclosing the square (diamond) signifies the heavens surrounding the earth. The cardinal points mark entrances, one on each side of the square, and enhance the transfer of energy between heaven and earth.

Harnessing this energy brings happiness, joy, ancient wisdom and the incredible ability to change the status quo through good fortune, new beginnings and dynamic opportunities. Take action and fulfill life-long dreams by manifesting positive vibrations.

Labyrinths offer infinite possibilities for creative expression and expansive knowledge. Walking the circuits focusing on aspects of the current astrological sign provides a different perspective.

Such an astrology walk took place in June 2008 concentrating on Gemini attributes. A mutable air sign ruled by the planet Mercury overseeing the arms, hands, shoulders, lungs and nervous system. Symbolized by twins, Gemini's key phrase is "I think and thus know."

Gemini rules all communications, written and verbal, thoughts, attitudes, mental activity, basic reasoning and electronic channels (media, television, internet and computers). As guardians of our minds, Gemini determines the capacity for learning and accepting new information. The Gemini nature is to be flexible, versatile, adaptable, open-minded, mentally agile and clever.

This sign of the twins controls dualities and polarities — yin and yang, male and female, judgments of good vs. bad. Evolved expressions of Gemini perceive dualities with neutrality. One side is not better than another. Objectivity allows open access to higher consciousness, expands intuition and leads to increased receptivity.

Gemini also governs the wind, air and human breath. Partaking of the life force through the breath of acceptance affects how the chi circulates and cleanses the body's energy centers and meridians. Exhaling rigidity releases pent-up emotions and frees the flow of respiratory restrictions.

The capacity for life itself can be influenced by the relationship of Gemini and Mercury in individual and family astrological charts. Afflictions can present challenges to the enjoyment and healthy fulfillment of any life force. Destiny rules even when certain planetary aspects think they are in charge and the only regulatory agency with a voice.

Studying each month's astrological impact can provide beneficial information for all signs of the zodiac. Whatever is transpiring skyward affects everyone. Plus, all 12 signs occur somewhere in each person's natal chart. Current focus on any sign activates that area.

Having done your homework and taking the above knowledge into the sacred circle, the astrological labyrinth walk reveals the following message:

• Honor neutrality and equanimity. Stay non-attached, be receptive to others and to new ideas so growth and change become natural states of being.

• Assimilate new information unconditionally so it evolves into knowledge, understanding and wisdom.

• Increased Gemini influences can lead to blocked energy. Give agitation and worry to God.

• Stay focused. Communicate clearly to avoid confrontations and misunderstandings.

• Overstimulation stifles awareness and leads to boredom.

• Forget the gossip; preach only to yourself.

• Balance mental, physical, spiritual, emotional, social and community activities.

• Slow down and breathe.

• Walking, yoga, tai chi, dancing, stretching, gardening, swimming, knitting or reading help release nervous energy.

• Take short trips to renew inspiration.

• Elevate your perspective.

• Recognize the unity in duality.

• Release judgment and outdated beliefs.

• Entertain new ideas and concepts.

• Open yourself to fresh perceptions and higher truths.

• Wear lots of blue this month to accentuate the spoken and written word.

• Above all, believe in yourself and handle all communications with love.

Tulsa

The mandala of hope and creative expression splashed its colorful labyrinthine design on a grassy slope with interlocking pink bricks and interesting geometrical shapes inviting walkers to enter a sacred circle where positive expectations interact with conscious creation.

Gracie cordially invites walkers to experience the beautiful 7-circuit Classical grass labyrinth adorning the Tulsa back yard of Gala and Bill McBee. Built in 2006, this magnificent sacred circle was part of the 15th Annual Wildlife Habitat Garden Tour sponsored in June 2008 by the Tulsa Audubon Society. This spacious 2-acre yard reflects the natural beauty of its wooded surroundings and peacefully hosts humans as well as bunny rabbits, butterflies, hummingbirds, blue jays, cardinals, robins, dragonflies, and many varieties of indigenous flora and fauna.

Hunter Park (open 8 a.m. to 9 p.m. daily)
5804 E. 91st Street, Tulsa, OK
(between Sheridan and Yale on 91st)
Bob Hendrick, (918) 596-2488, BobHendrick@cityoftulsa.org
Located near the picnic shelter in the back of the public park
11-circuit Chartres, outdoor pavement, 62 feet, half-mile path
wheelchair accessible, built May 2005

What better use of two abandoned basketball courts than a 62-foot pavement labyrinth marked with yellow lines and a massive 1,000-pound stone perched in the center. Not something one would expect to find at a south Tulsa public park.

All the more reason to build one there. Each labyrinth offers a unique experience. This labyrinth provides an unusual setting on slightly higher ground than its park perimeter, wooded background and scenic residential setting.

Bob Hendrick, Tulsa Parks Special Events Coordinator, spent a week in late May 2005 chalking and painting the design for the permanent, outdoor concrete, 11-circuit, medieval labyrinth patterned after the Chartres model in France.

Uncertain what the response would be to building a labyrinth on the cement slab of two former basketball courts, Hendrick said remarks have been positive with walkers describing their experience as healing, meditative, peaceful, cleansing and spiritual.

"Parks have lots of sports facilities and other aesthetics, but nothing like this," he said.

"Prior to building the one at Hunter Park, I had the chance to walk a labyrinth. I was a bit skeptical and was humoring a friend. But when my friend started walking and began crying, I knew there was something to it."

Hendrick said people who walk labyrinths describe a feeling of peace and serenity, stress release, healing or any combination thereof.

The Hunter Park labyrinth has a walking path of one-half mile with a reflecting stone in the center.

"We strapped the rocks to the end of a bulldozer and lifted them in position so people could have somewhere to sit and reflect after walking the circular paths.

"It was important the rock be square and have sides facing north, south, east and west," Hendrick added. "One of the features of labyrinths is that the layout faces all directions."

The bottom rock serves as a solid foundation with a huge flat rock cemented on top. There's room to sit, lay, stand or dance on the granite, tabletop rock. Or even have a picnic.

It's a friendly, inviting rock full of ancient wisdom connecting humans to primordial roots and forgotten knowledge. A place to sit and contemplate the layers of intuition it enfolds.

Or simply enjoy the picturesque view of the landscape. The park has a nice duck pond and clean, playground and picnic areas in a scenic area of Tulsa. The south end of the park (where the labyrinth is located) cul-de-sacs and parallels the Creek Turnpike in a secluded setting with woods to the southeast and homes to the south and southwest.

Bicycle tire tracks glistening in the hot sun after a recent rain emphasized movement and transcendence. Much like the energy of the former basketball court. Connecting with this brisk pace, one walker, a former captain of her high school basketball team, expressed the desire to run through the paths, pivoting, twisting, turning... dribbling an imaginary basketball. Weaving in and out of the lanes, positioning atop the key, balancing for a undetected pass to a teammate or executing a perfect jump shot. Swish, nothing but net.

Imagination can run rampant in a labyrinth. Not everyone noticed the outline of Buddha in a water puddle in path seven or the cloud figures the rain water had created in the shape of a man kneeling in prayer with his wife and kids standing next to him overlapping nearby paths.

However, everyone did appreciate the lovely message spoken from the Hunter Park labyrinth "court." Originally designed for ordinary physical activities (hoop/shooting practices and pick-up games), then abandoned and given fresh meaning when someone saw a large concrete slab with new eyes and designed a totally different use for it.

The circular paths of the labyrinth painted in yellow signifies intellect, earth, will power and balance — the solar plexus (middle) chakra color and the bridge between upper and lower chakras. This labyrinth represents a bridge between the mundane and mankind's divine connection. On the surface, it seemed this place was no longer useful. A human being followed an inspiration and something novel was created.

The Hunter Park labyrinth speaks of the importance in seeing things with "fresh eyes" and asking for guidance on "new uses" for what was earlier considered worthless. No longer can we, as children of the 2012 awakening, view the forms, rituals, heritages and/or people of earth with outdated viewpoints. We have accepted a mission to nurture the primal energy of oneness, balance, respect for our planet, its inhabitants and resources. Any preconceived ideas about things, places, beliefs, vocations and people require re-evaluation. We must open our hearts and minds and be receptive to the vast legacy of wisdom we have been gifted from the Creator through the Loving Spirit of Truth.

This labyrinth said it did not start out as a sacred place, but was honored to fill that function. It is not the place that creates holiness, but the intention and attention of the people who frequent it that develops a sacred consciousness.

Tulsa

Phillips Theological Seminary
901 N. Mingo Rd., Tulsa, OK 74116, www.ptstulsa.edu
Mady Fraser, Seminary Chapin, mady.fraser@ptstulsa.edu
7-circuit modified Santa Rosa design, painted concrete
Built 2004. Call for availability, (918) 610-8303

A beautiful landscaped meditation garden is the serene setting for the 7-circuit, modified Santa Rosa labyrinth at Phillips
Theological Seminary in Tulsa.

Four natural wooden benches comfortably surround the
38-foot circle with its hidden question mark in the center. Dark
red and white paint on concrete is a perfect match for the foliage,
flowers and light-colored rock enclosure.

The trees and plants are indigenous to Oklahoma yielding
healthy and attractive growth throughout the year. Arranged to
provide a restful, contemplative environment, these native trees
and plants also symbolize the seminary's roots and permanence
in northeastern Oklahoma.

Phillips Theological Seminary is a graduate-level school affiliated with the Christian Church (Disciples of Christ) and has an
enrollment of about 250 students representing more than 20
denominations. Its rich 100-year history has trained thousands
through a master of divinity program that leads to ordination and
congregational ministry. The school also grants master's degrees
in Theological Studies and Ministry and Culture and a doctorate
in ministry.

Part of the former Phillips University in Enid its first 80 years, the Tulsa seminary offered classes for 20 years in the state's Oil Capital before the donation of its present 7.5 acre Mingo Road site in 2003.

The labyrinth is inside the Tabbernee Conference Center Yetter Meditation Garden. Dedicated on April 4, 2004, to the memory of Frank Augustus and Lanella Whitlock Yetter of Tulsa, this garden is open to any who desire to use it. Person's outside the seminary community may make arrangements to walk the labyrinth or utilize the Tabbernee Conference Center and Yetter Meditation Garden by calling or visiting the reception desk in the Cadieux Building from 8 a.m. to 5 p.m. weekdays.

Water, sustenance for all life, flows freely in the fountain on the path towards the labyrinth. As each season lapses, growth and beauty increase in the garden for the enjoyment and tranquility of visitors. Spiritually retreating into the depths of the labyrinth, many find peace, vision, solitude and stillness.

The labyrinth design is based on the Santa Rosa model, developed in Santa Rosa, California, in 1997. The modifications have intentionally created wider paths to allow access for persons in wheelchairs or using other ambulatory assistance to negotiate the turns.

It also has another distinct feature that few recognize. As with all lofty issues, it's easier to see from a higher perspective.

A student approached Seminary Chaplin Mady Fraser one day while she was eating lunch in the student commons and asked if she knew what was at the center of the labyrinth.

"It's a question mark!" the student exclaimed. A picture of the labyrinth, taken from the roof of the conference center, was on the cover of the catalog that year and when the student looked at it, the question mark jumped off the page at her.

Mady explained the question mark is formed by the spiraled center and the small circle just to the right of the first turn on the path which is part of the Santa Rosa design.

"We agreed this was quite appropriate for our setting since the seminary journey is full of so many questions and so few absolute answers," Mady said. "The journey, through seminary and the labyrinth, continues as we explore who God calls us to become."

This sacred circle is regularly utilized by ministry students for their own personal spiritual discipline in addition to serving as a resource for spirituality classes, one of which is specifically focused on labyrinth walking.

Mady said occasionally students are suspicious of walking the labyrinth in an introductory class as if she were asking them to do something anti-Christian.

"For most of them, it proves to be a moving and unexpectedly spiritual and treasured experience and leads to a continued willingness to enter this sacred space. Several formerly suspicious students have even taken the labyrinth walking class."

Mady said that class is focused on the labyrinth as a means of enhancing the spiritual life and ministry of students. It meets on two Saturdays, six hours each, and provides opportunities to focus on how the spiritual life inspires, supports and otherwise affects the work of ministry in the Christian church.

Different types of guided walks, as well as discussion of the reading assignments and a presentation on the history of the labyrinth, are part of the course curriculum.

Students are required to walk the labyrinth 12 times during the semester, at least half the time with other people, and to write short reflections on their journeys. They also read and study the book, *Labyrinths from the Outside In, Walking to Spiritual Insight, A Beginner's Guide,* by Donna Schaper and Carole Ann Camp.

Applying resources from the book and seminar experiences, the final class project requires students to create a labyrinth ritual for a ministry community in which they are involved.

"My most powerful walk was one I took alone," Mady recalls. "As I entered, I began to think about a very difficult time in my life which I thought I had fully processed. It turned out I hadn't and my time in the center was an encounter with God of cleansing and forgiveness. Exiting the labyrinth, I truly felt renewed and knew I would now be able to share my time of difficulty with others in a way that might contribute to their healing."

Labyrinths help elevate, consecrate, illuminate, enrich and deepen commitments to ourselves, generate healing and alleviate emotional pain and fatigue.

They frequently ask as many questions as they answer. In theory, students seek knowledge at an institution of higher learning. Inside the labyrinth, answers often appear in the form of a question. Perhaps, the meaning of the poignant question mark hidden inside the design's center.

As students of life, maybe the goal is not so much to analyze answers, but to question them.

St. Andrew's Presbyterian Church
3601 S. Yale Avenue, Tulsa, OK 74135, (918) 627-9600
http://www.standrewstulsa.org, office@standrewstulsa.org
4-circuit Chartres, built spring 2003

The footprints of individual soles led to the creation of a new spiritual path for collective souls at St. Andrew's Presbyterian Church in Tulsa.

In October of 2002, Rev. Ann LaMar sketched and engineered plans for a 4-circuit Chartres labyrinth in the church's Memorial Garden. Originally painted on the lawn, the labyrinth houses rocks donated by church members who brought a collection of stones to place in the labyrinth while walking its meditative path.

"Many consider the labyrinth primitive, but it's actually a very innovative design for spiritual renewal," LaMar said. "It's a great tool to employ in a congregation's walk with God."

St. Andrew's labyrinth is a gift to the congregation as well as the entire community. Non-church members are welcome — and encouraged — to walk its circular paths for personal, psychological and spiritual transformation.

"My purpose in creating a labyrinth here is to help us individually discover God's will for our own lives and for the life of this congregation," the minister noted, folding her hands in prayer.

LaMar said the recent resurgence in the popularity of the labyrinth can be attributed to individuals longing for deeper spirituality "and to a connection to something greater than themselves."

Modern walkers can still use the labyrinth as a pilgrimage or journey for divine guidance, she said, symbolically viewing the turns of the labyrinth as the turns of their lives.

Although several people use the terms "labyrinth" and "maze" interchangeably, they are not the same, LaMar said. "A labyrinth generates peace. A maze is meant to befuddle, confuse and hinder with obstacles. It's a very significant difference."

The minister said the answer to a troubling question or problem has often been revealed after a walk in the labyrinth. "Taking time to reflect is also important."

Three benches in the center of St. Andrew's labyrinth provide a resting place for those who desire to pray or meditate before completing their walk.

Three also signifies the Holy Trinity and a deeper communion with the Creator.

St. Dunstan's Episcopal Church
5635 East 71st Street, Tulsa, OK 74136, (918) 492-7140
http://www.stduntulsa.org, jjosborne@cox.net
11-circuit Chartres, portable indoor canvas, 32 feet,
purchased 1997
Available throughout the year for scheduled walks

Thirty-three of the 70 Oklahoma labyrinths are located at religious or spiritual institutions. Churches host 25 including United Methodist (12), Episcopalian (6), Christian (3) and one each at Presbyterian, Unitarian, United Life and Unity.

Sancta Sophia Seminary at Sparrow Hawk Village in Tahlequah built the first permanent outdoor labyrinth in the Sooner state, November 13, 1992. St. Dunstan's Episcopal Church in Tulsa purchased the second indoor state canvas portable labyrinth in 1997, a few weeks after St. John's Tulsa Episcopal obtained an 11-circuit Chartres.

Jane Osborne, chair of St. Dunstan's Labyrinth Ministry, shares their labyrinth story:

The labyrinth was introduced to St. Dunstan's in 1996 by long-time church member and parish administrator Carolyn Strickland Combs. Thanks to the unrelenting efforts of this lovely, tenacious woman, St. Dunstan's was the first church in Oklahoma to establish a Labyrinth Ministry.

Carolyn had a chance labyrinth encounter during a visit to Grace Cathedral in San Francisco. She watched as others walked the labyrinth path and became more and more curious. Being a cautious person when trying something new, particularly in public, she had questions. What was its purpose? How was it correctly walked? Of what use was it? Drawn by the answers she received, she walked the path herself and was amazed and deeply moved by its spiritual benefits.

Upon her return to Tulsa, Carolyn shared this labyrinth experience with her friends at St. Dunstan's, especially those in her Education for Ministry class. Carolyn was a graduate of its four-year program and a class co-mentor. To illustrate the labyrinth's use, she led the class in the construction of an outdoor labyrinth using sticks and twine.

Although the construction was crude, the labyrinth's concept and potential advantages were quickly recognized. The dream of a permanent outdoor labyrinth was born.

In August of 1996, six months following Carolyn's introduction to the labyrinth, she attended facilitator training at Grace Cathedral conducted by the Rev. Lauren Artress, president and founder of Veriditas, the voice of the U.S. labyrinth movement. Inspired by this training, Carolyn committed herself to creating a labyrinth ministry at St. Dunstan's.

Though her dream was of a permanent outdoor labyrinth, it was not an affordable vision in 1996. An alternate route presented itself and a 32-foot, 11-circuit Chartres portable canvas labyrinth was obtained with funds from a private donor. The labyrinth was received August 6, 1997, dedicated Sunday, August 17, 1997, and walked for the first time in October 1997.

St. Dunstan's Labyrinth Ministry was established.

Due to its portability, this labyrinth is offered not only by St. Dunstan's during the year, but has also become extremely popular throughout Oklahoma. Churches of various denominations and a variety of organizations in the Tulsa area frequently request its use. The labyrinth has become a constructive tool for youth groups, special workshops and interfaith functions.

In the first seven months of 2007, St. Dunstan's labyrinth was utilized by St. Paul's Cathedral in Oklahoma City, a youth workshop at St. Crispin's in Seminole, and the May Sacred Activism Conference held in Tulsa and attended by more than 700 people. A Tulsa non-profit organization employs its positive influence in prison ministry workshops.

When the white canvas labyrinth painted in purple is presented at St. Dunstan's, candles are placed at each of the points of its octagon shape. The color of the candle holders coordinate with the color of the church calendar: purple, ruby and green. Two white candles sit at each side of the entrance. Meditation music is played softly in the background. Silence is maintained in the area of the labyrinth and an attendant is always present.

When the scheduled walk concludes, each of the three labyrinth sections (held together with Velcro stripping) folds into a bundle approximately 18 inches wide, 24 inches long and 10 inches high. The canvas labyrinth stores in a large Rubbermaid container with wheels.

St. Dunstan's dream to have a permanent outdoor labyrinth is not forgotten. In 1996, when the idea of a permanent outdoor labyrinth was enthusiastically discussed, Educational Ministry class member and architect Brad Griffin volunteered to draft plans for its "dream" design. Other students shared ideas for the "ideal" outdoor labyrinth and Brad sketched the blueprint. It was important the permanent labyrinth be fully accessible, and conducive to prayer and meditation. An especially pertinent requirement was that it be compatible in construction to St. Dunstan's Memorial Gardens.

The path should also be in the same pattern as the portable labyrinth: the 11-circuit Chartres replica. A terrazzo path surrounded by stone walkways with benches, trees and shrubs was far too expensive an undertaking for the Tulsa church at that time. So plans were framed and hang to this day, just outside the church office. The vision is still alive and not forgotten. Cost estimates have recently been requested and plans are currently underway to take the first steps toward fulfilling this dream.

Every time St. Dunstan's labyrinth is walked, we remember this precious ministry is possible because of the tireless efforts of a lovely lady and dedicated parishioner. Carolyn made every effort to develop and enrich her own spirituality. She discovered the labyrinth benefited her in achieving this goal and believed it would be a divine instrument to offer this gift to others. At the edge of the entrance to the labyrinth, we honor her with the words: "Dedicated to the Memory of Carolyn Strickland Combs."

Carolyn died in October 1998, due to a terminal illness diagnosed in early 1997. Much of what she achieved in establishing this outreach program was done despite the enormous difficulties of her illness. The Labyrinth Ministry at St. Dunstan's continues through the efforts of committed volunteers, many of whom are driven by the inspiration of Carolyn's unselfish, determined efforts.

Tulsa

St. John's Episcopal Church
4200 S. Atlanta Place, Tulsa, OK 74105, (918) 742-7381
www.sjtulsa.org, info@sjtulsa.org
11-circuit Chartres, portable, purchased 1997
Call for availability and scheduled walks
7-circuit grass, built spring 2008, always open
Corner of 41st and Atlanta Place

The forerunner of the portable, canvas 11-circuit Chartres labyrinth purchased by the Oxley Foundation for St. John's Episcopal Church was a classical 7-circuit model spray painted on a vacant parking lot in late 1996.

"That may have been the first labyrinth in Tulsa," said Nancy Harbaugh, St. John's labyrinth facilitator. "Another girl and I knew of the little used lot, grabbed some spray paint and decided to go for it."

The labyrinth was popular with a woman's group who walked it on a regular basis "often under a full moon," Nancy said. "Many other people enjoyed it during the several months it was there before the lot was resurfaced."

Less than a year later, the church purchased a portable, canvas labyrinth and 12 years later, a modified 7-circuit Classical grass replica graces the corner of 41st and Atlanta Place.

The large, peaceful center of the grassy sacred circle is in direct antithesis to the ongoing traffic buzz. Far removed from a vacant parking lot, walkers connect to the heartbeat of Mother Earth massaging their feet as they travel the shaded circuits.

Bounded by a colorful playground, two streets and the church diocese house, the new permanent, outdoor labyrinth has elm and magnolia tree companions. Elm signifies strength of will, intuition and acknowledgement of the unknown. Magnolia trees convey idealism, pleasantness, fulfillment and blossoming to fragrant prosperity and completeness.

The simplicity and coolness of the area were greatly appreciated as the walkers needed some simple shade in the humid 92-degree Oklahoma heat at 4 p.m. on the sixth labyrinth walk of the day.

A welcome breeze accompanied the traffic noise, joining the rhythmic drumbeat of creative song swirling in our heads, connecting humans to All That Is.

The message from today's walk: Sometimes, it may be hard to decide which direction to take or path to travel. It doesn't matter as long as we stay together, and lovingly support each other.

"That's what St. John's parishioners do — support each other and join together on various projects," Nancy said. "That philosophy and nourishing assistance has led this diocese to a journey of precedence."

Presently, St. John's Episcopal is the only Oklahoma church with both indoor and outdoor labyrinths.

Nancy believes in dancing to the beat of a different drummer as she was an original pilgrim to the first public labyrinth prayer service at San Francisco's Grace Cathedral in July 1995. "That hooked me on these sacred circles as a beneficial tool for healing, renewal and connecting to a higher power," the Tulsa resident said.

Traumatically moved by this experience, and wanting to share it with others who might find relief, support, guidance and comfort from its spiraling circuits, she invited Rev. Dr. Lauren Artress to bring a canvas labyrinth to Oklahoma City in April 1996 on the first anniversary of the Murrah Building bombing.

Several parishioners from Tulsa's St. John's Episcopal Church traveled to Oklahoma City to attend Dr. Artress' presentation and a keen interest was generated in securing a canvas labyrinth.

"We decided the best space for its use would be in Powell Hall, a beautiful chapel-like room with stained glass windows and fine woodwork," Nancy recalled. Since Powell Hall measured 29 feet across, the size of the labyrinth in the Chartres pattern was determined.

Tulsa

In July of 1997, St. John's had the first portable indoor canvas labyrinth in Tulsa. A few weeks later, St. Dunstan's Episcopal Church purchased an 11-circuit Chartres.

"I was also fortunate to have participated in the initial labyrinth facilitator training conducted by Rev. Artress at Grace Cathedral in August of 1996," Nancy added.

That training helps her guide people as they walk, enhancing their experience, releasing emotions, assisting with grief, loss or mourning. "Many first-time walkers are unsure how to embrace a labyrinth and want to make sure they are walking it correctly," Nancy said.

In addition to making its labyrinth available periodically at Powell Hall, the St. John's Chartres has traveled with Nancy to various sites for walks and educational presentations. In the past decade, churches (Unity, Methodist, Christian, Episcopal, First Christian, Presbyterian, Fellowship Congregational, United Methodist), spiritual centers, seminaries, youth groups, peace rallies, hospitals, universities, student associations, hospices and women's retreats have enjoyed a labyrinthine adventure.

"We racked up frequent traveler miles in Tulsa, McAlester, Bartlesville, Enid, Sand Springs, Ponca City, Jenks, Muskogee, Claremore, and even traveled to Fayetteville, Arkansas, Ft. Worth, Texas, and Great Bend, Kansas," the certified Veriditas facilitator laughed.

Hillcrest Hospital housed the St. John's labyrinth for several months at its Chapel exploring its benefits as a healing tool, spiritual counselor and stress reducer.

"We displayed the labyrinth in the conference center auditorium during Spirit Week activities to give staff, patients, families and visitors the opportunity to experience a labyrinth and to help balance personal health issues, stressful situations and spiritual concerns," Hillcrest Chaplain Ron Nofziger said.

Tulsa will have two more permanent labyrinths soon at Hillcrest Hospital and Clarehouse, a new facility providing dignified end-of-life care for the terminal ill and their families. The hospital has an indoor Chartres included in the next phase of its two-year remodeling plan. Clarehouse will offer an 11-circuit labyrinth in the summer of 2009.

Cindy Ritter, director of Support Services for the non-profit organization, said the Clarehouse labyrinth will be ideal for "walking through" the grieving process.

"Walking the labyrinth as a meditation or prayer exercise

mirrors the grief journey. The grief process involves traveling between the way things used to be and how things will be in the future. It is an interior process of coming to terms with a new reality by letting go and saying goodbye in such a way that emotional healing occurs," Ritter said, adding the grief process connects "what was" with "what will be."

The Clarehouse labyrinth will not only offer support to guests and families, but will also provide a meditative space and experience for the northeast Oklahoma community as well as increase the care ability of staff and volunteers by reducing the stress and demands affiliated with end-of-life care.

Ritter said the 11-circuit Chartres will facilitate staff development and team building. "It will be an advantageous development tool for staff and volunteer orientation and continuing education. The Clarehouse goal is that each person and those closest to them receive loving, compassionate care during the dying time and grieving process. The labyrinth will enhance and support this goal by providing a quiet space and regenerative method for actively walking through grief as a journey resulting in comfort and healing."

The first portable, canvas labyrinth in Tulsa has also been used by Saint Francis Hospice in a memorial remembrance service for families and friends of persons who passed away during the previous year. People gathered at All Souls Unitarian Church and walked the St. John's labyrinth as a memorial to departed loved ones.

"Both tears and laughter were expressed and shared," Nancy said. "Children who had lost a parent and widowers found the labyrinth path to truly be a healing event."

Barbara Bilderback, Bereavement Supervisor for Saint Francis Hospice, said walkers found the labyrinth experience "peaceful" during the Annual Service of Remembrance.

"It is traditional for hospices to offer opportunities for family members and staff to come together to remember loved ones and renew acquaintances through this type of service. It is not a funeral, nor does it focus on dying. It is about new methods of relating and working with grief to overcome stagnation and identify hidden or missing joy."

Bilderback said the service is planned to present gentle comfort and compassionate assistance to help survivors deal with grief and loss. "A labyrinth fits right in with this philosophy," she said. "It can allow people to discover new life in their grief or pinpoint fresh ways of remembering their loved ones.

"People walk a labyrinth at a memorial service for varied reasons," Bilderback added. "We never try to limit to a particular reason or need the ways in which one works with grief. Walking a labyrinth could be an act of gratitude, a request for forgiveness, an answer to a thus-far unanswered question, a desire to feel closer to the deceased, a request for help in making a decision, or a prayer.

"There are many customs to describe a labyrinth. It is a path of prayer, a walking meditation, a crucible of change and a watering hole for the spirit," Bilderback said. "No matter where one is in the grief process: feeling burdened and overwhelmed, seeking to release a painful part, realizing needed adaptations, or aware of a desire to move on, they can share the labyrinth walk with a loved one. It nourishes all who enter its sacred circuits."

Nancy spoke at the 2003 hospice remembrance service introducing the labyrinth as a healing tool. That year's program featured a labyrinthine theme. "Life is a Journey" was read and the songs "Simple Gifts," "Now I Walk in Beauty" and "We are Marching in the Light of God" were sung.

Psalm 16 was also read which refers to the "Path of Life."

"The St. John's canvas labyrinth has traveled far and wide, opening its pathway to hundreds of people," Nancy, who is also a Feldenkrais (Awareness Through Movement) counselor, said. "I am constantly amazed at how the labyrinth really does function as a spiritual tool, whether your feet are walking the path or you are introducing it to others."

Private Front Yard — Michelle and Clark Wiens
3730 Terwilleger, Tulsa, OK 74105
mkwiens@swbell.net, (918) 747-3398
11-circuit Chartres, mortared stone on concrete, 38 feet
built 2001, wheelchair accessible
Always available for visitors to walk
Call ahead for group or night visits

Walkers come full circle in a labyrinth and that's exactly what Michelle and Clark Wiens have accomplished with the exquisite 38-foot mortared stone labyrinth built in their front yard in 2001.

The Wiens say it is okay to come unannounced to walk their labyrinth during daylight hours, but call ahead if planning an evening walk and "we'll turn the light on for you."

"It illuminates the entire labyrinth in a soft glow," Michelle said.

They even have a handout welcoming visitors to their home. It explains the history of labyrinths and gives directions on how to walk them. Two diagrams on the back page show a Classical 7-circuit and an 11-circuit Chartres.

The Classical 7-circuit is ancient — thought to date back at least 3,500 years. Found in many civilizations throughout the world and associated with the design of the Hopi medicine wheel and Tibetan sand mandala.

"Ours is an 11-circuit Chartres — a later and more complex version of the seven circuit based on a labyrinth still existing today in the floor of the nave of a 13th century French cathedral."

The handout explains the labyrinth experience is simultaneously unique and universal. Everyone travels the same path, but may experience it differently — just like life. People often describe labyrinth walks as peaceful, centering, healing or insightful. Some say it increases perception, intuition or empathy. Many focus on a question, repeat a prayer or mantra while walking.

Michelle said the goal of walking a labyrinth is not so much to get to the center of it, as it is to get nearer to the center of oneself.

Labyrinths teach humans how to successfully walk in both worlds, overcoming the illusion of a material environment while embracing the truth of a spiritual realm. Duality merges into a circle of absolution where compassion meets forgiveness.

Glistening with rain, this magnificent mortared stone creation appeared even more majestic and dazzling. Unique, impressive, brilliant ... does not do it justice. A cornucopia of divine generosity, the only mortared stone labyrinth we discovered in Oklahoma nourishes the soul as well as the other five senses.

Beautiful rocks and stones in a variety of colors and shapes adorn the 11 circuits, their presence speaking to each walker depending on perspective and need.

Three reddish-brown boulders provide a resting place under spacious shade trees near the entrance to this extraordinary sacred circle. Solidifying a strong, vigorous foundation, these dynamic "bones of Mother Earth," convey a compelling connection of permanence, strength and integrity, orchestrating the architecture of our lives.

Several eye shapes in varying rock patterns winked mischievously through the mist. Perhaps, the message is to open both eyes and enjoy the continuous, breathtaking beauty surrounding us. Or brush away the sleep and connect with inner eloquence. Develop the third eye of spiritual perception, omniscience and rebirth viewing what cannot see, but know is there. The color fades on shiny, moist stones, concealing a prelude to revelation.

Some stones mimic life, reflecting a need for repair. Foundations may still be solid, but the veneer desires restoration. The original luster is neither radiant, nor distinctive. A glossy sheen no longer portrays quality, playfulness, iridescence. It requests a return to former stylish, polished, glazed surfaces. A renewed jest for life, enthusiastic, grateful, sensual, intense, exciting the senses.

What do you see? Or are willing to admit?

A crisp breeze encircled walkers as twilight approached, casting an etheric glow and providing charm and grace to the scenic splendor. The spectacular arbor furnished a natural fortress of picturesque protection. A fitting place for a rite of initiation.

Wandering woodsy trails, lost in a forest or navigating any place of mystery, danger, intrigue... facing trials, tribulation or uncertainty is a powerful metaphor for the pains of inexperience and the achievement of knowledge.

Finding one's way through the complex world of form, solving problems, uncovering solutions or locating a missing piece of the puzzle often lead to self-discovery. "Know thyself" is a timeless admonition spoken in the Bible and advised by Greek oracles.

The complete inscription over the Oracle of Delphi in ancient Greece once proclaimed: "Know thyself and you will possess the keys to the universe and the secrets of the gods."

A living stream of consciousness flows along its passageway circumnavigating the beautiful circuits of multi-colored mortared stone. Gray dividers accent the scalloped edges highlighting a six-pedaled lotus blossom center.

Four small rocks from Chartres, France, placed in each cardinal direction, connect with the small feather that floated towards Michelle as she entered the cathedral housing the famous 800-year-old labyrinth after which hers is patterned. The feather is buried under the center stones.

Feathers have ascension symbolism and are emblematic of prayer. Their association with air, wind and thunder signify freedom, purity and spiritual life. The wind is a potent messenger of divine forces, natural extension of creative expression and a powerful symbol of change.

A distinctive feature of the Chartres labyrinth is the beautiful radiating petals of the lotus blossom decorating its center. The glory of creation springs eternal as the water lily emerges from primeval slime in the muddy river of life flowering into untapped inner potential. Its resplendent elegance unsurpassed as immaculate petals unfold to the sun basking in the knowledge that leads to spiritual awakening.

Tulsa

Enlightenment germinates spontaneously as humans harmonize with the soul's budding evolvement and harness the flow of cosmic energy to attain divine perfection.

Cleansing, refreshing, washing away mud and debris, water is an essential element of life, a building block of nature. The primordial point of origin, limitless, formless, inexhaustible, full of possibilities.

Three holly trees near the labyrinth expound on these attributes symbolizing hope and joy. Textured varieties of clover wave a passionate greeting of wellness and wholeness. Clover characterizes luck, love, fidelity, kindness, living a life of ease and luxury.

A few moss-covered rocks at the perimeter of the property connect to the concrete foundation of the mortared stone labyrinth. Their velvet adornment accentuates the aristocracy of this sacred circle. Its well-defined paths with strong turns allow effortless traveling, promenading in natural grounded rhythm. Shades of gray interspersed with sunshine amid flecks of shiny marble create pictures within pictures, patterns within patterns and worlds within worlds.

Dancing feet swirl to the delightful edges of the circumambulation as walkers stop, look and listen to the joyous heartbeat of holistic intelligence within and without. Talented designs of artistic décor form in the mind's eye as well as underfoot.

Each labyrinth has its own distinctive beat just as each walker has an individual step, pattern, rhythm, purpose, musical note, orchestration, direction. The labyrinth of life has brought us full circle. Our journey is complete. We have learned:

Life is meant to be enjoyed, not endured.

Vian

Dwight Mission Presbyterian Camp, Conference & Retreat Center
Route 2 Box 71, Vian, OK 74962, (918) 775-2018
Allison Beavers, allison@dwightmission.org
11-circuit Chartres, outdoor in wooded area, 74 feet, built 2001
Available to on-site campers, guests and general public

An arbor entrance marks the trail leading to the 11-circuit Chartres labyrinth at Dwight Mission Presbyterian Camp. The peaceful gravel path provides protection from the outside world as one meanders its wooded passageway preparing to explore the inner universe of Creation on a divine odyssey of self-reflection.

Camp Director Allison Beavers said the rediscovery of the medieval labyrinth, a 13th century mystical tool, may be one of the most important spiritual developments of the last decade.

"We teach campers about the historic practice of making a spiritual pilgrimage — a search for the holy," Beavers said. "Hebrew Scriptures refer to God's people journeying to a land of Promise, to Zion, to sacred places. The Psalms witness to this deep yearning within. Early Christians were called 'people of the Way,' as they tried to follow the path Jesus set before them.

"That's what we desire to instill in those who use our

facilities," Beavers added. "That and a sense of gratitude."

The year-round conference, retreat and camping center offers an atmosphere conducive to spiritual growth for people of all ages. Located on 176 acres approximately 11 miles northeast of Vian and 10 miles northwest of Sallisaw, Dwight Mission serves individuals, churches, families, organizations and community groups.

Representing the three presbyteries of Oklahoma, Cimarron, Indian Nations and Eastern Oklahoma, this ministry was originally founded in 1820 as an Indian mission and later became a vocational school. Since 1952, it has existed as an extension of the Christian education programs of Presbyterian churches featuring fellowship, study, recreation, prayer and worship for thousands of children, teens and adults at a peaceful, secluded site nestled in the beautiful hills of eastern Oklahoma.

The labyrinth and 8-station Prayer Trail feature hidden adventures in the northwest corner of the camp.

Patterned after the labyrinth found at Chartres Cathedral in France, the Dwight Mission model was completed in 2001 by volunteers (primarily the Memorial Presbyterian Church Youth Group from Norman, Oklahoma).

"Labyrinths are an ancient spiritual tool, used for the purpose of prayer, meditation, reflection and contemplation," Beavers stated. "It is a universal image representing the path of life; and its winding trail in toward the center and out again symbolizes a pilgrim's walk with God, an epic journey in the form of a walking meditation. Traveling the path is a sacred ritual that can provide insights, courage and understanding in facing life's challenges."

The Presbyterian Cross graces the center of the labyrinth and each of its designs are explained in the Prayer Trail, located northeast of the 11-circuit Chartres replica. A source for prayerful contemplation, the Prayer Trail winds around a small creek with benches for campers to sit and reflect on the eight stopping points. The stations explain the meaning of the individual parts of the church's symbol, present a thought to ponder, recommend scripture to read later and suggest actions to consider while walking to the next pausing spot.

Stations represent the flame of the burning bush, a fish (one of the earliest signs for Christians), an open Bible, the Crucified Christ, a cup signifying the sacrament of Holy Communion, baptismal font, descending dove and pulpit.

Imagery, imagination and inspiration abound inside a sacred space — or anywhere else one truly listens to their inner sanctum. Passionately connecting with nature reaps it rewards. Leafy branches swaying in a gentle breeze cast shadows in the moist shade. Natural tree stumps invite weary travelers to rest and release their burdens.

A towering sandstone precipice presents a background stage as birds, cicada and tree frogs fill the air with a joyful cadence. Water drips from the rocky expanse creating a cooling sensation. Mountains sprout in the distance overshadowing an expansive field of green, white and yellow wildflowers. The coolness from the boulders and the heat of the sun offer a refreshing respite.

In quiet contrast, a train echoes in the distance telling humanity to slow down. "You will get there, maybe a little later, but much less stressed. Sit a spell, visit with fellow travelers, share a few hours of tranquility, and view the lovely scenery out the window of your soul."

The train sound fades leaving vibrational gradations bouncing in earth tones, a purple mist swirling in the distance.

Although no campers were scheduled to use the labyrinth that late June morning, the authors were blessed when one counselor decided to take his charges on a spontaneous walk. Four adults and seven kids shared a moment of suspended time in a holy space communing with their inner divinity and its Source.

Before ascending onto the sacred circle, the counselor took a few minutes to impart some knowledge.

"The labyrinth is found in various forms in all religious traditions around the world and throughout history. It is not a maze; there are no tricks to it, and no dead ends. Only one path leads to the center and out again. If you make a misstep, you will simply end up at the center or at the beginning. The path winds throughout and becomes a reminder of the way we live our lives; it touches our sorrows and releases our joy. So walk it with an open heart and mind."

After the walk, an astute eight-year-old boy who had never walked a labyrinth before, said it was like life and death. "The center is heaven," he said.

Another boy said "you seem to turn your back on God as you travel the circuits, but if you keep on truckin', you will reconnect with Him as he is waiting for you when you reach the center or come back home."

Vian

"It seems the closer you get to obtaining the goal, the farther it is to come full circle and meet God in the center of the labyrinth," a nine-year-old girl shared.

The authors also learned about squeeze prayers from the church group. We formed a circle holding hands and bowed our heads. The two counselors spoke first giving thanks for the day's activities. Fortunately, the prayers circled to the right and we stood to the left.

A couple of youth spoke elegantly, preceding a brief silence. Then a girl two campers down said her prayer. Now, we were confused and stole a quick look with eyes open, heads still bowed, to assess the situation before it became our turn.

After the girl finished voicing her prayer, she squeezed the hand of the camper next to her who chose to pray in silence. As did the next youth when his hand was pressed. The boy next to us, smiled a friendly greeting as he squeezed the adult hand holding his. We knew it was our turn to either pray aloud or silently.

Just like the Bible says, we were led by a small child... and have shared the squeeze prayer concept a couple of times since with other adults who had no clue as to the meaning of this simple way to dialogue with Our Creator.

Ancient wisdom awaits in this natural sanctuary as we rediscover the forgotten practice of communing with our divine essence inside a sacred circle of creation.

P_Bar Farms
Rt. 2 Box 92-G, Weatherford, OK 73096, (580) 772-4401
Loren and Kim Liebscher, www.pbarfarms.com
7-circuit Classical, grass, 75 feet, built 2006

Kim Liebscher said the family decided to build a grass labyrinth in 2006 to add eye appeal and to complement other points of interest at the 320-acre P_Bar Farms.

A design was selected off the internet, everyone headed out to the South 40 and an hour later it was done. They used rope and spray paint to create a 75-foot diameter labyrinth with seven circuits, four rocks and Round-Out to clear the paths.

The Weatherford corn maize farmers were particularly attracted to making the labyrinth due to its spiritual aspect and offering a place for prayer and meditation.

"Our guests enjoy walking the labyrinth, young and old alike; many find it relaxing and some just think it is fun. Kids love to run around the circuits, often racing through them."

Future plans include placing smooth river stones along the paths to make the design more permanent. Currently, two huge rocks designate the entrance and another large boulder rests at the approach to the center, providing a place to sit for those who want to take time to reflect.

"The center rock can be symbolic for getting to the center of a problem or anything the walker wants it to be," Kim said, adding there is a short explanation on labyrinths at the entrance. "We let guests experience the labyrinth as they desire.

"It's an added attraction at the maze, there is no charge for walking the labyrinth, we just ask that folks respect and enjoy it."

A 5-foot limestone monolith stands in dignified silence inside a keyhole center speaking volumes to any who will listen. This grooved orator stone recommends we listen to our hearts while grazing in the center of agriculture country, taking nourishment from the Source of Creation.

Farm equipment dots the spacious surroundings reminding walkers to partake graciously of life-giving sustenance, enjoy newfound freedom in gratitude and employ the tools of their trade wisely.

The keyhole outline suggested by the grass walking path around the center affords a glimpse of the reward waiting inside but one has to open the door (travel the next path) to stand tall inside the keyhole and take center stage (complete the journey).

Red boulders inside the labyrinth say honor the earth, live your passion and rest on a solid foundation.

The entrance sign to the labyrinth has green type on a yellow background symbolizing freshness, healing, power and knowledge. "Many recognize the labyrinth as a metaphor for the path we walk through life and use the path to encourage mental focus through meditation and prayer."

P_Bar's maize has been in operation since 2000. The farm offers field trips for school groups, organizations and tour buses during the fall and spring. Party packages are available year-round for family reunions, conferences, corporate parties and wedding receptions.

Fall is the busiest season with Cornstock, the annual Christian concert, and a "haunted maze" the last two weeks in October.

Facility rentals are located in six acres near the farm entrance and the corn maze usually spans 10 acres. A new one is created every year. The 2006 design helped kick-off Oklahoma's centennial celebration. P_Bar was the official centennial maze.

Last year's puzzle contained more than 95 decision points, 300,000 corn stalks and 3.5 miles of twists and turns. Mazes are usually open from Labor Day to Thanksgiving. Oklahoma currently has six maze farms in Sayre, Crescent, Tulsa, Shawnee, Blanchard and Weatherford.

Even though the farm's motto is "Get lost in the fun," it's not hard to find. P_Bar Farms is located off I-40 along the north service road to Old Route 66, about an hour west of Oklahoma City.

And, yes, the farm also has a variety of crops... pumpkins, milo, sunflowers and a huge garden. But don't tell the pigs, sheep, goat and baby bunnies.

Weatherford

United Methodist Church of the Good Shepherd
10928 SW 15, Yukon, OK 73099, (405) 324-1900
Joan Brodmerkel, jebrodmerkel@netzero.net
11-circuit Classical, patio stone spiral on turf, 45 feet
built spring 2003

When you asked Joan Brodmerkel what gave her the idea to build a labyrinth at the Church of the Good Shepherd in Yukon, she shrugs her shoulders and replies with a sly grin, "I'm the one who got the hint from God.

"I know God works in mysterious ways, but when He put the idea in my head to build a labyrinth at our church, that was the furthest thing from my mind."

Joan said she had very little knowledge and "no want or need for labyrinths," so it came as a great surprise to her when the idea literally popped into her head one day while sweeping the kitchen floor.

After researching labyrinths on the computer, reading about the why, how and where of them, Joan said she "became a bit obsessed with the idea of building one at my church."

When presenting the idea to Pastor Rusty Williams, she discovered he had been wanting such a place and praying about it.

"He actually jumped up and down and clapped his hands

(kind of like a cheerleader) when I proposed the idea of building a labyrinth," Joan chuckled.

Rusty took Joan to an area on the church grounds where he had been kneeling in prayer and meditation about adding this sacred spiritual tool to the church's ministry. He encouraged Joan to meet with the Good Shepherd trustees and the Methodist Men's group to seek permission and aid in fulfilling this "hint from God."

The trustees said "go" and the men's group eagerly accepted the project. Music Minister Bob Macemon and Scott Schuermann, church member and landscaper, were instrumental in the pattern design and securing workers and the spiral, 11-circuit labyrinth was created over a few weekends in the early spring of 2003.

"We learned to lay out the classical pattern from a book and also from a web site," Bob said. "I practiced drawing the design on paper, then made one in the field with a lawnmower. It was only seven circuits and didn't have sufficient room in the center for the bench and tree. So, we modified the 'seed-space' and chose 11 circuits to better fit our space."

More than 1,100 patio stones grace several hundred square feet of turf, twisting and turning for about three-quarters of a mile. A small oak tree and white stone bench occupy the center and a forest of magnificent trees, fragrant flowers and ornate benches frame the area.

The tree in the middle is not just any oak; it is a "Survivor Tree" sapling from the 1995 Murrah bombing site. A significant reminder that with proper sustenance and loving care, anything grows well in God's garden.

Joan serves as the maintenance crew and several church groups assist with mowing and weed-eating.

"The youth group has been a great asset in helping maintain the beauty of the labyrinth garden," Joan said. Additional trees and flower gardens have been planted in the last four years to enhance the surroundings.

The "gardener for God" said when she gardens there, she experiences a real sense of peace and love. "It's a beautiful and serene place to praise our Lord, walk and talk to him, meditate or just get away from the world for a little while," she said.

There's certainly nothing monotonous about this labyrinth, it keeps you guessing as you spiral around on the four-colored, hexagon-shaped stepping stone path. No analytical mind required or allowed.

The unusually long circuits provide sharp twists and surprising turns, throwing in an off-centered curve to test the walker's balance.

Sometimes it's best to get off the beaten path, traverse backwards to move forward, meeting unexpected challenges with disciplined focus. These surprises demand immediate attention.

An adjacent creek had recently overflowed its banks submerging the labyrinth and bordering garden. A natural cleansing reminding us to remove the clutter from our minds and wash away obstacles to attain cherished goals.

Much like the message Joan received while sweeping her kitchen floor that day. Clear cobwebs, debris, anything out of place disturbing the focal point of life. The kitchen signifies nourishment, a family gathering room, a place of provision where laughter is shared and creative dishes served.

A tiny frog hopped in a nearby flower bed and onto the outer circuit hiding in leftover clippings from the freshly mowed grass. Several butterflies perched on flowering bushes, gracefully flapping their colorful wings.

Tantalizing surprises greet the walker on this labyrinth, keeping one off-balance, often traveling in the opposite direction than anticipated. Sharp focus and attention to detail is the name of this game.

It's a walk of faith. Just like the way it was built.

Oklahoma Labyrinths by Year Created or Purchased
(alphabetical by year of known dates)

1992
Sparrow Hawk Village/Sancta Sophia Seminary, Tahlequah

1997
St. Dunstan's Episcopal Church, Tulsa
St. John's Episcopal Church, Tulsa (indoor)

1998
St. Luke's Episcopal Church, Bartlesville

1999
MoonShadow Herb Farm, Muskogee (feminine)

2000
First Christian Church, Edmond
First United Methodist Church, Edmond
    (11-circuit canvas, 11-circuit nylon)
First United Methodist Church, Stillwater
McFarlin Memorial United Methodist Church, Norman
    (11-circuit)
Our Lady of Mercy Retreat Center, Oklahoma City
Private Edmond Back Yard — Carol and Harry Woods

2001
All Souls Unitarian Church, Tulsa
Dwight Mission Presbyterian Camp, Vian
MoonShadow Herb Farm, Muskogee (masculine)
St. Matthew's Episcopal Church, Enid
Standing Bear Native American Park, Ponca City
United Life Church, Oklahoma City
Private Edmond Back Yard — Diane and Rich Rudebock
Private Tulsa Front Yard — Clark and Michelle Wiens

2002
Camp Okiwanee, Sapulpa
Prairie Peace Path Labyrinth Sculpture, Norman
Private Edmond Back Yard — Beth and Robert Huntley
Private Stilwell Mountaintop — Lela Samargis

2003
Mercy Health Center, Oklahoma City
Quail Springs United Methodist Church, Oklahoma City
Red Plains Monastery, Sisters of Benedict, Piedmont
St. Andrew's Presbyterian Church, Tulsa
United Methodist Church of the Good Shepherd, Yukon
Private Edmond Lake Property — Raine and Blair Benham
Private Shawnee Back Yard — Lisa Sponseller

2004
Phillips Theological Seminary, Tulsa
Private Edmond Acreage
Private Lawton Combination Labyrinth Medicine Wheel
Private Tulsa Area — Jan Lowell

2005
Camp Christian, Chouteau (indoor)
First United Methodist Church Youth Ministry, Fort Gibson
Hunter Park, Tulsa
McFarlin Memorial United Methodist Church, Norman
    (7-circuit)
St. Stephen's United Methodist Church, Norman
Unity Spiritual Center, Oklahoma City
Windsong Innerspace, Oklahoma City
Private Edmond Back Yard — Barbara Henthorn
Private Shawnee Lake Cabin — Diane and Rich Rudebock

2006
All Saints Episcopal Church, Duncan
Clear Creek Wellness Center, Hulbert
First United Methodist Church, Edmond (7-circuit)
P_Bar Farms, Weatherford
Private Jenks Back Yard, Viola Rollins
Private Tulsa Back Yard, Gala and Bill McBee

2007
Harding Charter Preparatory High School, Oklahoma City
Heart in the Park, Tonkawa
Private Oklahoma City Back Yard — Gail Peck
    Wisdom Wheel Directional Labyrinth

2008
Bethany Christian Church, Tulsa
Camp Christian, Chouteau (outdoor concrete)
St. John's Episcopal Church, Tulsa (grass outdoor)
Private Oklahoma City Back Yard — Shantel Carr

2009 (projected)
Blanchard Healing Center
Clarehouse, Tulsa
Hillcrest Hospital, Tulsa

In Prayer Development
St. Dunstan's Episcopal Church, Tulsa (outdoor)
St. Matthew's Episcopal Church, Enid (outdoor)
Stillwater First United Methodist Church (outdoor)

The Oklahoma Labyrinth Team

Gail Peck graduated from the University of Oklahoma in 1976 with a BA in journalism. She started writing for the *Capitol Hill Beacon*, a weekly newspaper in south Oklahoma City, at age 14 and has worked for the *Oklahoman and Times*, *Oklahoma Daily*, *Oklahoma Living Magazine* and the Mental Health Association in Oklahoma. Actively involved with statewide Holistic Health Fairs and EarthWind Holistic Center, the Oklahoma City resident incorporated 7 Hawks Publishing Company in September 1998, and recently published "The Napkin Series," a book of inspirational poetry written on napkins at fast-food restaurants. This is her third book.

Registered nurse **Linda Yeingst** graduated nursing school in 1981, specialized in orthopedics and neurology for 10 years, worked six years in psychiatric nursing and is currently part of an Oklahoma City flex pool which offers challenging work in all fields of nursing. The former director of the Oklahoma City School of Metaphysics is studying for a Doctor of Naturopathy and is a Past Noble Grand in Rebekahs and Past Matron in the Order of the Eastern Star. Linda actively participates in Oklahoma Holistic Health Fairs and is Kundalini Director for EarthWind Holistic Center.

Phyllis Pennington has degrees from both the University of Oklahoma (BA in psychology, 1968) and Oklahoma City University (BS in biology/chemistry, 1974). She studied commercial art at Oklahoma City Community College and has taken courses in computer graphics and web design from vo-tech centers in both Houston and Oklahoma City. Phyllis is the webmaster and graphic designer for the Graduate College at the University of Central Oklahoma in Edmond. The Oklahoma native possesses a keen celestial insight, which she shares weekly with "A Course in Miracles" study group.

Graphic designer **Lloyd Matthew Thompson** is a self-taught artist, photographer and writer born and raised in Oklahoma City. His spiritually inspired writings, designs, paintings, sketches and photographic artwork can be seen and purchased at www.InvisibleSoul.com. Lloyd's work reflects a luminous transcendence of both tangible and intangible awareness, resonating a radiant emergence and continuous evolution.

Oklahoma Labyrinths — a path to inner peace is the first book in a three-part series. *Sacred Circles of Creation Encircling the Oklahoma Landscape* will feature additional labyrinth experiences and highlight mandalas, rose windows, medicine wheels and zen gardens. The series will conclude with *A Mystical Journey Exploring Oklahoma's Sacred Sites*.

Activate those senses...

That's how you experience a labyrinth.